# THE EDUCATIONAL WELCOME
# OF LATINOS IN THE NEW SOUTH

# THE EDUCATIONAL WELCOME
# OF LATINOS IN THE NEW SOUTH

## EDMUND T. HAMANN

Foreword by Guadalupe M. Valdés

Westport, Connecticut
London

Library of Congress Cataloging-in-Publication Data

Hamann, Edmund T.
    The educational welcome of Latinos in the new South/Edmund T. Hamann.
       p. cm.
    Includes bibliographical references and index.
    ISBN 0-89789-882-6 (alk. paper)
    1. Hispanic Americans—Education—Georgia. 2. Georgia Project.
    3. Multicultural education—Georgia. I. Title.
    LC2674.G46H36  2003
    371.829'9680758—dc21     2003054721

British Library Cataloguing in Publication Data is available.

Library of Congress Catalog Card Number: 2003054721
ISBN: 0-89789-882-6

First published in 2003

Praeger Publishers, 88 Post Road West, Westport, CT 06881
An imprint of Greenwood Publishing Group, Inc.
www.praeger.com

Printed in the United States of America

The paper used in this book complies with the
Permanent Paper Standard issued by the National
Information Standards Organization (Z39.48–1984).

10  9  8  7  6  5  4  3  2  1

## Copyright Acknowledgment

The quote on page xiii comes from the *History Matters* website (http://historymatters.
gmu.edu/d/5745/—accessed 1/3/03). *History Matters* is a joint project of the American Social History Project Center for Media and Learning at City University New York and the Center for History and New Media at George Mason University.

*This book is dedicated to two mentors:*
*Erwin Mitchell*
*and*
*Theodore Sizer*

Both are accomplished. Both have dedicated a substantial portion of their lives to trying to make schools more responsive to kids and parents (whatever the background of either), and both share an inspiring mix of confidence, insistence, and humility that has meant they have welcomed the scholarly scrutiny of their endeavors with a faith that such scrutiny, though perhaps uncomfortable, ultimately makes their work better. I feel lucky to have learned at the side of both of them.

The Georgia Project is about all ethnic groups living, working, suffering, laughing, and prospering together. The Georgia Project is about every person being important and every child being equal. The Georgia Project is, in fact, a spirit, a spirit of equality, a spirit of cooperation, a spirit of mutual respect. The Georgia Project is about every man, woman, and child within its influence knowing that divided there are no possibilities, but united there are no impossibilities. The Georgia Project is about the future of thousands of new Americans; therefore the Georgia Project is about the future of America.

—*Erwin Mitchell*

# Contents

## Part Three: A Novel Binational Partnership: From Launch to Consolidation    93

## Part Four: Ephemeral Opportunity or Inclusive New Order    211

# Foreword

This book, *The Educational Welcome of Latinos in the New South,* by Edmund T. Hamann, offers a unique view of the challenges faced by a Georgia community and its school district as they sought to respond to the educational needs of a newly arrived Mexican-origin population. As a first-rate ethnography of educational policy, it provides a detailed and nuanced narrative of the roles of community leaders in initiating (and in several cases abandoning) the region's first bilingual education program. What is unique about this volume is that, by describing the efforts of the local elite to respond to the presence of Latinos (through the formation of an innovative binational partnership between the district and a Mexican university) and by describing the district's final rejection of bilingual education, it brings to light ways in which competing values, beliefs, and identities impact the policy process.

Hamann's account is a reminder that what constitutes best practice is not always readily or easily answered, as the answer is contingent upon the judging party's sense of what should be. Thus, in this case, best practice appears to be viewed alternatively as maintaining a district's favorable popular reputation, helping newcomers attach their new learning to previous linguistic and cultural experiences, and figuring out ways to preserve host-community residents' sense of what *their* community should be in the face of cultural and demographic challenge.

One of the best things about cultural anthropology (and this book firmly identifies itself in that tradition) is the priority given to representing the emic, the worldview and modus operandi, of the people being studied. While Hamann indicates his own frustration and discomfort when some of the tenets of a bilingual-education grant proposal that he authored were not pursued by certain school-district administrators and when other portions of the binational partnership were unfulfilled, he successfully conveys the sincerity rather than capriciousness of those who ultimately turned away from the plan. He documents well how those who intended to collaborate unwittingly talked past each other until misunderstandings grew into disagreements, then rivalries, then uncomfortable public disputes. Perhaps even more emphatically than he does, I share Hamann's sense that a golden opportunity to change the way schools welcomed and responded to Latinos was, at best, only partially realized. Yet I admire his insistence that the perspectives of the educators described here not be dismissed and that the gains, though less than what was promised, not be ignored.

Yet Hamann represents not only the viewpoints of the key administrators who ultimately became skeptics of the partnership. He provides an intriguing opportunity to also consider the motives and rationales of the scholars from a private Mexican University and a wily former congressman who played a central role in both initiating and sustaining the partnership (even expanding it into other nearby districts). The Mexican scholars were quite conscious of the unorthodoxy of the North (the United States) soliciting expertise from the South (Mexico) and thus were careful to operate effectively and graciously too. They knew they were guests, even as they were insistent that many of the Mexican newcomers on whose behalf they were advocating were not. In turn, the former congressman insisted on his status and prerogatives as a committed resident. If the schools in his community were not going to rise, unprodded, to a challenge, then by golly he was going to prod them. As he did so, he mobilized an impressive array of supporters.

This book is more than the detailed account of several individuals. As a work of anthropological scholarship, it documents how individuals' actions shape and are shaped by the milieus and meaning systems in which they take place. Yet Hamann does not only label this an anthropological text, he also convincingly labels it a policy study. More specifically, he helps extend the nascent field of ethnography of educational policy, pushing the reader to see how individuals draw selectively from larger scripts and discourses as they create the rudimentary structure of every policy: a problem diagnosis and a strategy of action to solve it. He also clarifies how those problem diagnoses are related to their advocates' positionality and worldview. In so doing, he provides an unusual window into understanding why Latino experiences in school are what they are. To the extent that we want them to be different and better—and I've devoted much of my career to insisting upon that point—we need nuanced depictions like Hamann's so that we can know where and how to direct our interventions. Ultimately, I found *The Educational Welcome of Latinos to the New South* to be an outstanding contribution both to the study of educational policy and to the literature that focuses on the education of Latinos. I trust other readers will as well.

Guadalupe M. Valdés

# Acknowledgments

Though the limitations of this volume are clearly my responsibility and mine alone, the very existence of this book and its importance and utility are products of the work of many. No doubt I will unwittingly overlook some people. However, I want to express my gratitude first and loudest to my family: to my partner Susan for her patient insistence that this book could be done; to my children Megan and Alex who might find that "Daddy writes books" is slightly more tangible than "Daddy is an education researcher;" to my grandfathers who both established family precedent to pursue studies at a doctoral level; to my grandmothers who joined my parents in financially supporting the many many years of my schooling that culminated in my dissertation about the Georgia Project and thus the foundation for this book; to my father who doggedly keeps reading my publications even though they are far from his professional interest in estate law and personal interests in *Forbes* and *Foreign Affairs* magazines; to my mother who came to see the presentation by Georgia Project leaders that I organized in Providence in April 2000 so she, too, could get an idea of what I was pursuing; and to my brother who, long before Nike, insisted that I could "just do it," with "it" referring to anything I set my mind to.

As importantly, I am building on the work of many teachers, including Drs. Fred Erickson, John Puckett, Kathy Hall, and Ken Erickson, who each sat on my dissertation committee, and many who came before them: Martha Allexsaht-Snider, Jude Preissle, Doug Massey, Sheryl Gowen, Don Stull, Akira Yamamoto, Allan Hanson, Jane Gibson, Lucie Barron,

Laurie Orum, Regina Cortina, Rick Lear, Adie Becker, Charles Thomas, Chris Zamore, Margaret Guerriero, and Norma Marsh.

I have been encouraged and buoyed by many colleagues. Guadalupe Valdés and Amanda Datnow have been particularly welcome sources of encouragement. Through the Council on Anthropology and Education I have exchanged ideas, been intellectually challenged, and been supported by James Mullooly, Norma Gonzalez, Sofia Villenas, Enrique G. Murillo, Stanton Wortham, Tim Mahoney, Lisa Rosen, Enrique Trueba, Bradley Levinson, and Catherine Emihovich. Here at the Education Alliance at Brown University the support of several colleagues—Julie Nora, Gwen Jordan, Joe DiMartino, Mary-Beth Fafard, Deborah Collins, and Brett Lane—has been particularly welcome, as has the mentorship and support of four other Brown colleagues—Cynthia Garcia Coll, Evelyn Hu-DeHart, Liza Bakewell and Carl Kaestle. Though they are harder to categorize, Scott Beck and Melissa Cahnmann, both at the University of Georgia, have also been sources of energy, ideas, and purpose.

Several people provided important logistic support for me as I carried out this research and they often became sounding boards for my emergent ideas. Beth Arnow, Coordinator of ESOL in Gwinnett County, recommended me to educators in Dalton to assist their preparation of the *Title VII—Systemwide Bilingual Education* grant proposal that became my entrée to the school district and community. She also introduced me to a number of educators at and formerly at the Georgia Department of Education and to her husband, Steve Weisbrod, who hired me to teach ESL in Atlanta while writing and researching. Bob Blakely, Rebecca Dameron, and Ann Colloton helped me find a temporary home at Georgia State University's Center for Applied Research in Anthropology when I first moved to Georgia, with Sheryl Gowen and Gayle Nelson helping me find temporary teaching positions. Subsequently, Martha Allexsaht-Snider, Carl Huberty, and Steve Olejnik helped me find a home at the University of Georgia for a year. John Keyes and Rosemary Henze shared their Dalton research with me on topics overlapping with mine. When I had a question about higher education in Mexico, David Lorey who is an expert on that topic patiently fielded my phone call. Back in Philadelphia, Bryant and Carolyn Tolles frequently opened their home to me as I returned to give research updates to my dissertation committee. Ruth Ebert was a willing copy editor and consistent friend. Lynn Taylor of the Greenwood Publishing Group offered me the original contract that led to this book; then, after she left, Marie Ellen Larcada provided useful encouragement and welcome flexibility with deadlines. I also thank Elizabeth Potenza for editing assistance and Larry Goldberg and his team at Shepherd Incorporated for their editing and production expertise.

My final thanks go to the dozens of people in Dalton and Monterrey who shared their experiences and ideas with me, allowed me to observe their practice, and endured my scrutiny. I particularly want to thank Lisa Goode whose dissertation was so useful to my updating the Georgia Project story. I knew the district very well and was a regular presence there in 1997 and 1998. She, along with others, has allowed me to keep up from afar.

Bradley Levinson and Peggy Sutton recently wrote, "Too often, research inspired by critical theory ignores the inescapable need for administrative techniques in modern societies. It is easier, and far too tempting, to raise a critique without venturing into the messy business of policy formation" (2001, 16). The following long list of those who directly assisted me and their hundreds of colleagues all are sincerely addressing the challenges of trying to raise a new multiethnic generation of Daltonians. They deserve credit and respect for that attempt. In alphabetical order I owe explicit thanks to each of the following: Francisco Azcúnaga, Tom Bartley, Frankie Beard, Sandra Benitez, Billy Bice, Fredda Bulger, Jennifer Carlisle, Sylvester Carrington, Carolyn Couch, Elaine Davis, C. Dempsey, Irma Diaz, Nancy Doss, Tom Durkan, Ghada Elnajjar, Zenhya Escamilla, Sheila Evans, Brenda Garcia, Rocio Garza, Tomas Gonzalez, Lupita Gracia, Loretta Guthrie, Dian Hall, Angela Hargis, Craig Harper, Amy Haynes, Rubén Hernández-León, Lynnda Higgins, Amy Huggins, Fernando Iturribaria, Vanesa Iza, Gwen James, Karen Lee, Linda Lozano, Homero Luna, M. Mackey, Dalia Martinez, Monica Martinez, Nora Martinez, Betty McLure, Linda Miller, Erwin Mitchell, Ximena Molina, Zenaida O'Bryant, Laura Orr, Francisco Palacios, Diana Perez, David Perry, Sue Phelps, Rita Pierson, Judy Pontonio, Dawn Sanders, John Schaerer, Janna Shadduck, John Shaheen, M. Sharp, Bob Shaw, Jo-Anne Schick, Daniel Stack, Fred Thomason, Blanca Treviño, Marioly Villareal, Ann Warren, Leigh Watson, Robert Webb, Nancy Westrup, Angela Wheeler, Burt Wingfield, and Victor Zúñiga.

## THE NEW SOUTH

The vision of a "New South" was heralded by Southern landowners, entrepreneurs, and newspaper editors in the decades following the Confederacy's defeat in 1865 and the abolition of racial slavery across the South. These "New South" boosters argued that, with its plantation economy destroyed by the Civil War and Reconstruction, the South would develop a new economy more attuned to the industrial capitalism that defined the rest of the American economy. *Atlanta Constitution* editor Henry Grady was the leading exponent of a "New South" based on industrial development, giving speeches throughout the country and writing articles and editorials in his newspaper. Two speeches by Grady—one given in Boston in 1889, the other in New York in 1886—conveyed not only the message of industrialization as a panacea, but also Grady's fierce regional pride and his general moderation on racial issues, which were becoming increasingly contentious in these years. (From *History Matters*)

# Part One

# Introduction

# Negotiating a New Demography: Schooling and the "Latinization" of North Georgia

Perhaps the name Dalton, Georgia, rings a bell with a few Civil War buffs who note that General Sherman scorched a lot of nearby earth as he began his march across Georgia. In fact, according to a brochure distributed by the Dalton/Whitfield Chamber of Commerce, Whitfield County (of which Dalton is the county seat) has more Civil War–related historic markers than any other Georgia County.[1] Perhaps those inclined to read *People* magazine will recall that Dalton is the hometown of Donald Trump's ex-wife Marla Maples, though some city residents will clarify that she grew up outside the city limits and attended Whitfield County Schools, not Dalton's. Perhaps regional historians will recognize Dalton as a significant site in the creation of the New South economy, with its earliest industrialization occurring in the 1880s (Flamming 1992). Perhaps those who have recently gone shopping for carpet will remember that practically all domestically manufactured carpet comes from Dalton and nearby communities. None of these facts, except perhaps the last two, hint that from the mid-1990s through the writing of these words (in 2002) Dalton was host to a rapidly growing Latino population and to a dramatic, business-initiated, educational and community development program that had the espoused purposes of accommodating immigrant students, their families, and the broader interests of the community.[2] Particularly in its original design and initial implementation, that program reflected an intriguing and sometimes contentious blend of understandings regarding what Latino newcomers needed, how they should be schooled, and how they fit within a newly multiethnic community.[3] This book studies those understandings and the educational policies—the projects of the binational partnership—which they engendered. The vignette that follows presents one manifestation of the partnership.

### Vignette 1: Change Is an Opportunity

During his five-minute stop in this local, multigrade, multiracial, bilingual classroom (part of a fifty-minute visit to the school), the Fortune 500 executive worked the room like a politician, shaking hands, smiling, waving, and drawing students' genuine responses of delight. A Latino boy (age 6 or 7) brought over a child-size cap and placed it precariously atop the executive's head, then the student hugged him and paused to pose for a camera pointed at them.

Elsewhere in the room, a Mexico-trained teacher (who was compensated as a "parapro"—that is, an uncertified paraprofessional) interrupted her out-loud reading of "Buenas Noches Luna" (Goodnight Moon) to chat briefly with an esteemed local attorney, who was also a classroom visitor. The attorney and the executive had been instrumental in getting her and thirteen of her Mexican colleagues to come spend a year in this 4,500-student school district. Watching were the smiling principal, a smiling district administrator, an Anglo teacher, and a bilingual Anglo parapro. Three of these four had spent four weeks at a Mexican university the previous summer, attending an intense language, culture, and curriculum-training institute organized specially for educators from this district. I was also in the classroom, as were the twenty-eight students of Mexican, other Latino, African American, and Anglo backgrounds.[4]

In the hallway outside, just before his departure from the school, the Fortune 500 executive reiterated his belief that the schools and the community needed to see the ongoing local demographic changes (i.e., the influx of several thousand Latino newcomers) as an "opportunity" rather than as a "problem." His company was both a major employer of newcomer labor and a longtime practitioner of corporate paternalism for community ends.

Despite the Fortune 500 executive's optimistic interpretation, not all established residents in and near Dalton viewed the changing demography favorably. Nor was the willingness of some Anglo residents to abet and accommodate the Latino newcomers fully accepted. As the next vignette illustrates, for some, the presence of newcomers was cause for making violent and consequential threats.

### Vignette 2: Threats and a Multilateral Sense of Fear

A few weeks prior to the executive's celebrated classroom visit, in a nearby jurisdiction, a local employee of a state education program had been warned by a friend to fear for her personal safety because her work with so many Hispanic newcomer families was controversial. The friend had said something like, "You better be careful; there are people around here who would try to hurt you if they knew what your job is." For similar reasons, a different friend recommended that the state employee take the magnetic education program logo off the side of her car for safety reasons while she was traveling in their rural neighborhood.

After seeing several Hispanic parents visit the state employee's mobile home (where they thanked the employee for assistance she had given), the employee's landlord also stopped by the trailer, ordering the employee not to have any more "Mexicans" on his property. This threat prompted another friend of the state employee to advise her to move her mobile home to a different lot, warning that the landlord might get violent. Fearful and angry about the threats to her personal safety and bewildered that some people could be so hateful just because she worked with Mexican immigrants, the employee finally moved to a town a hundred miles away. Nonetheless, at the end of my study period, she still held her job providing outreach and school/home liaisons to many Hispanic families in dozens of Georgia districts.[5]

The response of the executive and the response of the landlord to the Latino newcomers are similar in one ironic way—both were atypical. But I start this book with them because both reactions were consequential in disproportion to their frequency. The unorthodox outreach to the newcomers by a few and the threatened and threatening xenophobia, also of a few, framed local policy formation as schooling strategies and community accommodations for the newcomers were considered. Moreover, both of these local events drew upon and were similar to the varied responses to Latino newcomers elsewhere in the nation. That is, they were both local and more than local.

Street protests and acrimonious letters to the editor were other examples of explicit and atypical local xenophobia, but most longtime residents avoided such overt displays of racism. Indeed many of these longtime residents claimed superior status to "those redneck" protesters. Thus the presence of Latinos became grounds for some Anglos to self-define themselves favorably in relation to other Anglos and to exclude those inappropriate other Anglos from policy discussions. The easy equation of overt xenophobia with racism obscured the much more subtle racism (e.g., the reproduction of the ethno-racial stratification of the local economy) that many in the mainstream seemed willing to allow to perpetuate, perhaps without recognizing it.

For the bulk of the established population of Dalton and surrounding environs, the demographic transformation of their community and the economic and political changes that were related to it compelled neither a response of benevolence nor violence. Rather, the predominant reaction was one of disquiet and unease. Established residents were not sure whether to be welcoming or cautious, whether to see in the newcomers proof of community renewal or proof of community decay (Suárez-Orozco 1998). The emergent interethnic interaction, which was undergirded by an ongoing power differential that favored established Anglo residents, was improvisational and uncertain. The only thing that seemed certain to longtime residents of Dalton in the mid-1990s and later was that previously clear boundaries had suddenly become blurred regarding both who was part of the community and what were the community's shared mores and values. The disquiet generated a nostalgic impulse.

### Vignette 3: Loss, Change, and Nostalgia

In 1960 the world was a different place. Coming into town on Highway 41 from the north, the initial greeting sat rooted into a piece of ground just off the railroad tracks that nestled behind Crown Mills. A sign of somewhat large proportions titled Dalton the Carpet Capital of the World and down below, near the bottom, in black lettering on white, was the local population.

It was no staggering figure, having learned of the droves of humanity in such cities as Chicago and New York, but it was a comfortable total.

The bulk of business took place downtown. Shops and banks thrived. Ten-cent stores were high on the list. The U.S. Cafe, right there on Hamilton in the center of this tiny universe, and Oakwood were ballyhooed for miles.

Glenwood, past the fairgrounds and Legion Field, was less populated. Walnut Avenue slept in residential bliss. The interstate highway had not yet cut a swath through the north end of Georgia, and the mail was still, for the most part, delivered on foot.

The fire department was on Pentz Street, there was only one bridge downtown, and you could watch movies at the drive-in every night of the week. The Wink Theatre was alive, as was the Crescent.

Driving the streets, it was difficult to see a passing face that a name could not be placed beneath. Needless to say, the face of this little town has changed, both in detail and expression. Now, even the language is in question.

With the growth of the carpet industry and the lack of adequate labor on several different levels, the need for a work force escalated. While many work arenas suffered financially, even to the point of extinction, Dalton continued to offer a valid job list.

It is a secret to no one that this town is now approximately 25 percent Hispanic as the border of this country offers continued hope for those seeking gainful employment and a new, better life. But change has its price.
— Larry Green (sports columnist), *The Daily Citizen-News,* May 1996

The three vignettes give glimpses into a complicated, unfinished story of one transnationally linked, Southern Appalachian community's efforts to negotiate the arrival (and occasional departure) of thousands of Latino families. In the mid-1990s, in response to this demographic change and, in particular, its effect on schools, a few community leaders joined with some Mexican partners to instigate a dramatic, far-reaching, novel, binational partnership that was nonetheless both controversial and imperfect. That partnership—known as the Georgia Project—linked Dalton Public Schools, surrounding Whitfield County Schools, and a new community organization (itself called the Georgia Project) with the Universidad de Monterrey, a private university in Mexico's third largest city.

The individuals who crafted and guided the Georgia Project were policy-makers, though not all were in positions that one would normally associate with educational policymaking for a school district in North Georgia. They embedded the Georgia Project with particular beliefs about the constituencies they were addressing, the struggles the community faced, the needs their program should attend to, and the strategies that could be pursued. Those who were Georgia certified educators also assured that state policy parameters and those policies' underlying assumptions were part of the calculation of local policy and practice. This book is a study of what those beliefs were, what the consequent strategies were (i.e., local policies), and thus, how the Georgia Project was conceived and launched.

The Dalton case is instructive because we can consider not just what has happened but why and with what goals. Thinking back to the vignettes, what traditions of civic engagement and local decision making compelled a carpet executive to weigh in on the process of newcomer schooling? Why were his input and the attorney's considered? What were their habits of problem diagnosis and action? In turn, why did the mobile home lot owner have so little expectation of inclusion in the formal policy process that he acted crudely and unilaterally, albeit with consequence?

In Dalton, one can consider the value, means, and consequences of importing bilingual teachers from Mexico, of sending Georgia-origin teachers to Mexico for training, of attempting to make the curriculum bilingual, of conducting a careful needs assessment of the newcomer community, and of initiating a newcomer political organization. All of these policies were strands of the Georgia Project. Like all policies, each was created with at least an implicit problem diagnosis that the policies were proposed to solve (Levinson and Sutton 2001; Shore and Wright 1997). Thinking of the Georgia Project, one can ask why these were the proposed policies (as opposed to others). How were they created? How broadly were they understood? And with what degree of consensus and confidence were they pursued?

At the time of this writing in 2002, the Georgia Project had attracted growing amounts of popular attention, resources, and praise, but careful analysis by just a handful of scholars. In the first five years of the Georgia Project, the partnership's initiators and the Dalton schools hosted more than a hundred visitors (from many parts of the country) and were invited to share their story in North Carolina and Rhode Island, as well as elsewhere in Georgia. The project had garnered two federal Title VII grants, substantial local financial support (both public and private), and in 2000–2001, a $600,000 noncategorical special federal allocation. On behalf of the Georgia Project, the attorney/founder had accepted multiple awards of recognition, including the 2001 "Citizen of the Year" award from the National Association for Bilingual Education and the

George I. Sanchez Memorial Award from the National Education Association. He had also accepted an invitation to sit on the advisory board of a major research and advocacy organization—the Center for Applied Linguistics—in Washington, D.C.

Still, according to economic, cultural, demographic, and education variables, Dalton was like a number of places at the turn of the millennium, differing only by detail and degree (Lamphere, Stepick, and Grenier 1994; Wortham et al. 2001). Like the "New South" of which it is part, Dalton's population and economy both grew rapidly and became increasingly intertwined with international flows of labor and capital in the 1990s, while traditions of anti-unionism persisted (Griffith 1995). Dalton was also part of the "old New South"; that is, though small, for more than a century it has been industrialized. Like the Appalachia that it is also part of, Dalton has remained disproportionately reliant on manufacturing, making it vulnerable to the international relocation of jobs if rising labor costs were ever to outweigh the economic advantages of nearness to markets and existing investment in physical plant (Gaventa 1990; Mencken 1996).[6] (See the map to gauge Dalton's proximity to markets and transportation links.) The locally dominant carpet industry's record profits (Barry 1997) in the 1990s did not eliminate this vulnerability. Nor was Dalton economically different from rural towns and small cities scattered across North America that are not large enough to have substantially diverse economies; like them, Dalton was vulnerable to the cyclic swings of a single dominant industry (Hackenberg 1995). The long economic expansion of the 1990s (that occurred concurrently with Dalton's demographic transformation) precipitated a national construction boom and a substantial demand for carpet. As in other boomtowns, Dalton's boom also supported a relative tolerance for diversification of the workforce (though not necessarily of the schools), as newcomers mostly moved into "Mexican-typed" jobs (Tienda 1989) that did not displace most established residents. Into such a context was the Georgia Project born.

Just as economic circumstances in Dalton were akin to those encountered in many other locations, schooling decisions in Dalton occurred in a context similar to that encountered by other communities and similar to those that still other communities will encounter. The new students in Dalton were Latino, often immigrant, often English language learners (ELLs), often highly mobile, often from economically vulnerable households, and usually of Mexican birth or descent. Nationally, each of these labels/categories describes a growing number of students. A recent map in *Education Week* (2000a) shows that hundreds of counties across the former Confederacy saw the proportion of Hispanic school-age children grow by at least 75 percent between 1990 and 1998.[7] The number of identified ELLs rose an estimated 95 percent nationally between 1991–1992 and 2001–2002 (NCELA 2002). Unfortunately, these labels/categories also describe students who perform less well and are served less well by schools than are "mainstream" students

**Dalton from a Regional Perspective**

*Source:* From Dalton's $500,000 *Title VII—Systemwide Bilingual Education* grant proposal (Dalton Public Schools 1997:1).

(e.g., Rumberger and Larson 1998; Súarez-Orozco and Súarez-Orozco 2001; Valdés 2001; Valenzuela 1999). By the mid-1990s it was increasingly apparent that a growing proportion of Dalton students would fare comparatively poorly unless schooling for newcomer students differed substantially from those encountered by similar students elsewhere in the United States.

In Dalton, like much of America, schooling decisions in the 1990s were influenced by concerns over standardized test scores (D'Agostino 2000; Madaus 1999; Packer 2001), by debates regarding reading instruction and the "scientific" basis for certain strategies (Coles 2001), by the promise and prospect of importing externally developed school reform designs (Hatch 2000), by the challenge of "hosting newcomers" (Dentler and Hafner 1997), and by the paucity of educators trained in bilingual and/or English to Speakers of Other Languages techniques (General Accounting Office 1999; Macias 1989; Varisco de García and Garcia 1996; Zhao 2002).[8] As Dalton Public Schools' Hispanic enrollment grew sharply—increasing from less than 1 percent in 1987 to become the first majority Hispanic district in Georgia by 2000–2001—the national debate about bilingual education became newly pertinent. So too did social phenomena such as the flight of middle-class white students from public to private school and from the city's school system to the county's. As anywhere, established residents of Dalton brought existing worldviews to their considerations of these new topics and, even as the new information and new circumstances modified those worldviews, patterns of belief and interpretation often remained consistent and little changed. Thus, by one rendering, the story of educational policymaking in Dalton in response to demographic change is the story of existing habits of interpretation being applied to new circumstances.

However accurate, that summary obscures the drama and importance of how a patrician, maverick attorney's career-long quest for racial/ethnic justice and two long-running community traditions—(1) community business leaders' personalized involvement in education and other civic affairs (Flamming 1992) and (2) hierarchical and centralized school district management—all compellingly affected the creation of educational policies for Latino newcomers. Moreover, that summary gives little hint that Dalton's locally developed, ELL-accommodating school reform initiative (i.e., the Georgia Project) had important and possibly replicable elements that other school districts also confronting demographic transformation might want to adapt and adopt.

The attorney's oft-retold account of how and why he decided to initiate the Georgia Project illustrates the link between storytelling, posturing, and policy formation: One day his monolingual daughter—then serving as a "parapro" at a pre-Kindergarten through Grade 2 elementary school on the poorer side of town—had described to him how difficult her and her colleagues' task was because they were monolingual English speakers and so many of their students and their students' parents were monolingual Spanish speakers. The two sides could not communicate.[9] Feeling compelled to try to remedy this mismatch, but not immediately sure how to proceed, the attorney visited the school where his daughter worked. Disconcerted by what he found and then learning that the school district had no action plan, he mentioned his daughter's complaint to the CEO of one of Dalton's largest carpet manufacturers. The CEO in turn contacted the head of one of his company's Mexican trading partners. That Mexican contact, who was also a lead supporter of the Universidad de Monterrey, telephoned the rector of the university. The rector then engaged one of his professors in a discussion about how the Universidad de Monterrey—in Nuevo León, Mexico—might be able to help the public schools in Dalton, Georgia. The attorney was given the professor's name and called him, closing the loop.

The attorney's story has a "gee whiz" nature to it, but is careful to embed the impetus for the project in the empathy-generating experiences of local educators at school and their broadly appealing goal of wanting to communicate. Through the story, the attorney positions himself as a mediator and effective advocate for improvement, as can be judged by his ability to rapidly mobilize such distant, but well-connected partners. In other words, his story rationalizes his own participation in the project. The story itself is not a policy, but like a policy it embeds a problem diagnosis—the inability for educators and students to communicate—and then suggests the partnership as the problem's solution. By referencing a chain of individuals seeking expert advice that starts with a locally prominent business leader who has a public record of efficacy and community concern, the story clarifies how an unlikely partnership was initiated and includes a locally salient rationale for welcoming the Universidad de Monterrey. (Somebody we trust went to somebody whom he trusts, who went to someone that he trusts, and so on.) The story embeds expectations about what listeners will find salient while proposing a course of action that listeners can agree with or more actively support. The story illustrates acute, if implicit, understanding of what is culturally meaningful. On such a basis are local policies created and on such a basis they become schema for action.

The research on the relative lack of school success for Latinos in the United States (lack of success in relation to other groups) is abundant and growing. It includes quantitative data, such as those from the National Center for Educational Statistics that show Hispanic dropout rates staying stubbornly above 25 percent since 1980. At the same time, the non-Hispanic white dropout rate has declined from 11.4 percent to 7.7 percent (in 1998) and the African American dropout rate has fallen from 19.1 percent to 13.8 percent (*Education Week* 2000a:44). Quantitative data also show Hispanics are less likely to attend college, less likely to stay in college long enough to obtain a degree, and more likely to be in lower-track classes, including special education, and that these trends have persisted over time (Brown et al. 1980; De la Rosa and Maw 1990; Garcia 2001; President's Advisory Commission on Educational Excellence for Hispanic Americans 1996a). The story is particularly dismal in Georgia where Hispanic children attending school are less likely than anywhere else in the country to graduate on time with a diploma (Salzer 2001).

There is also a growing and rich body of ethnographic depictions of the schooling of Latinos (e.g., Delgado-Gaitan 1990; Foley 1990; Pugach 1998; Valdés 1996, 2001; Valenzuela 1999; Vazquez et al. 1994; Wortham et al. 2001). Yet despite this growing abundance of scholarship regarding the education of Latinos, there is a dearth of research that considers how host community education leaders imagine Latino newcomers and, relatedly, how this imagining informs the thinking and decision making that results in the policies and practices encountered by Latino students and parents. Building on the work of Anderson (1991), Chavez (1994) has directed anthropological inquiry to consider how undocumented Mexican newcomers "imagine" themselves as part (or not part) of the communities in which they live and how that imagining is consequential for newcomers' decision making and cosmology. I seek to complement Chavez' proposition by instead looking at how long-term members of a community imagine newcomers. Are the newcomers welcome? Are they part of a newly expanded community? Are they welcome only to a certain extent and only in specific ways? And how does this imagining translate into what is acceptable as educational policy and what is enacted in schools? Of course, host community members are not the only ones shaping the answers to these questions. In the case of Dalton, scholars from the Mexican university and newcomers also contributed to the answers (even though the newcomers were not directly present at the formal Georgia Project policymaking table).

Crucial to an understanding of the pages and chapters that follow is an appreciation that both the formal and informal policymaking arenas are sites for elaboration and contestation of what it means to be educated. It is important to note that education and schooling are not fully synonymous, though it is often unexamined practice in the United States to treat them as such. As Levinson and Holland (1996:2) explain:

Anthropologists have long recognized the existence of culturally specific and relative definitions of the educated person. Although the degree to which cultural training is formalized, situated at a remove from the activities for which it is intended, and provided on a mass scale may vary, anthropologists recognize all societies as providing some kind of training and some set of criteria by which members can be identified as more, or less, knowledgeable. Distinct societies, as well as ethnic groups and microcultures within those societies, elaborate the cultural practices by which particular sets of skills, knowledges, and discourses come to define the truly "educated" person.

In a society like the United States, and in a microcosm of that society, such as a community like Dalton (with all of its particular idiosyncrasies and specific histories), there are processes by which certain people are trained more than others. Those same people are favorably marked as being more educated and deserving a comparatively privileged status within the stratified local and national order.

It also follows from Levinson and Holland's (1996:2) insight that host community members (typically Anglos) and newcomer Latinos would differ in their views of education and what it means to be educated, as they differ along other cultural dimensions as well. Though both groups might see schooling as a vehicle for education, Valdés (1996) and Villenas (2001), among others, have written poignantly and powerfully about Latina mothers' aspirations for *una buena educación* for their children, with that aspiration referencing not just literacy and numeracy, but also a sense of appropriate comportment—for example, good manners, respect for elders, and assuming responsibility for one's actions. This contrasts with the more straightforward equating of education, schooling, and academic learning that is a dominant conception in the United States.

Though perhaps few would acknowledge it, it follows that host community members might distinguish between what constitutes an "educated" Latino and an "educated" Anglo. An "educated" Latino, for instance, may be constructed as one who knows how to work hard and not complain or one who has fully assimilated, while an "educated" Anglo may know how to shape a corporate vision and engineer profitable practices. (Chapter 4 further explores this idea with its discussion of immigration scripts [Suárez-Orozco 1998].)

Even if schools are not the only site where the definition of "educated" is constructed, schools are key "mediating institutions" (Goode et al. 1992; Lamphere 1992) at which newcomers and established residents encounter each other and at which, through curriculum, pedagogy, and school structures, newcomers are required to negotiate the host society's dominant paradigms. Thus schools are key loci for rejecting, accommodating, and assimilating impulses (Wong-Fillmore and Meyer 1992). Schools are sites where definitions of community membership, community values, social status, and other social constructions are all defined, enacted, and accepted or resisted.

This study is an "ethnography of educational policy" (Levinson and Sutton 2001) that seeks, in part, to redress anthropology's long absence from policy studies (Shore and Wright 1997). This study takes a different tack than most of the growing number of reports on Latino education. It does not directly focus on Latino students in Dalton, nor the classrooms they were in, except as both were relevant to the research question of how corporate leaders, educational administrators, local politicians, and researchers based in Mexico understood and responded to the challenges in school and elsewhere of the changing demography. Thus, this study is about planning meetings, teacher trainings, executive tours of schools, and curriculum battles—including the main one resulting from the contradictory, simultaneous embrace of bilingual education and the DISTAR-derived Direct Instruction model.[10] (That conflict is described in greatest depth in Chapters 11 and 13.) Meier and Stewart (1991) claim that investigating the interaction between layers of the educational hierarchy (ranging from the links between the school board and central administration to individual instances of teacher/student interaction) provides the key to understanding the politics and prognosis for Hispanic education. That assumption is shared here.

After this introductory chapter, the book starts with an explanation of the ethnography of educational policy (Chapter 2), further identifying this rendering of that framework within the genre of "research as collective praxis" (Adams et al. 2001). Per the tenets of that genre, Chapter 2 thus includes my relationship to the story told here, highlighting my field work in Dalton in 1997 and 1998, my ongoing communication with educators and Georgia Project advocates in that community, and my influence on Lisa Goode, a Dalton educator, whose dissertation (Goode 2002) was also an ethnography of educational policy crafted as an updating and response to my own.[11] Given the importance of her observations and keen insights in the chapters that follow, perhaps this text can be read as an appreciative response to her response.

Per other tenets of the ethnography of educational policy that note the need to historically ground educational policy studies (Levinson and Sutton 2001:9), the third chapter offers a short history of schooling and economic and group relations in Dalton. The fourth chapter ties this description to local manifestations of American public sphere constructions of assimilation and accommodation. It uses Suárez-Orozco's (1998) model of "pro-immigration" and "anti-immigration" scripts, thus imitating Rosen's (2001) examination of the relationship between "myths" or "tropes" and cherished cultural ideals about education. Chapter 4 also describes immigrant-relevant Georgia education law and some actions by the administration of State Superintendent of Instruction, Linda Schrenko, who presided over the Georgia Department of Education when the Georgia Project was being launched. Her administration was clearly hostile to native language instruction or any other accommodating pedagogical approach that was not by purpose subtractively assimilative (Beck and Allexsaht-Snider 2001).

Chapters 5 and 6 are both largely biographical, with the former providing background on the Georgia Project's founding attorney and three key Dalton educational leaders and the latter offering background on the two most important shapers of the Georgia Project from the Universidad de Monterrey.[12] Chapter 6 also briefly explores the institutional history of the Universidad de Monterrey.

Chapters 3 through 6 together form the second part of the book and are collectively titled: "Places, Scripts, and People: The Particularities of People and Settings." Chapters 3 through 6 remind us that Dalton residents and educators were negotiating a changing, contested, complicated environment of which the Georgia Project was only a part. Educationally, pressures to enact the Georgia Project competed with public pressures for improved test scores, safe schools, back-to-basics reading instruction strategies, a stanching of white flight from the district, and the augmentation of various honors programs (e.g., an international baccalaureate program at the high school), to name just a few. Often it competed just for attention with these other agendas, but at times realization of the Georgia Project conflicted with the strategies being used to realize other ends. More broadly, the Georgia Project needed to negotiate Dalton's century-old fault line between the poorer East Side and the wealthier West Side, Dalton's equally long-standing presumption that its schools were preeminent in relation to the county school district, and the reality that historic forms of injustice in the community—notably "legal" segregation—were not yet completely redressed. To the extent the Georgia Project was labeled as "for Hispanics" it encountered a muffled but real complaint from some: "Why should *they* get what *we* never got?"

The book's third part looks in depth at the Georgia Project, relating primarily the period from mid-1996 to mid-1998 that overlapped with or just preceded my field study. However, these chapters also include updated information through this writing in 2002. Chapter 7 more fully details the partnership's origin. It describes the maneuvering of the attorney who, with the help of the Fortune 500 executive, founded the partnership; it offers an analysis of the Dalton superintendent's first contact with the Monterrey partners (which had a potent effect on shaping their expectations); and it describes changes initiated at one elementary school that did much to convince school district leaders that the changes proposed as the Georgia Project were promising and viable. Chapter 8 describes the first three face-to-face encounters between Monterrey and Dalton-based project planners in 1996 and 1997. The last of these meetings was the accord signing ceremony that formally created the partnership, committing it to the four-component structure that had been negotiated over the previous months. Chapter 8 also describes how even at the very moment the rationale for the project's proposed structure was being articulated, a competing and narrower interpretation of the project's purpose was introduced: to teach newcomers English. This alternate rationale figured centrally in the subsequent fates of each component and matched the official priorities for the education of ELLs in Georgia. These four components are detailed in the following four chapters.

Beginning with a review of research that found Latino students performed better academically when there were more Latino teachers in their school (Meier and Stewart 1991), Chapter 9 describes the visiting instructor component that brought Monterrey-trained teachers to Dalton where, because of Georgia law, their credentials were not formally recognized. Recruited as professionals but compensated as "parapros," the chapter describes how Georgia-based educators and parapros responded to the new instructors, alternately treating them as threats, subordinates, and expert partners. The chapter clarifies that there are more dimensions to the policy decision to import bilingual educators than just the issue of increasing the number of adult Spanish speakers at a school. It ends with the June 2001 decision by the Universidad de Monterrey project leaders to suspend the visiting instructor program in Dalton, occasioned by that district's decision to stop providing living quarters, vehicles, and other in-kind support in addition to their compensation as parapros.

Chapter 10 describes the learning, adventurousness, and enthusiasm of the first cohort of Georgia teachers to head to Mexico for a four-week rigorous summer training. It also describes the challenge to centralized district curriculum decision making that this training posed. As the expertise of some school-based instructors to teach Mexican-origin students grew, the rationale of heeding the district's curriculum coordinator (who had no special training in immigrant education or ELL issues) became contentious. Again, a policy that seemed to be straightforwardly about increasing classroom instructors' capabilities was actually much more complicated than that.

Chapter 11 describes the fate of the bilingual education component that the visiting instructors were supposed to help implement. Complicated by changes in this component's leadership at the Monterrey end and then by the host community's new awareness of and resistance to bilingual education, as California's bilingual education-ending Proposition 227 was covered in the national media, the curriculum was never formally implemented. Ironically, the idea that the Georgia Project was a bilingual education program remained widespread. Political maneuvering related to this component was complicated, becoming a main reason for an emergent schism between school district officials and the attorney who remained the project's most dogged community-based advocate.

The Mexican scholars who led the Universidad de Monterrey's participation in the partnership were sociologists; they brought a more holistic framework to their Georgia Project goals than just consulting on K–12 issues. Chapter 12 describes several other projects (all under one component heading) that they embarked on as part of the Georgia Project agreement but for which Dalton Public Schools was not a main partner. These included a community survey, an assessment of adult education programs, and the initial organizing and training of a new local Latino political action committee. All three of these activities had direct consequences for Dalton and the fate of the partnership's more school-centric components. The community survey documented many Latino parents' mistrust and frustration at the school system. The adult education assessment, which included a critique of several carpet industry-supported workplace literacy programs, bombed badly, generating an angry reaction from several of the employers who had helped initiate the Georgia Project. Their message was stark: You can help us but not criticize us. Creation of the political action committee meant for the public identification of several local Latino leaders. This was consequential in several ways; as one example, it meant that community entities such as the schools could no longer plausibly turn to bilingual Anglos (e.g., a local Catholic priest) to serve as proxies for the Latino community. As another, it has meant that Dalton has now had two Latino candidates run for school board positions, though none successfully so far.

Though the time horizon reviewed in this book spans 150 years, this third part focuses on May 1996 through May 1998, an exciting time, a time when some powerful actors in Dalton and the Universidad de Monterrey started to recognize the immense challenges and opportunities that the new presence of Latinos put before Dalton. During these months over $1 million

worth of school district, city government, and federal funds were committed
to the Georgia Project's enactment. Private companies and individuals
provided hundreds of thousands of dollars of free logistic support, occa-
sionally anonymously, as well as tens of thousands of dollars of direct
financial contributions to the effort.

Each of the four chapters (Chapters 9 through 12) that consider the prin-
ciple project components details how in the attempt to implement the
Georgia Project's quickly sketched policies, several elements were resisted,
co-opted, and/or transformed. These chapters highlight some obvious project
successes, but they also reiterate how dramatically policies as enacted can
differ from policies as described on paper. Appraising the efficacy of any of
the project's strategies requires understanding what they were, not what
they were supposed to be. Chapter 13 describes a March 1998 celebration
of the Georgia Project that was acme of the project as a three-party partnership (between the school district, the Universidad de Monterrey, and the
attorney-led citizens group that was also called the Georgia Project). After
that point, the Georgia Project grew in fame and began a number of new
initiatives (e.g., a scholarship program) but more as a community-based
organization and less as a partnership. Chapter 13 also includes two more
vignettes and two figures that highlight the multiple and quite distinct ways
the goals of the Georgia Project were variously categorized. A third figure
quotes two U.S. Senators who were instrumental in securing more recent
support for the Georgia Project.

By the middle of 1998, as my field study was wrapping up, the initial window of opportunity for educational policymaking that the project-initiating
attorney had seized began to be closed as the school district leadership no
longer automatically deferred project decision making to the attorney and
often countered his actions. The Georgia Project was initiated with a hazy
consensus to help the schools and larger community successfully negotiate
change, but the superficiality of that consensus became apparent as project
leaders began to assert and enact differing visions of what a successful
response to newcomers should look like. The promulgators of the Georgia
Project were all sincere and efficacious, but they so substantively disagreed
on *how* the Georgia Project should be conducted and *for what* that by 2002
the Georgia Project and Dalton Public Schools were hardly partners. Yet the
Georgia Project had become a welcome presence in several nearby districts.

The fourth and final part is entitled "Ephemeral Opportunity or Inclusive
New Order?" and is just one chapter long. Using the metaphor of a "window
of policymaking opportunity," it reminds us of the drama and challenge of
Dalton's ongoing demographic transformation, considers how and why the
relationships between the six key project leaders profiled in Chapters 5 and 6
changed, and appraises the success of the Georgia Project on a number of
dimensions, including its use as a pilot of strategies that could be implemented elsewhere. Chapter 14 also considers how, from a school district

standpoint, as test scores were falling and the expensive Direct Instruction program was struggling, the Georgia Project came increasingly to amount to a choice between policies. On the one hand district officials could align with the espoused goals of the Georgia Department of Education (facing substantial pressure if they did not). On the other hand were policies that might have been more responsive to the newcomers, that might have matched the professional advice of the Universidad de Monterrey collaborators, and that might have been faithful to the text of the Title VII grant that I drafted, but for which there was little understanding among non-ESOL-trained educators and the dominant non-Latino portions of the Dalton public. Thus the final chapter returns to their key points of inquiry of an ethnography of educational policy—how various beliefs, taxonomies, and understandings interrelate with policies and practices, in this case the policies and practices that composed Dalton's recent response to its new Latino majority.

Policies embed problem diagnoses and strategies for their resolution. Consider two competing problem diagnoses: (1) Newcomers' existing skills and knowledge bases are assets upon which new schooling should build; the question is how. (2) Newcomers either lack skills or have skills that are irrelevant to living in Dalton; in any event, important deficit remediation work is needed, so the question to be answered is "How can that remediation be most efficiently rendered?" Both the diagnoses and the strategies are cultural productions, reflecting assumptions about what can be done and what should be done. This is true of Dalton and it is true of places like Dalton. The chapter and book end not with the question "what should be?", but rather with the questions: What is the problem diagnosis? What are the strategies? Who gets to decide? What considerations do the decision makers find salient? When we consider the educational welcome of Latino newcomers, these are the core considerations.

# The Ethnography
# of Educational Policy

The research frame one uses dictates, to a large extent, the way one
researches these problems, the policy options one considers, the
approach one takes to policy implementation, and the approach taken
for policy evaluation.

—*Young 1999:681*

Thirty years ago, Nader (1972:289) called on anthropology to change its
traditional focus of inquiry "to study the colonizers rather than the colonized,
the culture of power rather than the culture of the powerless, the culture of
affluence rather than the culture of poverty." Despite this call to "study up"
and despite the tradition in the first half of the twentieth century for leading
anthropologists such as Margaret Mead, Ruth Benedict, and Franz Boas to
comment on policy issues of the day, only recently has anthropology begun
to conceive of itself as being a policy science in the sense of overtly identifying formal policy and policymakers as a topic of study (Shore and Wright
1997). This "johnny-come-lately" status means that the framework for an
anthropology of educational policy is nascent and still rough; indeed
another rationale for the drafting of this book is to help further flesh out
what the anthropology of educational policy can entail. This late start also
means that much of what constitutes the anthropology of educational policy is either borrowed from complementary traditions (e.g., borrowing from
the sociology of Ball [1990] and Borman et al. [1996], or the critical theory
of Foucault [1977]), or developed as a critical response to theories and

methodologies from other traditions. Levinson and Sutton's observation fits into this latter category: "We maintain that in all the scholarly discourse around policy, there is little evidence of the sociocultural perspective: a locally informed, comparative account of how people make, interpret, and otherwise engage with the policy process" (2001:4).

Much of cultural anthropology is centrally fixated on studying how people make, interpret, and otherwise engage with ideas, each other, and the physical environment that surrounds us. It follows then that accounting for how people make, interpret, and engage with the policy process can be pursued as an anthropological inquiry. Moreover, through such accounting we can demystify the policy process and can lay bare its core components—the initial problem diagnosis, the strategies for problem solving, and the culturally and experientially informed suppositions that rationalize or explain why a given strategy is presumed to be appropriate to respond to the original problem diagnosis. As Levinson and Sutton (2001:11) explain, "In the processes of policy formation, problems are constructed for solution and thus the needs of individuals and societies become subject to authoritative definition."

They also assert that:

When we pay close attention to the frameworks of cultural meaning people use to interpret their experience and generate social behavior, we see not only the recipients of educational policy but also its authorized formulators and purveyors as cultural animals as well. By highlighting the place and role of values, beliefs, and identities in the policy process, we provide analytic tools to range across the spectrum of sociocultural activity. (Levinson and Sutton 2001:2–3)

Their advice rationalizes several of the methodological steps that I pursued both in my study of Dalton and in the organization of this book. First, through the use of several complementary ethnographic techniques—participant observation, semistructured interviews, collection and review of policy documents, the use of open-ended questions on questionnaires, and so on—I could pay close attention to various key individuals who were fundamentally consequential for the shaping of the Georgia Project. Indeed, through my additional roles in Dalton as grant writer of a *Title VII—Systemwide Bilingual Education* proposal (see Chapter 8) and later as a de facto consultant regarding the Georgia Project, I frequently had a formal excuse to share ideas with various "authorized" and self-appointed formulators of Georgia Project policy and to gain a sensibility regarding their values and beliefs.

Second, the contextual background information offered in the chapter on Dalton's history (Chapter 3), the review of recent public sphere discourse regarding the newcomers (Chapter 4), and the rendering of several short biographies (Chapters 5 and 6), highlight the place of values, beliefs, and identities as they pertain to the unfolding of this story. To render these contextual chapters convincingly, I had to gather a substantial amount of background data. Much of my research efforts in Dalton were expended to that end. Based on an understanding that policymakers' and educators' ideologies— their beliefs about teaching, schooling, community, and life, all through the lens of "what should be"—influence their actions (Datnow, Hubbard, and Conchas 2001), a central tenet of this book is that the Georgia Project's various shapers contributed to and responded to the partnership in the ways that they did because of how they understood their own roles; how they acted upon their values regarding community, place, and future; and how they understood the needs and proclivities of the newcomers. They did what they did because of what they understood and what they wanted.[1]

Shore and Wright (1997:8) maintain that, "Policies are most obviously political phenomena, yet it is a feature of policies that their political nature is disguised by the objective, neutral, legal-rational idioms in which they are portrayed. In this guise, policies appear to be mere instruments for promoting efficiency and effectiveness." They add that this masking of the political under the cloak of neutrality is a key feature of the contemporary display of power.

Let us consider these claims in turn. That policies are political seems relatively easy to establish. Whether one defines the purpose of the Georgia Project as a way to assure that Latino newcomers learn English or succeed academically or become biliterate and bicultural adults—and various stakeholders asserted each of these as goals for the partnership (see Chapter 13)— each of these purposes is a political purpose, proposing *what should be*. Yet it seems that there are at least two ways that the political nature of policies can be obscured. One, noted earlier, is that the language used to describe policy can appear objective and rational, rather than subjective. Defenses of both the bilingual curriculum proposed by the Universidad de Monterrey and of the English-monolingual phonics-based Direct Instruction program that competed with it were framed in terms of "what the research said." Research and its cousin *science* do not seem political (even if they are [Nader 1996]).

Another explanation for why the political nature of policy may be obscured is that policy can seem so normal, so familiar that the underlying problem diagnoses and purposes remain unconscious, cloaked in a naturalistic sensibility that that is just how things are done. Administrators making decisions that are in their formal purview may well neither self-reflect nor draw external scrutiny regarding those decisions' political nature. Acting normally may not feel political, even when it is.

Finally, because the discourse surrounding an educational policy obscures the political nature of policy through the use of scientific idioms, because the enactment of policy by those accustomed to being policymakers (e.g., superintendents, curriculum coordinators, and principals) is so routine as to be unquestioned, and/or because the creation of policy by those unaccustomed to seeing themselves as policymakers (e.g., professors) is unrecognized as policymaking, the fact that each of these three scenarios embeds the play of power is also obscured. Yet power is very much a part of the story rendered here.

Foucault, describing policy as a political technology for both the acquisition and expression of power, makes a distinction between groups and individuals who are "objects of information" and those who are "subjects of communication" (1977:200), noting that the former have substantially less power. Latino newcomers in Dalton were objects of information, the focal point of planners of the Georgia Project, but mostly they were not subjects of communication. Their voices were included only indirectly through, for example, the Mexican scholars' community needs assessment and their report on the initial effort to form a Latino leadership organization. (See Chapter 12 for more on these efforts.) The prerogatives asserted by Georgia Project planners—be they from the Dalton schools, the private sector, or the Universidad de Monterrey—were expressions of power. The planners had the power to determine a program of action for Dalton's Latino newcomers. Of course, that was not the only way power was manifested in this story.

Levinson and Sutton (2001:2) make a bow to Foucault and other critical theorists with their assertion that, "Policy serves at various levels of government as a legitimating charter for the techniques of administration and as an operating manual for everyday conduct; it is the symbolic expression of normative claims worked into a potentially viable institutional blueprint." Most of the case study considers the relationship between legitimating charters and techniques of administration.

Less obviously, but still crucially, several rationales in circulation ostensibly supporting the Georgia Project also had the power of expressing normative claims and providing an operating manual for everyday conduct. As two quick examples, consider the decision to have the trained visiting bilingual instructors from Mexico be classified as "parapros" (see Chapter 9). This was done in part because Georgia laws did not recognize Mexican credentials, but it had the consequence of allowing classroom teachers to treat the visitors as if they were paraprofessionals, rationalizing the consignment of the visitors to the most marginal spaces in Dalton's overcrowded schools (e.g., the corridor, or a broom closet converted into a tutoring space) and rationalizing a managerial relation between the classroom teacher and the visiting instructors that made the teachers' unilateral determination of lesson plans (which the visiting instructors were then to follow) seem natural and appropriate. Thus the visiting instructors' actual expertise in bilingual instruction and working with Mexican students was often neglected. Consider also the April 1997 editorial in the local newspaper (*The Daily Citizen-News* 1997c) that endorsed the Georgia Project as a way to teach newcomers English and thereby provided a highly particular lens through which the success or failure of the partnership could be judged (see Chapter 8).

In keeping with Shore and Wright's recommendation that the ethnography of policy should do more than study up, my research methodology was also consistent with Reinhold's notion of "studying through" (cited in Shore and Wright [1997:14])—that is, tracing the ways in which power creates webs and relations between actors, institutions, and discourses across time and space. "Studying through" entails multisite ethnography, as the actors in the "policy community" frequently operate in and are informed by different geographic spaces. In conducting this research, I visited administrative offices and classrooms in Georgia and Mexico. I sat in on the majority of the face-to-face encounters between Georgia and Mexico partners in 1997 and 1998, and I collected about 1,000 pages of documentation (e.g., faxes, letters) of much of their communication that was not face-to-face. I even invented a context for Georgia-based and Mexico-based project leaders to interact in April 2000, when, with my colleagues at Brown University, I co-organized a day-long seminar on the Georgia Project in Rhode Island as part of an institute on cultural and linguistic diversity that was attended by 150 educators and researchers. The attorney and the curriculum coordinator profiled in Chapter 5 were among the featured guests, as were a researcher/program coordinator from Monterrey, a teacher from the innovative elementary school (see Chapters 5 and 7), and a former employee of the Georgia Department of Education.

To better understand the Dalton context, I visited the workplaces of Latino newcomers and the corporate offices of their employers and pored through every issue of the daily local newspaper from 1993 through 1998. I drew from previous experience living and working in Mexican sending communities and teaching in bilingual adult immigrant education programs in U.S. receiving communities (in Kansas and Georgia). I also spent a lot of time in Dalton classrooms interviewing educators and observing instruction. In particular, I visited all of the classrooms of Dalton teachers who went to Monterrey for the first summer training institute in 1997 and "shadowed" all fourteen of the first cohort of visiting instructors from Monterrey. I conducted most of my fieldwork in 1997 and 1998, but have remained in contact with Georgia Project's founding attorney and with Dalton schools and Universidad de Monterrey-affiliated personnel. I have also benefited from the more recent ethnographic inquiry by Lisa Goode that resulted in a dissertation (Goode 2002) about the Georgia Project that focuses on the post-1998 period when my direct inquiry was reduced.

Thirteen years ago Rosaldo (1989:7) warned that, "If classic ethnography's vice was the slippage from the ideal of detachment to actual indifference, that of present-day reflexivity is the tendency for the self-absorbed Self to lose sight altogether of the culturally different Other." I acknowledge that warning and do not want to indulge in too lengthy an autobiography. But it is crucial for readers to have information useful for determining how credible they find me. That is to say, it behooves me to try to let readers know where I am coming from now as an author and also what it was that I was trying to do in Dalton. They can then account for the inevitable bias that influences how I have told this story. Erickson (1984:60) writes: "[As a researcher,] I should at least make explicit to you the point of view I brought to the site and its evolution while I was there, as well as the point of view with which I left." Conceding that I have a point of view does not mean that I neglected to be empirical. Accuracy—that is, descriptive and interpretive validity (Maxwell 1992)—was (and should have been) a paramount goal in this study. Still, from the beginning of my involvement in Dalton, I was intentionally more than just a doctoral student and even in my capacity as a doctoral student I brought with me my background experiences and related orientations. Toma (2000) suggests that being an interested party can be an important asset for conducting qualitative inquiry as it can help the interaction with research subjects to become more transactional and thus more substantive and intimate. I was an interested party in Dalton trying to help launch the Georgia Project and to help the schools be more responsive than other locations have been to their Latino newcomers.

For those trained in more positivist disciplines than contemporary anthropology, the nonchalance of my confession to bias may seem disconcerting, but in my discipline to feign an absence of bias would be more problematic. As Trueba and Zou, two educational anthropologists maintain, "If we had to identify the single most important departure from traditional research canons and practices at the turn of the twentieth century . . . we probably would have to say that researchers can no longer retain political neutrality or hide their political values behind the pretense of objectivity or the shield of methodological or theoretical purity" (1998:3). By acknowledging my politics and values I hope to position the reader to account for them. I am also following in the action anthropology footsteps outlined by Sol Tax more than half a century ago. The goal of action anthropology as developed by Sol Tax and described by van Willigen (1986) and Hackenberg (1993) is to improve a community's capacity for self-determination. Action anthropology is value-explicit, meaning the researcher states his or her own interests, including diagnoses of what ought to be.

If, as I posit, the larger framework for this study is the ethnography of educational policy, then the particular genre within that framework that characterizes how I have tried to engage in this study and to interact with people involved with the Georgia Project is the genre of "research as collective practice." According to Adams et al. (2001, p. 61):

Core assumptions of the "research as collective praxis" model are that (a) researchers acknowledge and act upon their political commitments and (b) they do so in the context of theorizing and practice (i.e., praxis) with both professionals and non-professionals, such as students and community members (Fine, 1989; Gitlin, et al.,

1992; Reinharz, 1984; Vio Brossi & de Wit, 1981). In this way, the line between "researcher" and "policymaker" or "practitioner" becomes blurred as those who identify (or are typified) primarily as playing one of these roles in fact play both. Not only do policymakers, administrators, teachers, students, and community members participate in research, but "researchers" become active participants in various settings, working with others to understand and change schools and society.

As I have alluded already, I first came to Dalton in the "active participant" role at the invitation of the curriculum coordinator who chose to hire me as an outside consultant and ultimately lead author for a *Title VII— Systemwide Bilingual Education* grant proposal (Dalton Public Schools 1997) that the district wanted to craft and submit. (It was the district's decision to seek money in the *Systemwide* category of the Title VII allocation.) Though I was always explicit about my intent to be a researcher (and welcomed as such), and though my notebook and/or tape recorder were consistently visible, I came to Dalton as more than a researcher, wearing the hats of policymaker (of whatever efficacy), employee, and advocate as well. When the grant was funded, in many circles I was not just the researcher, but also the writer who helped obtain $500,000 for the Georgia Project and the district. In other words, my roles blurred and some of them were overtly political. In the spirit of "critical reflectivity" (Young 1999:689), I need to remind myself to consider how these political roles might bear on what I saw and how I have rendered it here. I have tried to position readers to deliberate about the same.

I accepted the grant-writing appointment not just because it was "a way in," or because it was a way to earn $2,000, though it was both of those things. For me, the grant-writing effort itself was something I believed in. It was a continuation of a long series of efforts dating back to when I was in high school and restlessly, naively, and self-righteously trying to figure out a way "to make the world better."

At age 16, in 1985, I volunteered for a summer with a community sanitation project in the Darien rain forest in Panama. That was my first sustained contact with Latin Americans and Latin America. For six weeks, with just one partner from North America, I lived in a village of about 200 Panamanians along a spur road about ten kilometers south of the unfinished Pan-American highway. That summer and four subsequent summers of similar work in Ecuador and several parts of Mexico shocked and changed my worldview; I learned how to communicate in a different language (i.e., Spanish) and to negotiate and respect various cultural milieus with rules quite distinct from those of my suburban Boston hometown.

I acknowledge that there is quite a distance—physically, chronologically, and psychologically—from Panama to Dalton, Georgia, so I will also make quick reference to some key stops in between. Because of my work in Latin America, in college I majored in Latin American studies as well as education.

Because of the Latin American studies major, upon graduation I was handed a letter written by a recent alumna seeking candidates for a job teaching an experimental bilingual family literacy class at a public library in Kansas City, Kansas. I took that job and for two years worked with immigrant parents primarily from Mexico. For those same two years I attended professional development activities sponsored by the National Council of La Raza, a national advocacy organization for Latinos and the source of the experimental literacy curriculum.

I learned quite a lot from my literacy students including how much they did and did not know about the schools their children attended and how those same schools treated them. In particular I remember that many of my students could name the bilingual paraprofessional who was their key intermediary to the school and often an instructor for their child (in pullout tutorials), but those same parents often did not know the name of their child's regular classroom teacher. By virtue of the association with the National Council of La Raza, I interacted with educators from other Latino-oriented community organizations elsewhere in the country and became accustomed to thinking about what was particular to my Kansas City site compared to larger trends encountered by colleagues elsewhere. Clearly, many of the things I was looking for in Dalton were things that my Kansas City literacy students had taught me to think about. Equally clearly, I brought to Dalton a binary frame, noting Dalton as a particular place, with a particular history and mix of people, and noting Dalton as an example of an immigrant receiving community like many many others around the country.

As I was ending my stint as a literacy teacher and beginning master's work in anthropology at the University of Kansas, I met the coordinator of bilingual and ESL services at the Kansas Department of Education, who was also an anthropologist. That administrator took me under his wing, securing several minor evaluation contracts for me, including an evaluation of the state's use of a Title VII grant. He also arranged to pay me to study what bilingual paraprofessionals working in Kansas City, Kansas, elementary schools did and to assist with one of the six receiving sites—Great Bend Kansas—of a distance-learning course on alternative assessment for ELLs that was taught through the state's closed-circuit two-way television network. I later built on both of these experiences to write my master's thesis on bilingual paraprofessionals functioning as intermediaries between Spanish-speaking households and Anglo public schools (Hamann 1995). The six paraprofessionals who I most closely studied deeply and favorably impressed me in regards to how well they knew the students they worked with and knew the informal rules of interaction that governed the behavior of adults in their schools. I have little doubt that this favorable orientation toward "parapros" also affected what I saw during my multiple visits to Dalton schools and made me particularly disposed to be disturbed by the dismissive treating of the visiting instructors from Monterrey (formally classified as "parapros") by some Dalton educators (see Chapter 9).

My relationship with the coordinator at the Kansas Department of Education was consequential in two other ways. Prior to going to work for the state, he had been involved with the Ford Foundation-funded Changing Relations Project research team that had studied Garden City Kansas' response to a dramatic influx of Latinos (Stull et al. 1992). In Dalton I was predisposed to see community change through the lens of what I had learned from the coordinator and from the literature about the Changing Relations Project that he had directed me to (e.g., Grey 1991; Lamphere 1992; Lamphere et al. 1994; Stull et al. 1995). Because of the Kansas coordinator, when I moved to Georgia in 1996 one of my first stops was a visit with the then-coordinator of Migrant Education and English to Speakers of Other Languages (ESOL) at the Georgia Department of Education. This Georgia coordinator played an essential role in my entrée to Dalton, passing my name along as a potential grant writer. She and many of her colleagues also became important informants as I tried to understand the state-level policy response to Latino newcomers (Hamann 1997a).

It was with that experiential background that I came to the task of drafting the Title VII grant proposal that I prepared for Dalton in the winter of 1997. At the school district's invitation and using their collaboration and descriptions of the emergent Georgia Project, I crafted a vision of schooling that promised diverse community input, suggested extensions and adaptations of existing programs (e.g., teacher training activities and academic summer camps), expected thoughtful reflection, and developed two-way bilingual instruction capabilities eventually at every grade level for those who wanted it. That much of the strategic plan incorporated in the grant proposal was not enacted was a source of personal frustration that I have tried to check in the remainder of this document, though it no doubt slips through.

My frustration regarding the Title VII proposal was tempered by the fact that much of the initial promise of the Georgia Project was enacted. If inclusion of Latino parents in a Title VII community advisory committee never occurred because such a committee was never convened (despite the grant proposal's promise of this end), it was still the case that Latino newcomer parents and other Latino leaders were convening as a group for the first time under the auspices of the Georgia Project. The prospect of raised Latino community voices helping to shape the larger community was intact, if by a different means. Much of what I wanted (and obviously many others wanted) did happen.

Because I came to Dalton with a discrete and short-term purpose in hand (grant writing), my first and best contacts there were the leaders of the school district. Because chronicling local need was one starting point for our relationship, the generally optimistic leaders not only shared rosy scenarios with me but also acknowledged at least some of the struggles they confronted.

Thus my conversations with Georgia Project planners effectively high-lighted their evolving understanding of the challenges brought forward by the new presence of Latinos. A related starting point for our relationship was my need to understand the still sketchy structure and purported intent of the binational partnership they were creating so that I could write convincingly about how that partnership responded to local challenges and merited funding.

In Dalton I was privy to the tentative problem constructions engaged in by leaders. In my capacity as grant writer, I helped them articulate an authoritative, "official" policy in response. I was told that the Georgia Project would be their primary educational policy response to demographic change and to its related challenges to identity and community, though an alternative response—the broad introduction of fully scripted, monolingual, phonetics-oriented Direct Instruction program—later became a rival policy response as the coalition that created the binational partnership began to fracture.

I first met the Mexican partners before the $500,000 Title VII grant was approved and before the attorney who founded the Georgia Project had prevailed on the Dalton City Council to contribute $750,000 to the new partnership. My ability to speak Spanish (albeit as a second language), my background of having worked and studied in rural Mexico and with Mexican immigrants in the United States (which meant I was more versed in their area of scholarly expertise than anyone else they encountered in Dalton), my then-residence in Georgia (and relevant awareness of statewide currents of educational politics) and my shared status as an outsider to Dalton (though one familiar with the insiders) made me a useful sounding board for the Monterrey team. When I visited their university in Mexico for four days in 1998, my visit became an occasion for them to highlight their Georgia work within their university community—as I was asked to make a formal presentation. In turn, I was invited to stay at the home of one of the Mexican partnership leaders and I was given open access to all of the files the Mexican leaders kept regarding the partnership (except for individual evaluations of visiting instructor candidates sent to Georgia). I had an arranged interview with their university's president and I had a chance to spend a day at a private Mexican trilingual primary school with that school's director. That director became the second bilingual coordinator that Monterrey sent to Dalton who figures prominently in Chapter 11. I also met with the Mexican leaders during most of their visits to Georgia. In 2001 I was coeditor of a volume to which they contributed (Zuñiga et al. 2001).

One aspect of my political project in Dalton and in this book is to join others in problematizing the goal of assimilation for the newcomers. In taking such a stance I am using Grey's (1991:80) definition of assimilation: "Assimilation . . . is a one-way process in which the outsider is expected to change in order to become part of the dominant culture." By emphasizing the processual nature of assimilation, its unilateral orientation, and unequal power differential between outsider and insider, Grey's definition echoes Teske and Nelson's (1974) and that of the Social Science Research Council's Seminar on Acculturation of 1953, which declared, "Assimilation implies an essentially unilateral approximation of one culture in the direction of the other, albeit a changing or ongoing other" (Barnett et al. 1954:988).

Delpit (1988), an African American educational scholar, has famously warned of the hazards of liberal Anglos self-righteously declaring that non-white students should not be expected to master the tenets of the dominant culture at school. She notes that self-appointed advocates can contribute to the undereducation of those same students who we are allegedly advocating for. It was not my place in Dalton nor here to argue against new learning. In fact, I agree with Delpit's argument that such acculturation is important to newcomers' opportunity horizons. Rather my protest is against peda-gogical and curricular orientations that assume the linguistic and cultural "funds of knowledge" (Gonzalez et al. 1995; Moll et al. 1992) of the Latino newcomers are of little long-term use for those same newcomers and thus merit no acknowledgment or development at school. I am not opposed to the additive dimension of learning a new culture; indeed I think the oppor-tunity horizons of Latino newcomers in Dalton improve in proportion to their mastery of middle-class dialects, habits, and norms. Rather I am opposed to the subtractive expectation of assimilation.

I have consciously chosen to name my research site here for several care-fully considered reasons and not just because trying to hide the unique iden-tity of the "Carpet Capital of the World" would have forced fictionalizing or ignoring key details of my analysis. First, I never promised anonymity to the small group of Georgia Project leaders who could be identified here. (I did promise anonymity to the Dalton teachers and to the visiting instruc-tors from Monterrey who filled out surveys for me and their individual identities should be untraceable here.)

Second, though I do not use personal names (thinking it gratuitous in this instance), I do want those leaders who are familiar with the Georgia Project to be able to identify themselves and other leaders. Knowing that they will be able to do so puts pressure on me to avoid being slanderous and to push extra hard to see the emic rationale for their behaviors and actions. Echoing Sarason (1990) whose book *The Predictable Failure of Educational Reform* figures prominently in many of the following chapters, there were no vil-lains in Dalton. I refuse to characterize any of the individuals described here as having acted with malice. They did not. However, in honoring their sin-cerity, I do not want to pretend that actions they took were all in line with what I thought would be most helpful to Latino newcomers in Dalton and all other community members there as well. I want my collaborators in Dalton to recognize themselves here, to be proud of what they have attempted, and to see, when relevant, what I think were the existing or prospective limitations of some portions of their effort.

Furthermore, naming the research site strikes me as consistent with Nader's (1972) "studying up" orientation and with action anthropology (van Willigen 1986), meaning that the citizens who are affected by the Georgia Project, such as those who are leading it, deserve as unhindered access to an analysis of it as possible. I believe that hiding identities by obscuring or fictionalizing details interferes with that access. Doing so also interferes with Erickson's (1984:59) charge that "the ethnographer should provide readers with guidelines for the falsification of the analysis, should a reader decide to replicate the study." It is impossible to replicate a study if one does not know where the study was conducted or with whom the researcher interacted. Though Goode (2002) and I agreed on many points in our separate studies of the Georgia Project, the only reason she knew how to mark our differences is because she was able to know who I had talked to and what I had looked at as I assembled my dissertation, the precursor to this current volume.

On more than one occasion the attorney who began the Georgia Project, the superintendent, and others involved with the project asked me what I thought of the project, what I was finding, what they ought to do differently. This document and its predecessors, notably my dissertation (Hamann 1999), can be read as answers to that question. I hope it is accepted in the same spirit as those leading the ATLAS Project and those leading the Coalition of Essential School accepted the scrutiny of ethnographers (Hatch 1998; Muncey and McQuillan 1996; McQuillan 1998)—scrutiny that is uncomfortable perhaps or even embarrassing, but that can improve the project and thus help realize the project leaders' agendas.

In sum then, this book is an ethnography of educational policy, intended to capture the meaning making engaged in by the cultural animals (i.e., humans) who led the binational educational response to Dalton's changed demography. It follows that if I am going to label the key leaders of the Georgia Project as "cultural animals," then I should be willing to attach that label and its consequence to my own identity and perspective as well. In articulating how I was involved in Dalton, I have tried to position the reader to factor in details from my own biography that no doubt affected what I saw and learned from the Georgia Project and how I have rendered it here.

# Part Two

# Places, Scripts, and People: The Particularities of People and Settings

# 125 Years of Race, Class, and Corporate Paternalism in Dalton

Frederick Erickson has asserted that, "Educational research should search out sites in which the struggle for progressive transformation can take place" (1987:352). In the mid-1990s Dalton, Georgia, was such a place as various new and old and local and exogenous factors temporarily aligned in an unusual but potent formation. The ideologies, impulses, and understandings from local sources that were in play in Dalton's public sphere included ongoing pride in its long history of quality schooling, expectations of continued personalized corporate largesse (i.e., philanthropy), a transforming rivalry between the incorporated city of Dalton and the surrounding unincorporated expanse of Whitfield County, a normalized (i.e., largely accepted) stratification along socioeconomic lines with racial dimensions, and a growing disquiet about the substantial influx of Latino newcomers. Dalton and Whitfield were also affected by state, region, and national responses to the challenges of schooling Latino newcomers. Dalton was an atypically wealthy community in comparison to most of Appalachia and most of nonmetropolitan Georgia. In comparison to many "New Latino Diaspora sites" (Wortham et al. 2001), Dalton also hosted an unusually high preponderance of locally owned, Latino-employing businesses.

Durrenberger and Thu (2000:48) have argued that anthropology should "focus our attention on the relevant structures of the political economies that create the conditions to which individuals must adapt." The point of this chapter is to describe the origin of several of the dynamics noted in the previous paragraph and to clarify how each ties to the other dynamics and why each is salient for an understanding of the Georgia Project. However, primary consideration of the disquiet generated by Dalton's growing "Latinization" is deferred to the next chapter. The intent here is not to consider how Dalton and Whitfield County compare to various models in the social sciences literature, though some of that literature is referred to; rather the chapter's emphasis is on the specific circumstances (i.e., the history) that made Dalton and Whitfield County fertile enough locales for the Georgia Project to emerge and take hold.

## INDUSTRIALIZATION, EMPLOYEE RECRUITMENT, AND CREATION OF A SCHOOL DISTRICT

Dalton's formal settlement as the town of Cross Plains in the 1840s, less than a decade after the forced removal of the indigenous Cherokees in the Trail of Tears, meant that there were some local whites twenty years later to join the Confederacy's resistance to General Sherman's first incursion into Georgia. However, potent as the Civil War might still be for the general imaginary of many locals, the history of Dalton that is salient to the Georgia Project actually begins just a little later and has a little-noted Latin America tie-in.

Shortly after the Civil War, Dalton started to grow as an agricultural center as the importation of *guano* fertilizer (bat droppings) from Peru permitted local cultivation of cotton by sufficiently shortening the growing season (Flamming 1992). This production and Dalton's position at the junction of two rail lines made it a natural site for a few small-scale merchants to set themselves up as intermediaries between local cotton cultivators and the Northern textile industry. Though still a poor town in the midst of poor hinterlands, by the 1880s Dalton was home to several merchants with substantial savings. Hoping to protect and grow their wealth through involvement in other pursuits beyond cotton trading, these merchants decided to become part of the nascent industrial order of the New South. With little experience to guide them, they opened Dalton's first factory—the Crown Mill—in 1885.

The Crown Mill was a success, operating until 1969. From the beginning, the Crown Mill and the other mills attracted a white labor supply from the nearby Appalachian countryside, and Dalton grew as a consequence. In the Crown Mill's first decade of operation, workers came from rural parts of surrounding Whitfield County and five other nearby counties (Flamming 1992:32). During the decades after it opened, the mill was expanded on several occasions and a few other cotton mills were constructed in and near Dalton. While the Crown Mill was in operation, Dalton's population grew from 2,516 in 1880, to 4,315 in 1900, 5,222 in 1920, 10,448 in 1940, and 17,686 in 1960. (The 2000 U.S. Census counted 27,912 Daltonians and a total Whitfield County population of 83,525.)

In the introduction to his history of the Crown Mill, Flamming notes: "Dalton's black population is not much in evidence here because my focus is on the Crown Mill, a company that never hired a black person for any kind of job. Ever. Nor, so far as I can tell, did any of the other cotton mills in Dalton" (1992:xxx). In 1890, Dalton was about 30 percent black; by 1930 blacks were only about 10 percent of the population (Flamming 1992: xxix). In the 1990s, Dalton was about 8 percent African American, and there was some public sentiment that historic discrimination should be redressed.[1] Despite its relatively small African American population, Dalton had hosted a segregated African American-only school into the 1960s (i.e., more than a decade after the *Brown v. Board of Education* Supreme Court decision). Only in the 1980s did the century-long gradual decline of the local African American population stop. Despite Dalton's relative economic success in relation to most of Appalachia, African Americans have been historically excluded, first through "legal" segregation and since by inadequate amends—inadequate as measured by recent economic statistics showing that, for example, 7 percent of white households in Whitfield had annual incomes over $75,000 while only 0.7 percent of black households did (*The [Dalton] Daily Citizen-News* 1995).

Because Dalton/Whitfield's black population was historically small and proportionally declining, a second segment of the population was also materially marginalized and characterized as problematic in much public discourse.[2] Like the subjects in Gibson's Florida study (1996), in Dalton and surrounding North Georgia there was an identifiable population of low-income whites with limited school experience and high usage rates of welfare and other government aid programs. This population, which would be designated either *Appalachian* or *Southern* by those engaged in regional studies, was sometimes overtly stigmatized with labels like "redneck" and "poor white trash." Even when not referred to in such terms, this population was sometimes used as a negative referent by local Anglo white-collar professionals when contrasted with the growing Latino immigrant population.[3] I am getting ahead of myself, however.

Dalton's initial industrialization occurred nearly concomitant with the reemergence of the tufted bedspread homecraft.[4] Led by Catherine Evans Whitener, several Dalton women began sewing and selling tufted bedspreads for a profit at the start of the twentieth century. Because bedspread making diversified household income strategies, thus reducing economic vulnerability, the practice quickly caught on during the first decades of the twentieth century as new links to Northern and Southern department stores expanded the market and increased demand. In the 1920s and 1930s, bedspread production became more efficient with the introduction of various machines and the creation of some outside-of-the-home production facilities. The introduction of federal minimum wage laws as part of the New Deal hastened the transition to mechanization as the mandated labor costs associated with hand production became too high in relation to the price of the finished product (Deaton 1993).

These occurrences are relevant to the present study for several reasons. The opening of the mills marked Dalton's emergence as a small industrial center, while the production of tufted bedspreads was a precursor to the emergence of tufted rug and carpet production and an impetus for the invention of new machinery and the creation of additional types of tufted products. The mills and the tufted bedspread industry mark the beginning of the conversion of northwest Georgia from a primarily subsistence economy (with some cash crop production) to a wage-and-cash economy with national and international linkages. Both led to the emergence of regional labor recruitment networks, but not to the rejection of the preexisting racial hierarchy. In fact, echoing what Gibson (1996) found in Shellcracker Haven, Florida, Dalton's early industrialization may have exacerbated existing racial hierarchies as mill managers raised the status of mill work not by raising wages but by preserving such work as a privilege available only to whites. Early on and continuing through the period of my field research, these regional recruitment networks were strained by a finite local potential labor supply and the competition from the larger nearby markets of Chattanooga and Atlanta.

By popular account, the insufficient amount of available local labor in the 1980s led to the elaboration of transnational labor recruitment networks linking Dalton to Mexico. More accurately, there was an insufficient supply of local labor willing to work at the available wages. In the absence of Mexican migration, it is hard to project how the carpet companies would have adapted, but at least in the short term they surely would have raised wages (perhaps at the risk of losing their profitability and deciding to relocate production elsewhere).

As it happened, wages in the 1990s did not rise particularly. Instead, the labor supply expanded as thousands of Hispanics—mostly Mexican immigrants—came to Dalton.[5] The pioneer antecedents of this influx count back to 1969 when the first Mexican immigrants came to Dalton by way of Dallas, Texas, as part of a dam construction crew. By the late 1990s, several Anglo informants and a Latino newspaper editor were declaring that the Latino presence in Dalton had come to provide a crucial foundation for the city's continued economic security.

Because of the multinode nature of sending and receiving links, Dalton in the late 1990s was also connected through the same linkage processes to several pools of Hispanic laborers already located in the United States. Elsewhere in the United States labor recruitment strategies of poultry and meatpacking businesses have led to dramatic growth in local Latino populations (Broadway 1994; Griffith 1995; Hackenberg 1995; Stull et al. 1992). The presence of a ConAgra poultry processing plant seemed to facilitate the linkage between other Dalton employers and immigrant newcomers.[6]

In accordance with Tienda's (1989) observations about the maturation of migrant streams, in the 1990s the links between Dalton and Mexico meant the arrival not just of more laborers, but also, increasingly, of the children, spouses, and other relatives of the laborers. Job growth in Whitfield County averaged 4.2 percent from 1991 to 1996, more than twice the officially measured rate of population growth (Barry 1997).

"Popular account" is the most accurate way to describe the widespread, late 1990s belief that Hispanic newcomers had come to Dalton to fill vacancies in the carpet industry. (The role of ConAgra was usually not brought up.) But that belief may have been a simplification, or even a mischaracterization, of some of the dynamics driving Dalton's Hispanic influx. As noted, Dalton had to confront the challenge of attracting workers practically from the beginning of its industrialization; economic growth often outpaced population growth. In locals' conscious and subconscious, the story line, or script, of Dalton needing to look beyond its city limits and even the county and state lines to find workers, was deep and long established. Affirming the story line were explanations such as former World Carpet CEO Shaheen Shaheen's recollection that in the early 1970s there were 4,000 job vacancies in Dalton. He remembered that his company ran van pools to Chattanooga, Ellijay, Lafayette, and Summerville to bring in sufficient numbers of workers (Shaheen 1984:92). The murmured tales of alleged recruiting efforts in Mexico by Dalton employers would seem only to be logical extensions of this long-running need and the local story line.[7]

But it may not be that thousands of Hispanics came to Dalton just because of a shortage of workers. Most of the Hispanic influx into Dalton postdated the carpet industry's employment boom. In a mid-1990s Shaw Industries' Annual Report, the CEO noted that the carpet industry had become a mature industry; he even said the industry had been losing market share to other forms of interior decoration for the last ten years (1996:2–3).

According to Census Bureau business data, in March 1989 the carpet and rug industry in Whitfield County employed 15,752 workers earning a combined annual salary and wage of $336,276,000 (U.S. Department of Commerce 1991:231);[8] in March 1994 the industry employed slightly *fewer* people in Whitfield County—15,463—and their aggregate salaries/wages of $384,421,000 represented a total increase of only 16 percent per person over the five-year period, essentially no increase at all after factoring for inflation (U.S. Department of Commerce 1996:150).[9] Thousands of Hispanic laborers and their families came to Dalton in the last fifteen years of the twentieth century to take jobs in a mature industry with little job or wage growth. Why?

Perhaps the answer is that the carpet industry was in the midst of a dynamic similar to that occurring in some other mature, nonunionized U.S. manufacturing industries. (See Griffith 1995; Hackenberg 1995; Lamphere 1992; Lamphere et al. 1994). According to Mencken's (1996) analysis of employment trends in Appalachia from 1983 to 1988, Appalachian counties with significant labor-intensive manufacturing saw no discernible changes in manufacturing employment despite their exposure to increased global competition. Manufacturers appeared to have pursued a two-strand strategy of capital investment and reducing wages for unskilled positions. Mencken's analysis would seem to fit for the carpet industry. Dalton's leading producers invested hundreds of millions of dollars during the 1980s and 1990s as they automated large portions of the production process. Dalton's salary and wage numbers also suggest Mencken's de-skilling/wage-reducing hypothesis is plausible.

Hispanic laborers willing to work for lower wages, or at least to work for wages that were not growing, began replacing much of the carpet industry's existing workforce, though not necessarily displacing it, as unemployment figures in Dalton/Whitfield remained low. The departing carpet industry workers may well have been drawn to better jobs that were available because of Whitfield County's general job growth. Such a dynamic would explain the relative (though not complete) absence of complaints about workplace displacement. Also, a successful campaign by Dalton and Whitfield schools in the late 1980s for carpet producers to curtail hiring students not yet finished with high school might not only have reduced the dropout rate, it may have reduced the locally available entry-level job takers, also raising the demand for Latino newcomer laborers. Remaining longtime carpet employees, eyeing an ever-growing Latino labor pool, may have been too anxious about their own job security to press for higher wages or other improvements that would normally accommodate a tight labor market. In the latter scenario, some interethnic tension and misunderstanding would be a plausible if unfortunate outcome.

Ethnic or class tensions related to Dalton/Whitfield employment did not originate with the Hispanic influx, however. Nor did the various civic and private business efforts to avert such tensions and to safeguard the quality of community life. One long-standing dynamic with origins in Dalton's initial industrialization was corporate paternalism with its concomitant attention to education. Through the time of my fieldwork, this corporate benevolence was characterized by enlightened self-interest, a community orientation, and highly personalized implementation. As early as 1910, mill owners built the Crown Point School to serve workers' children in the growing Crown Mill village.[10] Perhaps one of their motives was recognition that their more literate employees were also more productive. Literacy seemed to correlate with an improved bottom line (Flamming 1992:116).

Flamming (1992) reports Crown Mill's bias in favor of hiring heads of household and its leaders' willingness to pay more experienced employees a higher wage (higher in comparison to other Crown Mill employees; Crown Mill salaries tended to lag in relation to those available in other Southern cotton mill towns). Both of these tendencies reflect a desire to retain employees rather than having to negotiate high employee turnover. In the face of the challenges of a limited local labor supply and competition for labor from larger nearby markets, positive corporate involvement in the quality of community life was a means to attract and hold families in Dalton, simultaneously improving the community and meeting the interests of the company.

The continuation of this pattern of corporate benevolence extended through the decades and was readily visible as the Georgia Project was organized. In the 1950s, 1960s, and 1970s, Gene Barwick—who through the now defunct Barwick Industries became Dalton's first major carpet baron—was noted for his generosity to employees, their families, and the larger community. Two thousand six hundred employees and their children were direct beneficiaries of Barwick's scholarship program. Barwick also supported the development of hospitals, schools, and public services in Whitfield County and adjacent Murray and Walker Counties (Deaton 1993).

At the time of my field research, World Carpet offered scholarships and tuition reimbursements to employees and provided in-house GED programs (Deaton 1993; Shaheen 1984). Mohawk/Aladdin, which promised $50,000 to the Georgia Project in 1998, provided after-hours GED tutorials and other types of adult education to employees and their families. In the early 1990s, Collins and Aikman executives donated money and time for the creation of a school-to-work apprenticeship program that drew enthused attention from the Appalachian Regional Commission (C. Hoffman 1993).

In its 1996 Annual Report, Shaw Industries—then the largest carpet manufacturer in the world (Jackson 1997a) and headquartered in Dalton—emphasized its belief in the importance of offering continuing education opportunities to employees and "providing exciting opportunities for long-term careers" (Shaw Industries 1997:6). In 1996, Georgia Public Television and the Georgia Department of Labor recognized the company as Employer of the Year because of the educational opportunities it provided its employees (Shaw Industries 1997:7). A whole chapter of the 1996 Annual Report was devoted to corporate citizenship, starting with the statement: "We cannot separate ourselves from the communities in which we have facilities. Our common success depends on helping each other" (1997:12). Practically by definition, reports to shareholders celebrate the financial attractiveness of a company, but it is telling that Shaw put such an emphasis on community relations and loyalty to employees as central tenets of their self-defined identity.

I witnessed executives from Shaw, World Carpet, Durkan, Mohawk/Aladdin,[11] and several other mills personally visit schools and make various offers to provide help and to be more assisting when a school needed to reach a parent at their work site. One carpet company, when it discovered that one of its Mexican immigrant line employees was a trained teacher, donated his services full-time to a Dalton school while keeping him on the company salary.[12] Another carpet mill helped pay for Dalton teachers to take week-long summer courses in "survival Spanish." It is within this context that the Georgia Project's originators initially proceeded, feeling some confidence that corporate endorsement and active support would be forthcoming if the project appeared viable and needed. Indeed, several carpet industry executives were among the early promulgators/facilitators of the Georgia Project, offering not just assent but material support.

That personal involvement by business leaders remained characteristic of the Georgia Project throughout my study. In February 1998 I attended one of the irregularly scheduled meetings of the ad hoc private leadership committee overseeing the Georgia Project. After the main meeting, which included a dozen local business executives (plus school officials from Dalton and Whitfield County Schools, all of the visiting instructors from Monterrey, and several invited others), there was a second, unannounced "executive committee" meeting; budget matters and other specifics were discussed by the Dalton superintendent, the attorney who began the Georgia Project, and leaders from four of Dalton's largest mills.

Historically, the habit of corporate paternalism may have originated as a way to attract, keep, and improve workers, but it also corresponded with the communitarian orientation sometimes attributed as a traditional Appalachian characteristic (Banker 1996). The personalization of corporate generosity also matched traditional Appalachian modus operandi (Plaut 1983). Moreover, the sustenance of corporate paternalism in Dalton seemed to be related to the fact that most of the corporate decision makers were members of the community and were willing to pressure each other to be philanthropic. The CEO of one of Dalton's largest carpet producers, a man who was born and raised in Dalton, remarked that, if it was not for carpet, he and everyone else in the community would be "poor red-dirt farmers" and that he was pleased that contemporary telecommunications permitted his company to remain based in Dalton rather than seek the advantages of larger cities such as nearby Atlanta. By staying in the community, albeit in a tony neighborhood, he and other executives seemed committed to living with at least some of the consequences of how their companies affected the life of the city.

The thread of sustained corporate paternalism linking the turn of the century to the time of my study is important in several ways and may suggest that other communities would face more challenges if they tried to imitate the Georgia Project. In most cities Dalton's size that have recently experienced unprecedented and dramatic growth—for example, Gainesville, Georgia (Griffith 1995), Garden City, Kansas (Stull, Broadway, and Erickson 1992), and Storm Lake, Iowa (Grey 1995)—the companies responsible for recruiting Hispanic newcomer workers were not locally owned or based. In those instances, the externally located senior executives did not have to deal much with the community consequences of their companies' actions. When leaders from Hall County (GA) Schools and the Gainesville/Hall County Chamber of Commerce came to see the Georgia Project in action in April 1998, they were impressed by what they saw, but believed there was no one in their community who could match the roles of the Georgia Project's instigating attorney or its corporate supporters.

This highlights the special environment that Dalton offered in the late-1990s for the nurturance of the Georgia Project. To give another example of the importance that most of Dalton's business leaders were heads of locally based companies, a manager of the Dalton branch of an Atlanta-based company admitted that as a vice-president she had personal latitude to be involved in the Georgia Project, but almost no capacity to volunteer any company resources for it. Such a donation, were it to come, would need to be directed from Atlanta.

Hackenberg, in his summary for an edited volume that describes many of the ways changes in the meatpacking industry have affected small town demographics and articulated new links between these towns and distant locales, notes that one challenge for such businesses is to figure out ways to "externalize their indirect labor costs" (1995:238)—the costs of housing, health care, language instruction, skills training, and other human services. From a corporate profit standpoint, such a company's goal is to let others carry these costs (Griffith 1993). Mencken (1996) and Gaventa (1990) have noted Appalachia's disproportionate reliance on manufacturing and the region's resultant disproportionate exposure to the effects of the globalizing economy. Competing with manufacturers in lower-wage countries, Dalton business leaders would have further incentive to try to externalize as many costs as possible. At the time of my study, Dalton business leaders faced a dilemma of being pressured to boost/maintain profits in a mature industry by reducing and externalizing costs, but also to be responsive to community needs. Regarding the latter, as bearers of the region's communitarian cultural (i.e., Southern Appalachian) history and as community members who also had to live with the community consequences of externalized costs, they also had impetus to avoid the most crass of cost-cutting measures.

Not all of the corporate history of Dalton has benign or benevolent implications for the Georgia Project. The history of Dalton's industrialization also laid the roots for an important fracture that posed a special challenge to the Georgia Project. As in other industrializing locales, the leaders of Dalton's early industries held themselves as more worldly and otherwise culturally separate from much of Dalton's laboring population (Flamming 1992). Certainly they were financially distinct. This early bifurcation never fully healed and it explained, in part, both the continued cultured, cosmopolitan air of Dalton's business leadership and the correlated split between Dalton's mostly upper- and middle-class West Side and the working-class East Side. The two sides of town were literally split by railroad tracks, and the catchment areas of the six elementary schools followed the split. At the

TABLE 3.1   East Side/West Side DPS Catchment Areas (Grades Pre-K through 6)

| Student category | East Side numbers | East Side, total catchment area, % | West Side numbers | West Side, total catchment area, % |
|---|---|---|---|---|
| Black students | 162 | 13.1 | 106 | 7.5 |
| White students | 220 | 17.8 | 1,119 | 78.7 |
| Hispanic students | 835 | 67.4 | 147 | 10.3 |
| Asian students | 3 | 0.2 | 33 | 2.3 |
| American Indian | 3 | 0.2 | 3 | 0.2 |
| Multiracial | 15 | 1.2 | 14 | 1.0 |
| All students in catchment area | 1,238 | 100 | 1,422 | 100 |
| ESOL students | 232 | 18.7 | 31 | 2.2 |
| Free/reduced lunch eligible | 1,057 | 85.4 | 409 | 28.8 |
| Gifted program | 17 | 1.4 | 147 | 10.3 |
| Visiting instructors from Monterrey | 8 | N/A | 1 | N/A |

time of my study, the three "Title I" (i.e., low-income) schools in Dalton all served just the East Side catchment area. The East Side was also home to Dalton's three majority Hispanic schools; the West Side schools were still predominantly white, though their Hispanic populations were growing. While the Georgia Project officially included the entire city (and county), the first two years of Georgia Project programs were concentrated on the East Side.

Comparing the two sides of town is instructive. It highlights the city's most important fracture line, a line that long predated the Georgia Project, but that the Georgia Project nonetheless had to negotiate. Table 3.1 quantifies the difference between the two sides by showing racial/ethnic breakdowns, the number of students enrolled in English to Speakers of Other Languages, or ESOL (an imperfect tally of students with limited English proficiency and from language-minority backgrounds), the number of students who qualified for free/reduced lunch (a poverty indicator), and the number of students labeled as "gifted" and enrolled in a supplementary program of the same name.

The data presented are aggregates (grades Pre-K through 6) from Dalton's three East Side elementary schools—Roan, Morris St., and Fort Hill—and three West Side elementary schools—Westwood, Brookwood, and City Park. Representing the final year before the Georgia Project had a direct impact on Dalton schools, the original data were from the *1996–97 Georgia Public Education Report Card* (Georgia Department of Education

1998), except for the gifted program enrollments, which were obtained from the district directly in May 1998.[13] The number of visiting bilingual instructors from Monterrey serving in these schools in the spring of 1998 has been added to the bottom of the table.

Table 3.1 indicates that poverty and racial, ethnic, and linguistic minorities were concentrated in the East Side catchment area, while indicators of early opportunity, such as the gifted program, were concentrated on the West Side. Several East Side teachers and administrators who had previously taught on the West Side reported that their previous West Side colleagues had seemed bewildered by the informants' choices to take a job on the East Side. This suggests that accompanying the higher poverty rates and the higher enrollment rates of racial, ethnic, and linguistic minorities on the East Side was a sentiment held by at least some Dalton educators that the East Side was a less-desirable work environment. It was also the case that at least a few Dalton educators (i.e., some of my informants) were attracted to the East Side because of its perceived greater need.

Ironically, because of the East Side residents' historic lack of political power, the comparatively smaller changes in the Hispanic enrollment on the West Side disproportionately affected the beliefs, understandings, and political activity of Dalton's predominantly white mainstream. As Dalton became a "majority minority" district in 1997–1998, the continued buy-in and support of the school district (including the support of the Georgia Project) by the largely white mainstream was increasingly in question. Dismantling the gifted program, making it more equitable, and otherwise challenging the inequities between the two catchment areas might have been in the interest of most students (see Oakes 1985), but it would have further risked this tenuous middle-class buy-in.

Dalton business leaders had complicated and intertwined ties to their local community. Habits of generous corporate paternalism, particularly corporate involvement in education, were well entrenched in Dalton as was a darker corporate legacy of socioeconomic bifurcation marked geographically and reflected in the differences between the two school catchment areas. One legacy of this community bifurcation was the differing response by longtime community residents to the influx of Hispanic newcomers. Wealthy Daltonians, who were both more formally educated and better positioned to financially benefit from the influx of Hispanic laborers, sought alternately to ignore, avoid, and/or embrace Dalton's newcomers. Many of these Daltonians were also readily critical of the working-class and poor whites who responded with nostalgia and sometimes overt racism to Dalton's changing demography. Ironically, the nostalgic impulse of Daltonians of many classes—remembering a time when everyone knew each other, for example—mostly denied or ignored the long-standing community schisms that distinguished East Side from West Side, dropout candidate from college-bound student, and laborer from manager.

## DALTON VERSUS WHITFIELD COUNTY SCHOOLS:
## A CHANGING RIVALRY

Corporate generosity, personalized involvement, and the just-noted bifurcation were not the only consequential habits and legacies of the Dalton business community's involvement with the schools that had implications for the Georgia Project. Local support and input were central to the operation of the Dalton school system since the district was created. All the way back in 1886, a year after the Crown Mill was opened, the local leaders who were promoting Dalton's nascent development exploited a loophole in Georgia public education law that permitted cities to establish public school systems using local taxes. They established Dalton Public Schools. That same year a Baptist academy—the Joe E. Brown Institute—was acquired and reopened as Dalton's first public school (Thomas 1996).

Because of an 1872 Georgia law requiring all counties to operate a public school system, there were a few scattered public schools in the area prior to the creation of the Dalton system, but they functioned erratically and with limited resources. The 1872 law generally proscribed counties from collecting local taxes and from finding other forms of revenue, yet the state's capacity to pay for public education was also quite limited as Georgia's financial and infrastructure bases had been decimated by the Civil War. Consequently, many things competed with county schools as budgetary priorities and the total amounts available were quite small (Thomas 1996).

At the end of the nineteenth century, as Whitfield County schools limped on serving the rural population with meager state-provided resources, Dalton used town monies to serve only those children who resided within the incorporated limits of the city. So began Dalton schools' reputation for being superior to those in the county system. By necessity and opportunity, strong links of financial support and involvement were forged between Daltonians and their schools. Vestiges of these habits remained strong and obvious over one hundred years later. Though at the time of this study Dalton received substantial state funds and some federal money, $17,561,683 or 59.3 percent of Dalton Public Schools' General Fund was still provided from local sources in 1996–1997, equivalent to $3,917 per student. In contrast, the larger Whitfield County district received $17,964,921 or 34.2 percent of its General Fund from local sources, equivalent to $1,679 per student. Total expenditures per student in 1996–1997 for each district (excluding Bonded Debt, Capital Projects, and School Nutrition) were $7,189 in Dalton and $5,076 in the county (Georgia Department of Education 1998).[14] In the 1980s, Whitfield County sued to reduce the financial inequality between its school system and Dalton's, ultimately getting an increased state allotment that somewhat narrowed the gap. However, during my study period, Dalton still had a larger local allocation and that allocation was reflected in its higher rate of expenditures per student.

This proportionally high local contribution was facilitated by the City of Dalton's successful annexations of nonresidential industrial spaces, increasing its tax base without needing to increase its mill rate. This occurred at the expense of the county. Citing the high level of local tax support from business—1996 city numbers indicated that approximately 73 percent of Dalton's tax base was business (commercial or industrial)—several carpet executives suggested that their additional contributions to the Georgia Project would be modest, as they already viewed themselves as major contributors to the schools.

This raised several intriguing issues. First, though Dalton was becoming a "majority minority" district with increased risk of middle-class white flight to private schools and to improving county schools, the fact that businesses provided the bulk of tax support for the city system meant that the school district's funding base seemed somewhat less vulnerable to possible future funding reductions that would reflect middle-class residents' disenchantment with Dalton's offerings. Second, if businesses conceived of their tax payments as their primary form of support of the schools, then perhaps the Georgia Project leaders' should have been rethinking their hopes of gaining major additional financial support from businesses and instead have concentrated on converting existing school budgets to support Georgia Project programs. Indeed, early corporate support of the Georgia Project (e.g., donated frequent flier tickets supporting the Summer Institute) waned over time, as did project leaders' rhetoric about expected corporate support.

Though higher expenditures per student are, at best, a crude or blunt estimator of better schooling, Dalton's obvious prioritization of public education was historically a point of civic pride. Willing to pay for the best, in 1994 Dalton Public Schools ranked first among Georgia's 180 school districts in terms of the training and experience of its teaching force (Hamilton 1994b). This reflected, in part, the district's willingness to pay for the cost of professional graduate study and its requirement that certified teachers earn a master's degree within eight years after they started with the system. It also suggested that Dalton had a veteran teaching force, many of whom came to the district and gained significant experience prior to Dalton's ongoing demographic transformation.[15] At least some of these teachers would have been faced with a mid-career paradox: being less certain how to teach many of the students before them than they had been earlier in their career when the student population was largely white.

Until the late 1990s, Dalton residents' pride in their public schools limited the use of private education in Dalton and made living within the city limits superior to living in unincorporated parts of the county. However, as Dalton crossed over into being a majority minority district, this connection between the local citizenry and the schools appeared to be weakening. Dalton's corporate leaders began sending their children to some of the elite private schools in Chattanooga and other whites also left the system.[16]

Three years prior to the start of my study, the Dalton schools were stunned when voters rejected a school finance bond issue that was to pay for the updating and replacement of several facilities (Hamilton 1994a, 1995a). In 1997, however, Dalton voters approved a Special Purpose Local Option Sales Tax (SPLOST) to pay for the same school improvements. This suggested that the long-standing civic support of public education had not disappeared, only that it was wavering or more cautious.

In turn, the demise of a proposed merger with the larger Whitfield County system suggested some in the county no longer thought of Dalton schools as stronger. In the mid-1990s, a Dalton/Whitfield County Chamber of Commerce report entitled "Target Tomorrow"(n.d.) had recommended a merger, rekindling an on-again-off-again discussion. Considerations about merging Dalton's schools with the Whitfield County system were complicated by the different relationship city and county residents had with their respective school systems and by a history of tense relations between the two systems. City residents were accustomed to paying a little more for their schools, secure that their schools were better. The city millage rate was $18.98 in 1996–1997, ahead of the county's $17.10. However, the belief in the superiority of their system was threatened as the Georgia Project was getting started. In 1996–1997, Dalton's average SAT score of 1063 (second in the state) still bettered Whitfield County Schools' average of 1051 (fifth in Georgia) (Georgia Department of Education 1998), but not by as wide a margin as in previous years.[17]

The discrepancy between the systems had been so wide in the 1980s that the county system sued to establish a more equitable funding formula. At that point, a principal of one of the county high schools also spearheaded an intensive dropout prevention campaign that continued into the early 1990s. To remove the dropout inducing "pull" factors of prospective work, that campaign's centerpiece was the forging of agreements with dozens of local businesses to agree not to hire recent dropouts.[18] Though the campaign benefited both districts, it helped Whitfield more (because Whitfield historically had more dropouts), narrowing the quality gap between the two districts as measured by dropout statistics. (It may have also tightened local labor markets, contributing to the demand for newcomer labor.)

Though immediate plans for a school district merger were dropped when a July 1998 ballot on the proposed merger was scrapped (allegedly by the Dalton/Whitfield Chamber of Commerce when polling revealed that the plan was strongly opposed), the responses to the idea before it was dropped are revealing. In both city and county, the debate became an occasion for cultural reproduction as residents made overt their senses of community, the purposes of schooling, and their relations to each other. City residents seemed to fear a reduction in school quality if the proposed merger went ahead, while county residents eyeballed Dalton's ethnic diversity with trepidation that was epitomized by a 1995 newspaper article (Hamilton 1995c). That article, which raised the prospect of Dalton becoming a majority Hispanic district and suggested that this would raise district costs, had a headline that read: "Merger may be Dalton's last chance at education."

Prior to the 1998 ballot initiative being rescinded, rumors related to the merger discussion about forced busing and forced ethnic mixing were common and largely negative. Before the initiative was postponed, dozens of local leaders, including one Hispanic representative, contributed hundreds of hours to the assembly of an impact study related to the merger proposition. Their study, however, was released after the proposition had been pulled from the ballot. Committee members—many who did not personally support the merger—felt frustrated that their efforts had been dismissed. There was also popular frustration about being denied the chance to vote.

The popular interpretation, reiterated candidly by Dalton's superintendent in his regular column in the school district's March 1998 monthly newsletter, was that the business community, through the Chamber of Commerce, had pulled the measure from the July ballot. That interpretation was both indicative of and contributive to a sense that popular and business interests related to the schools were at odds. This increasingly conscious fracture was highly relevant to the Georgia Project as it suggested a different fault line than just middle class versus poor and city versus county. As Chapters 7 and 8 will outline in detail, the Georgia Project was created and sustained by the business community (though not the business community alone). If the popular trust of the business community erected through years of corporate paternalism was being called into question, it was not too much to suggest that the business community's support of the Georgia Project could trigger a skeptical reaction to the project. Yet the business community was also being called upon to be involved. As an editorial in Dalton's local newspaper put it:

[The] former superintendent of Dalton Public Schools said more than once to our reporters that business and industry here must get more involved with solving community problems related to the rapid growth of the Hispanic community. . . . After all, our Hispanic neighbors are here because local businesses gave them jobs. . . . Business leaders here must accept some responsibility beyond handing out a regular paycheck. (*The Daily Citizen-News* 1997a:4A)

The merger discussion was relevant to the Georgia Project in one more way. The discussion occurred at the same time as the creation of the Georgia Project. This temporal relation positioned the merger discussion to serve as a distraction from the Georgia Project, an alternative to it, and an agent that mobilized public activism (and teacher activism) regarding schooling. This activism could be redirected, favorably or not, as attention to the Georgia Project.

## WHO WERE THE NEWCOMERS

The ultimate corporate legacy salient to this book, of course, is the way business hiring practices changed the demographies of both Dalton and Whitfield County. Absent the hiring of hundreds and then thousands of Latino laborers by local businesses, there never would have been a Georgia Project. While this book is less a description of the newcomers themselves and more the tale of the Georgia-based and Mexico-based educators and leaders who mobilized to respond to the new demography, it still makes sense here to at least sketch who the newcomers were. (Readers seeking further description are directed to Zuñiga and Hernández [2001].)

There is a rich literature on transnational migration, the relations between "sending" and "receiving" communities, and the processes that drive both this movement and the meaning various people make of this movement. That whole literature does not need to be summarized here; however, two points from it bear mention. Migration streams mature (Tienda 1989) and they become self-sustaining (Massey et al. 1987). The initial Latino arrivals in Dalton were workers, practically all single males or males traveling unaccompanied. Some of these initial Latinos did not stay long in Dalton, but other pioneers did and slowly accumulated sufficient money, job security, and supportive social networks that they could start families or send for spouses and children to join them. From the late 1980s through the end of my study period, an increasing portion of Latinos coming into Dalton were not arriving for work at all. They were children, spouses, elderly parents, and other kin. As this maturation of the migration stream became more significant, the habits of industries that were externalizing their indirect costs became more obvious and costly to the larger community, generating the disquiet and occasional xenophobia previously referenced and elaborated on in the next chapter. The maturation of the migration stream also made more plausible the claims of Georgia Project advocates and others that Dalton's new Latino community was a permanent community.

In March 1997, the Dalton school system compiled data specifying the place of birth of all Hispanic students in the system for the *Title VII—Systemwide Bilingual Education* grant proposal (see Table 3.2).

As one might expect, Table 3.2 shows that younger Hispanic students were more likely to have been born in the United States and in Georgia. That so many Hispanic students were born in the United States but not in Georgia problematizes (but does not discard) the notion held by some that Dalton Hispanics all come directly from Mexico. Clearly many Dalton Latinos had more than brief experience with other parts of the United States, leaving open the complicated question of how those experiences informed their expectations regarding both school and society in Dalton. That the majority of Dalton's Hispanic students were born outside the

TABLE 3.2   Hispanic Students' Birthplace*

| School and grade levels | Total number of Hispanic students | Born in Mexico or other Latin American country, number (%) | Born in U.S., number (%)* | Born in Georgia number (%)* |
|---|---|---|---|---|
| Westwood (pre-K–2) | 82 | 26 (32) | 56 (68) | 15 (18) |
| Brookwood (3–4) | 37 | 18 (49) | 19 (51) | 7 (19) |
| City Park (5–6) | 33 | 19 (58) | 14 (42) | 2 (6) |
| Roan (pre-K–2) | 438 | 178 (41) | 260 (59) | 95 (22) |
| Morris (3–4) | 137 | 72 (53) | 65 (47) | 16 (12) |
| Fort Hill (5–6) | 222 | 170 (77) | 52 (23) | 12 (5) |
| Junior high | 207 | 162 (78) | 45 (22) | 2 (1) |
| High school | 251 | 192 (76) | 59 (24) | 6 (2) |
| District total | 1,407 | 837 (59) | 570 (41) | 155 (11) |

*The information in these two columns is overlapping. Those born in Georgia are also counted as being born in the United States.

United States—59 percent—highlights the general newness of Dalton's Latino influx. This was corroborated by data from the one school that examined the birthplace of Hispanic students' mothers. That school found that more than 80 percent of mothers were born in Mexico with the remainder born in the United States; no mothers of students at this school were from other countries in Latin America.[19]

Reviewing the data in Table 3.2 helps locate where on the migration continuum most Dalton Hispanics were (i.e., immigrant or first generation), which in turn has implications for both the likely school success and the school needs of Hispanic students. If we consider the findings of Padilla (1996), Portes (1996), Suárez-Orozco and Suárez-Orozco (1995, 2001), and Valenzuela (1999) that second generation Hispanics in the United States tend to do less well in school than immigrant and first generation Hispanics, likely because of the emergence of alienation and oppositional cultures among many second generation Hispanics as well as the loss of a Mexican reference point (Gibson 1997b; Ogbu 1987). We can see how timely the Georgia Project was.[20] In terms of the chronology of migration, the Georgia Project was positioned to stave off the emergence of oppositional cultures among Latino newcomers and thus inhibit the entrenchment of alienation and poor school performance.[21]

4

# Of Immigration Scripts and the Conceptualization of Latino Newcomers

Marcelo Suárez-Orozco (1998) recently asserted that we in the United States are living in a time of dislocation. Dislocation refers to the cultural malaise and anxiety that seems dominant both in the United States and Western Europe. The anxiety is related to the instability of postmodern employment and to a simultaneous sense of lost community and lost shared values. To quote political theorist Michael Sandel (1996:1):

Two concerns lie at the heart of [U.S.] democracy's discontent. One is the fear that individually and collectively, we are losing control of the forces that govern our lives. The other is the sense that, from family to neighborhood to nation, the moral fabric of the community is unraveling around us. These two fears—for the loss of self-government and the erosion of community—together define the anxiety of the age.

Sandel also notes that the dominant political discourse has failed to relieve this anxiety, sometimes even cynically fanning it instead. The nostalgic newspaper article (Green 1996) quoted in part as Vignette 3 in the first chapter reflected this sense of dislocation and lost community in Dalton, but the political discourse statewide echoed and abetted this sensibility.

As Anderson (1991) and Chavez (1994) use the term, *imagining community* refers to the sense through which people identify as sharing community membership, including both those they know and many they do not know, "yet in the minds of each lives the image of their communion" (Anderson 1991:6). When a president says "my fellow Americans" or some such, the appeal is to an imagined community; that is, to many the president does not know who are still "fellows." Community can be defined at the local, regional, or national level and beyond.

Just as people imagine community (i.e., who is part of their group) they also imagine non-community (Barth 1969). They imagine an *Other.* As semi-otician Tzvetan Todorov defined it, the Other is "a specific social group to which *we* do not belong" (1984:3, italics original). Thus there can be many Others. It is the purpose of this chapter to clarify how Latino newcomers were "imagined" in Georgia and Dalton—sometimes as an Other, sometimes presumed not to be—particularly as this imagining relates to community membership and schooling. Like the history reviewed in the previous chapter, this imagining is a crucial contextual factor that shaped the Georgia Project.

The following disconcerting quotes from school board members offer one version of imagining Latino newcomers as part of the community, though, given the simultaneous cultural erasure made in the quotes, it is unclear whether many Latino newcomers would feel particularly included by this assertion.

The Dalton Board of Education discussed the issue of serving Spanish-speaking students during a recent work session. Board Vice Chairman Chip Sellers, taking an informal poll of students in the lunchroom of Park Creek Elementary, which is 83.2 percent Hispanic noted about half the kids he talked to were born in the United States. "I think the perception is, if they're Hispanic they don't speak English," said board Chairman Tommy Boggs.

Bill Weaver, interim superintendent, agreed. "We forget that a majority of these children have been born in this country. It's a perception problem, I think."

"I don't think it's fair to classify them as Hispanic," said board member Jim Wink. "They're born in Dalton, GA." (*Starks-Winn,* 2000)[1]

In this case, the *we* is defined as those born locally. Because Hispanic is not imagined as a local identity, the final quoted school board member suggests resolving the inclusion dilemma by not identifying the newcomers as Hispanic. The snippet also illustrates claims made about the tie-in between language usage and community membership.[2]

Whether Latinos in Dalton were viewed as part of the *we* or part of the *they* varied during my study, according to who was doing the determining, and by what criteria. For the bulk of the established population of Dalton and surrounding environs, the demographic transformation of their community in the 1990s and the economic and political changes that were related to it compelled a response of disquiet—rules of interaction and presumptions of social station were in flux. Established residents were not sure whether to see in the newcomers proof of community renewal or proof of community decay (Súarez-Orozco 1998). Interethnic interaction, though subject to a power differential favoring established Anglo residents, was improvisational and uncertain and often incorporated elements from broader discourses, for example, the reception accorded Latinos across the state, elsewhere in the South, and nationally.

These discourses were generated or reproduced by the popular media and then understood through the lens of many Daltonians' direct experiences. Naturally, many statewide issues were debated locally. Noting these statewide dynamics, particularly regarding the education of Latino newcomers and related issues, adheres to Hackenberg's (1997) recommendation to heed the political ecology. Hackenberg wants anthropologists to tend to the distribution of resources, people, and opportunities as a product of artificial jurisdiction marking of, in this case, a state boundary. This chapter tends first to statewide dynamics and then focuses again more locally.

## REGARDING THE NEWCOMERS—A STATEWIDE EDUCATIONAL PERSPECTIVE

Despite overt hostility to immigration by many Georgia political and educational leaders (Beck and Allexsaht-Snider 2001), including Dalton-area U.S. Representative Nathan Deal (Sherman 1997), immigration into Georgia from Mexico and the rest of Latin America soared in the 1980s and 1990s as the economic and transportation links between Georgia and Latin America grew rapidly.[3] Georgia's Hispanic student population rose from less than 2,000 in 1976 (Brown et al. 1980) to more than 33,600 in 1997 (Georgia Department of Education 1998), to 66,625 in the 2000–2001 school year (Georgia Department of Education 2002). This ongoing influx and concomitant demographic transformation (Hamann 1997b) was the result of: (1) the emergence of Atlanta as an international city with ample professional positions at multinational corporations and even more ample service sector positions—for example, construction, restaurant work (Dameron and Murphy 1996; Sassen 1988); (2) the expansion of the poultry industry concurrent with efforts to reduce wages in these industries (Griffith 1995; Griffith et al. 1995); (3) the near disappearance of African American and Anglo migrant farmworkers simultaneous with expanded recruitment of U.S.-born and immigrant Hispanics (Griffith and Kissam 1995) to work Georgia's sixteen crops that use migrant labor (Winders et al. 1995); (4) the relocation of the U.S. Army's School of the Americas from Panama to Fort Benning, near Columbus, Georgia; and (5) the carpet manufacturers of northwest Georgia turning to international labor recruitment networks as expansion and cost control demanded more labor than was locally available (Hernández-León and Zúñiga 2000).

All of these processes were supplemented or even supplanted by the increase in family reunifications and the starting of new Latino families as the migration stream to Georgia matured (Massey et al. 1987; Tienda 1989). Several of these dynamics converged in Dalton and made that city's school district the most proportionally Hispanic district in the state. All of these dynamics except the movement of military personnel and the recruitment of international professionals put Hispanic heads of household and other working family members in what some economists (e.g., Piore 1979) call the secondary sector.

What matters here is that the bulk of Latino newcomer workers in Georgia in the 1990s found secondary-sector jobs. According to Piore (1979) and Spener (1988) such jobs serve as buffers for the primary sector, with both wages and job security being vulnerable to the boom/bust cycles inherent to capitalism. Educational attainment tends not to matter in the secondary sector, affecting neither compensation nor job status, nor job security. In turn, the increasing "Latin Americanization" of the secondary sector (Griffith 1995; Hackenberg 1995) has multiple implications. The reactions accorded to Latinos in Georgia were likely to reflect their position in the political economy. If class structures tend to reproduce themselves unless interrupted, then it can be said that most Latino students in Georgia in the late 1990s were likely to enter the secondary sector in which their parents worked. These students were also likely to be living in households in which, regardless of how much formal education was valued, formal education had not contributed to economic security.[4] Of course, the Georgia Project was positioned to interrupt this trajectory.

The number of Latinos in Georgia and the number of Latino students in Georgia schools were both rising quickly at the time of my study, making the state and its schools part of the "New Latino Diaspora" (Wortham et al. 2001). However, in a state that has long struggled to provide adequate school opportunities for African Americans and low-income Anglos, the question of how Hispanics were faring in Georgia schools was infrequently asked and more rarely answered.

A review (Hamann 1997a) of quantitative data gathered by the Georgia Department of Education (1996a, 1996b) suggested that Hispanic students en masse were not doing so well in Georgia schools as measured by graduation rates. This point was reiterated four years later by an *Atlanta Journal-Constitution* article reporting that Georgia was last among the thirty-nine surveyed states in the proportion of its Hispanic students who graduated from high school (Salzer 2001). In district after district, the Hispanic proportion of enrollments significantly exceeded the Hispanic proportion in the class graduating from high school. Since Census Bureau data revealed no more Hispanic 8-year-olds than 17-year-olds in the state, the logical conclusion was that younger Hispanics were attending Georgia schools but that older Hispanic adolescents were not finishing. For the 2000–2001 school year, official state figures recorded that Hispanics made up 4.7 percent of Georgia public K–12 enrollment but just 2 percent of graduates (Georgia Department of Education 2002).

Looking still closer at those figures, in 2000–2001 Hispanics earned 2.5 percent of that year's General Diplomas, 2.2 percent of the Diplomas with Vocational Endorsements, 2.1 percent of the Diplomas with College Prep Endorsements, and 1.6 percent of Diplomas with Both College Prep and Vocational Endorsements (Georgia Department of Education 2002). This suggests that even the Hispanics who were successfully negotiating Georgia's public education system were doing so disproportionately in its lower tracks. To the claim voiced in Dalton and elsewhere that Hispanics' relatively low graduation numbers reflected only the late arrival of immigrants into the school system and too little time for them to meet all of the distribution requirements attached to a Georgia diploma, that only 4.2 percent of those leaving high school with Certificates of Attendance were Hispanic suggests this was, at most, a limited explanation.

In 1996–1997, when the Georgia Project began, the Dalton school district was proportionately the most Hispanic district in the state. Numerically, Dalton had the state's sixth highest Hispanic enrollment despite being only the sixty-eighth largest district in the state according to total enrollment (Georgia Department of Education 1998). For clarity, readers should know that all 159 Georgia counties operated school districts in 1998, while twenty-one incorporated cities in Georgia, including Dalton, operated school districts separate from the county systems, meaning there was a total of 180 public school districts in Georgia.

Despite the availability of data that showed that the Hispanic graduation rate in the state was only 60 percent of the enrollment rate and that the arrival of Hispanic newcomers was ongoing, meeting the needs of Latino newcomers was not a Georgia Department of Education priority. Reflecting the requests of the department's leadership, the 1998–1999 Georgia education budget included a $1.7 million cut in ESOL funding (Kurylo 1998a). This created an estimated $4.3 million shortfall in that program because the number of ESOL students expected to be eligible for special programs looked as if it would grow by more than 2,500 students (Kurylo 1998b). It is worth remembering that ESOL was the main state education budget category underwriting transitional programming for immigrant and other language minority students; it was the only state program of significance intended to help districts respond to the new presence of Hispanic students and families.[5] Meanwhile, practically all other education budget categories were increased in the 1998–1999 budget as the state enjoyed the record revenues resulting from growth and economic good times.

While not all ESOL students were Hispanic and many Hispanic students were not in ESOL, Dalton ESOL teachers and former employees of the Georgia Department of Education were dubious about the Georgia Department of Education's 1998 claim that ESOL student numbers were either declining or were previously overstated. The impression of some Dalton ESOL teachers, former state education employees, and researchers was that the attempted cuts in ESOL funding were consistent with the anti-immigrant sentiment popular (in some circles) nationwide and in evidence at the state education department.[6]

Given the ideological gap between the centrist foundations of the Georgia Project and the reactionary conservatism of the leadership of the Georgia Department of Education (Beck and Allexsaht-Snider 2001), it seemed likely that any possible activist contributions from the Georgia Department of Education after the end of my study would challenge the existing enactment strategy of the Georgia Project rather than support it. In early 1997, the efforts of the only Georgia Department of Education employee to positively respond to the Georgia Project were curtailed when a deputy superintendent of education blocked an invitation for that employee to attend the first meeting in Dalton between Dalton school officials and representatives from the Universidad de Monterrey. He inaccurately claimed the invited employee had a schedule conflict and then failed to convey the invitation.

Apart from initial discussions regarding bilingual education research and various ESOL strategies by the ultimately silenced former Department of Education employee, there was little participation by the Georgia Department of Education in the Georgia Project during the period of my study. The important exception was that the resigned employee ensured that Dalton's 1997 *Title VII—Systemwide Bilingual Education* proposal was officially supported in the department's mandated review. At the invitation of the attorney who originated the Georgia Project, two Georgia Department of Education employees did attend a March 27, 1998, exposition and celebration of the Georgia Project, but their participation in the event and subsequent response to it were minimal.

In June 1998, a Georgia Department of Education employee did send a letter to the Georgia Project's founding attorney in response to the attorney's concern that pending federal legislation—H.R. 3892, the "English Language Fluency Act"—in the U.S. House of Representatives threatened to eliminate Title VII as a budget category and end all currently funded Title VII efforts (including the one that was partially supporting the Georgia Project).[7] The state education employee's letter was precipitated by a letter from the attorney to U.S. Representative Nathan Deal. The state employee claimed it was premature to comment on the possible loss of Title VII monies, but added that the pending legislation seemed to support the idea that methods used in English language education programs should be managed from the state and local level, not the federal. That oblique comment conveniently ignored that Title VII funding was voluntarily applied for by local school districts and thus left intact local districts' prerogatives to manage their language education programs. It also ignored the state department of education's hostility to Title VII, which is clarified momentarily. A subsequent letter from Rep. Deal to the attorney repeated the state employee's misleading claim saying that it was "time we allow States and local schools and parents the right to select the method of English language instruction most appropriate for their children." Rep. Deal's letter also did not comment substantively on Dalton's possible loss of Title VII monies.

State superintendent of education, Linda Schrenko, did visit Dalton in September 1997, touring the school that had most embraced the Georgia Project and espousing her praise for it (Deck 1997). In April 1998, the state superintendent, then a candidate for reelection, returned for two additional visits less than a week apart. The newspaper headlines regarding her visits were contradictory. The first declared: "State Super Wants Focus on Teaching English" (Surpuriya 1998b:1A), while the second said: "State Superintendent Backs Bilingual Education" (Surpuriya 1998c:3A). Perhaps eyeing the power of the Georgia Project's local backers, she even declared her support for the Georgia Project in response to a direct question about it from the principal who is profiled in Chapter 5 (and whose school is profiled at the end of Chapter 7). However, her administration's policies did little to actualize her claim.

As Goode (2002:123) points out, Georgia is officially an English-only state with no state funds available for adopting a bilingual curriculum or even purchasing bilingual textbooks. Moreover, no assessments are allowed in a language other than English. Though not all of these policy postures were created by the Schrenko administration, they were endorsed by it and they have implications for any district operating within the state. As a point that is returned to in the final chapter, Dalton school officials in a sense had to pick sides when these state policies and the policies and goals promised by the Georgia Project were in conflict.

In general, the Georgia Department of Education was not supportive of the Georgia Project or any other effort that included any two-way Spanish/English bilingual curriculum or native language support. A 1998 *Title VII—Developmental Bilingual Education* grant proposal, called "Project B.A.B.E." and developed by Hall County Schools (1998), was challenged by the Georgia Department of Education in its mandated review of the proposal. The proposal included a two-way bilingual education component. The department explained that the proposal was contradictory to the goals and intents of the department. In a confusing letter intended to clarify their rationale for not recommending the proposal, the Georgia Department of Education reviewer wrote:

The goal of the Georgia Department of Education is to ensure that Limited English Proficient (LEP) students acquire English language skills as quickly as possible. The expeditious acquisition of the English language will ensure the effective functioning of students in American society. Given this goal, Project B.A.B.E. provides contrary educational strategies to students in its proposed plan.

Project B.A.B.E. seeks to implement a two-way language immersion program for LEP Spanish speakers and native English speakers. It is our belief that a strong English to Speakers of Other Languages program with effective methodology and materials will result in quicker proficiency of English language skills. While the concept of teaching Spanish to English-speaking elementary school children is worthy of consideration, it is the goal of the Department to promote English proficiency programs to LEP students. Since Project B.A.B.E. apportions significant teaching time to programs for students other than LEP, the Department cannot support Project B.A.B.E.

Given that the department had nothing directly to lose from a district writing a successful federal grant proposal (no state funds were involved), the department's reaction should be viewed as both extraordinary and indicative.

The academic needs of ELLs were singularly conceptualized as the need to gain English as fast as possible so they could function "in American society." Even though the proposed two-way bilingual model matched the instructional strategy that Thomas and Collier (1997), Ramirez (1991), Cloud, Genesee, and Hamayan (2000), and others have found as the most effective means to ensure the long-term academic success of initially LEP students, any virtues of two-way bilingual education or any form of native language support were summarily ignored in the Department of Education's response. Had Dalton sought Title VII support for the Georgia Project in 1998 instead of 1997, it is probable that the proposal I wrote would not have been supported by the Georgia Department of Education. The department's claims of wanting to emphasize more local control of schooling were false when local goals did not match those of state leaders. Moreover, at the same time ESOL was being praised as the single solution for the academic needs of LEP students by Georgia Department of Education officials, those same officials were seeking to reduce the ESOL budget. Ironically, TESOL, the international professional organization of Teachers of English to Speakers of Other Languages, at this time also asserted in its statement of standards that native language instruction is appropriate (Short 2000).

To further problematize the educational supports for Latinos in Georgia available in the late 1990s, another element must be considered in addition to school districts' Hispanic graduation records and the prevailing attitudes of the leaders of the Georgia Department of Education. At the higher education level, Georgia public universities offered few training programs and credentialing opportunities specifically responsive to the state's growing need for educators versed in particular strategies inclusive of and responsive to Georgia's increasing ESOL population. This lack of infrastructure did not mean there were no requests for support. Georgia elementary school principals surveyed by Beard (1996) claimed that they felt undertrained and insufficiently prepared to meet the challenges of Georgia students' increasing linguistic and cultural diversity.

In a 1996 letter from the chancellor of the University System of Georgia, the attorney who initiated the Georgia Project was told that state universities had no bilingual teacher training programs, that no bilingual education certifications nor endorsements were available, and that the regents were awakening to the needs for such programs, but that it would be some time before any programs were organized and put in place.[8] Though ultimately this letter was used by the attorney and other Georgia Project proponents to explain the shortage of locally available bilingual educators and to rationalize their efforts to recruit Mexican university-trained teachers, it is further illustration of the state's limited capacity to respond to the newcomers and low prioritization of developing that capacity.

At the time of my study, the statewide discourse concerning what to do about the growing Hispanic presence in the schools and various communities was passionate, confused, contradictory, and uncertain. There were, however, some themes to it. From a funding priority standpoint, newcomers were viewed as less deserving than other populations (not undeserving, just less) and the favored orientation for response was colonialism (though no one ever called it that), unfortunately colonialism with its "subtractive" implications (Valenzuela 1999). To clarify, as Albert Menni has summarized in the *Encyclopedia of Political Economy* (Diwan 1999), "Colonial ideology had two propositions: . . . (a) everything of the colonizer is superior, therefore 'good' and 'desirable'; (b) everything associated with the colonized is inferior, hence 'bad' and 'undesirable'." The goal was to help Latino newcomers learn English and master the existing curriculum. There was no overt attention to valuing/acknowledging any skills, linguistic or otherwise, that the newcomers brought with them. As discussed subsequently, this orientation is consistent with both Suárez-Orozco's (1998) "pro-immigration script" and its counterpoint, the "anti-immigration script."

## WHITE VERSUS WHITE, ANTI-IMMIGRANT SENTIMENT, AND A DISCOURSE OF NOSTALGIA

According to Suárez-Orozco (1998) a "pro-immigration" and an "anti-immigration" script both emerge from the sense of dislocation noted at the beginning of this chapter that he says pervades the contemporary United States. The pro-immigration script casts immigrants as familial, hardworking, self-sacrificing, and loyal. The pro-immigration script derives much of its appeal from its ironic stability. In an age of anxiety and upheaval, it reiterates the important domestic myth that America is a land of opportunity, a land where hard work, even in trying circumstances, can lead to success, and thus that America is essentially fair. Immigrants, through this lens of interpretation, offer the prospect of validating and rejuvenating America, but not of fundamentally changing it.

Given the appeal of this script as myth (Rosen 2001), those who espouse it do not easily tolerate messy deviations from it. Resistance to forgetting a first language (different from the oft-alleged but rare resistance to the idea of learning English), characterizations of employment conditions as less than fair, or seeking work that natives *do* want all violate the script and thus bring enmity to those who voice such complaints. In its full assimilationist presumption, the pro-immigration script embeds the colonialist conceits that were previously mentioned; the alleged virtues of the newcomers are imagined as American virtues.

This myth/script, of course, had a complementary local manifestation in Dalton in its self-image as a place where entrepreneurial pluck and hard work had created a concentration of carpet production and wealth (Deaton 1993; Patton 1999; Shaheen 1984). Moreover as the Georgia Project was getting underway, this local myth was under a kind of duress as the carpet industry consolidated. The consolidation accelerated between the end of my field study in 1998 and this writing in 2002, as Durkan, World Carpet, and Shaw were all bought out (Shaw by the Warren Buffet's Berkshire Hathaway). So the local myth's imperiled status became further impetus for some to project the pro-immigration script onto the newcomers.

The pro-immigration script is most apt to be embraced by those who gain from the presence of newcomer laborers. (While practically all consumers benefit from the presence of newcomers in the sense that we all enjoy lower produce prices, cheaper carpets, and so forth, this reference is to those whose benefit is more obvious and direct.) If the employment hierarchy can be equated to a pyramid, anyone in a position above those who are directly contested by newcomer laborers benefits from the expansion of the employment base below them. This means immigration is often eyed as a good thing by most people in management, as well as those who share their class level, such as spouses, doctors, lawyers, and so forth.

In contrast, articulators of the anti-immigration script look at the same change in demography and see threat rather than reassurance. Immigrants become illegal aliens, welfare cheats, criminals, and job stealers. (The contradiction between government dependency and stealing jobs is left unexplored.) As Suárez-Orozco (1998:296–297) summarizes, "Anti-immigrant sentiment—including the jealous rage that 'illegals are getting benefits instead of citizens like my friend'—is intertwined with an unsettling sense of panic in witnessing the metamorphosis of 'home' into a world dominated by sinister aliens."

Because the two scripts contradict each other (even as both ignore the actual voices of newcomers), those who espouse the different scripts tend to talk past each other, often heatedly, over a wide gulf. This miscommunication leaves the anxiety untouched, but dehumanizes the espousers of the opposite view such that their viewpoint and rationale can be readily dismissed. Because the pro-immigrant script was typically used by the more powerful while the anti-immigrant script is typically uttered by the less powerful, the powerful's rejection of those articulating the anti-immigrant script is consistent with hegemonic reproduction.

When their script is dismissed, those articulating anti-immigrant views feel even more disempowered, more anxious, and, not surprisingly, even more anti-immigrant. The self-defeating likelihood of articulating the anti-immigration script in an unacceptable fashion only increases. Plaut (1983:277) notes a long-standing dynamic in Appalachia where communitarian voices of marginal locals are first ignored and then, as the expressions of disenchantment take on less and less appropriate forms, the marginals' hostility becomes a rationale for excluding them. Thus the festering disenchantment of the disenchanted becomes a rationale for the reproduction of their marginality.

To the pro-immigration powerful, the increased shrillness of the anti-immigrant xenophobes not only rationalizes their dismissal, it also creates an opening in the pro-immigration script for immigrants to be characterized in comparative and favorable terms in relation to the xenophobes (i.e., low-income, anxious whites). This violates an important tenet of self-identity for low-income whites—the sense of white privilege—and perpetuates the deflection of working-class Anglo (and to a lesser extent African American) rage toward immigrants instead of at the community's power brokers.

In a study of a low-income white community in rural Florida that in many ways paralleled the pre–Hispanic-migration demography of North Georgia, Gibson (1996) noted how important the construction of racist attitudes was for local poor whites' sense of identity and community. She followed this observation with the claim that this was how low-income whites unwittingly contributed to the construction of their own marginality (as elites dismissed them as racists), thereby perpetuating the advantages of the powerful. As Gibson put it (1996:387), "Representations of whites as singularly successful thus serves the interests of the privileged group because it hides the real social and economic disparity between privileged and poor whites and so obstructs identification with similarly situated minority members." Thus, the one "privilege" that low-income whites have—their whiteness—is phantasmagoric.

A script that constructs certain whites as lower status than non-whites— for example, below the status of Latino immigrants—then is centrally threatening. This portion of the pro-immigration script keeps the anti-immigration script shrill enough that the espousers of the anti-immigration script can see no common cause with the immigrant newcomers. When low-income Anglo women married Mexican men in northwest Georgia (Kelley 1996) their Anglo peers ostracized them. Ironically, this xenophobia by others serves the class interests of most espousers of the pro-immigration script. Moreover, the shrillness of the anti-immigration script perpetuates the continued self-righteous assertion of the pro-immigration script. The scripts continue to be directed at each other in a self-sustaining loop that, through their twin dominance in the public sphere, crowd out third and less familiar ways of responding to the newcomers.

Since becoming a local trading center more than one hundred years ago, Dalton's intra-community social relations have been complicated, inter-dependent, and stratified. One constant theme has been the inverse relation between increased community wealth (not necessarily evenly distributed) and a decline in familial autonomy for most households (as families individually controlled less and less of the production required to keep their households viable). Given the disaggregative forces of market capitalism where labor and management interests are at cross purposes—management wants to maximize the profit it can realize per employee, while employees want to minimize the difference between the value of their work and their compensation—Dalton like any coherent community has needed to invent communitarian forces that counter social fracture along class lines.

According to one school district informant, the influx of Latinos into Dalton was displacing low-income whites and blacks from Dalton's East Side, where the bulk of the city's lower-cost housing was located. According to the same informant and consistent with the pro-immigration script, Latinos were gaining a reputation among local landlords for being more prompt with rent payments and better at keeping up properties than other types of tenants. Whether this informant was factually accurate, it is important that there were perceptions by some in Dalton that Hispanics were more meritorious than low-income whites and blacks.[9]

Local Hispanics were often cast in preferable terms in relation to other low-income populations. Matching Suárez-Orozco's (1998) pro-immigration script, a December 1996 editorial in *The Daily Citizen-News* celebrating the vision of the Georgia Project's founding attorney claimed that "For too long Dalton and Whitfield County have walked by the growing Hispanic community, rarely offering substantial help." It characterized local Hispanics as "hardworking," "filling some of the toughest manual labor jobs around," and "an example of intensive familial ties."[10] Having praised local Hispanics, the editorial writers thus exempted themselves from the following charge, also in the editorial: "Meanwhile [Hispanics] have been virtually ignored—even hated by some—simply because of their presence."

If Hispanics were the primary group referred to in the editorial, there was also a shadow referent: the unnamed group(s) that was allegedly not hardworking, not willing to take on the tough manual labor jobs available, and not exemplars of intensive familial loyalty. If local Hispanics were meritorious because of their family and work habits, then those from other backgrounds who lacked these virtues were not deserving of support or sympathy. The closest the editorial came to mentioning the shadow referent was with the vague pronoun *some* in the phrase "even hated by some."

A brief retelling of local history, particularly as it involves the local newspaper, clarifies who "some" refers to. In 1995, before the Georgia Project had been suggested by anyone, several citizens began a slow stream of letters to the editor questioning and complaining about Dalton's changing demographic face. The writer of an early letter sarcastically wrote:

Am I to understand that people in our community are upset Dalton has become a haven for uninvited guests? . . . Just because the crime rate in Dalton has risen considerably in the past couple of years. Just because the local law enforcement is overburdened by a whole new (to them) criminal subculture. Just because native Daltonians prefer to retain their own language—poor English or not—is no reason to be uncivil to guests.

Several components of this letter merit highlighting: Latinos were labeled as a criminal subculture; Latinos were characterized as guests (not part of the imagined community) and contrasted with natives; and they were labeled as uninvited, which illuminates a distinction among longtime Daltonians between those who "invited" Latinos (by employing them) and those who did not. With a leap of logic, the author implied that the presence of Latinos had imperiled the retention of English by English speakers. Finally, the author made claims about her socioeconomic status and group membership with the self-denigrating reference to "poor English." Plaut (1983) found similar expressions of embarrassment about values and way of life by white Appalachians in his study. Though as the letter itself shows, the author's English was generally fine, she distinguished herself from the presumably more schooled, better speakers of English who perhaps were not threatened by the Hispanic influx. Her loyalty was with native-born, "law-abiding" Daltonians, who might not be so accomplished according to schooling (or who, per the dynamics of the secondary sector, did not have their school experience rewarded), but who nonetheless had the right to express their concern about how Dalton was changing.

Later in 1995, the trickle of anti-immigrant letters to the editor became a torrent. Claims such as that in a May letter that "We're losing control of our borders" became increasingly common. In the fall, shortly after an INS raid at a local carpet mill led to the arrest of several hundred undocumented workers (Rehyansky 1995a, 1995b), the letters became especially virulent. *The Daily Citizen-News* responded by declaring a temporary moratorium on letters to the editor that mentioned Latinos.

Though the local paper has long been identified with advocating local business leaders' points of view (Kelley 1996) and not supporting more nativist or reactionary perspectives, the letter to the editor moratorium blocked access to one of the few public forums through which populist doubt about immigration could be expressed. Was a major portion of the local population dubious about accommodations to Hispanic newcomers? Yes. Were they welcome to express these doubts publicly? No.

The point here is not to defend a racist discourse, which is what the letters to the editor largely were. Rather what needs highlighting is that many members of Dalton and Whitfield's less educated, predominantly white working class—a 1995 Education Is Essential Foundation study found that 33 percent of the employees in the carpet industry had not finished high school or obtained a GED (Hamilton 1995b)—had serious doubts about how immigration was changing their community. They felt geographically displaced in a more acute way than Dalton's wealthier residents who primarily

lived on the West Side. They also felt ignored. Their resistant voice was
largely excluded from Georgia Project planning and implementation, which
was one reason the project moved forward so quickly. But it also meant
that an existing community fracture line was exacerbated and a major
impediment to the project's ultimate success was not dealt with during my
study period.

Dislocation, the contextual condition Suárez-Orozco (1998) identified as
supporting the two immigration scripts, implies previously being located,
that something was disrupted or lost. Whether the remembered past was
mythic or real, articulators of both scripts appear nostalgic for something
lost. As noted, the newspaper article (Green 1996) cited in the first chapter
about Dalton circa 1960 serves as one example of a nostalgia discourse.
A September 1997 controversy about a planned change in a local AM radio
station's format serves as another (Jackson 1997b, 1997c).

In that second instance, local citizens became upset by a proposed conversion to a Spanish-language/Mexican music format at Dalton's first radio
station, WBLJ-AM. The change was proposed because of a steady decline
in listeners to its adult contemporary music format. Though the controversy
was ultimately sidestepped when WBLJ-AM's owner—the North Georgia
Radio Group—decided to switch another of its stations (WDAL-AM) to a
Spanish-language format, a burst of public outcry preceded the revision of
plans and provided another opportunity for residents to articulate their attitudes and impressions regarding Dalton's changing demography and how
they imagined their community. In the controversy, both the pro-immigration
and the anti-immigration scripts (Suárez-Orozco 1998) again were visible.

Though the 1997 radio station controversy was of lesser degree than the
1995 controversy, many of the themes in letters to the editor were similar.
One woman wrote: "Well, well, the Hispanics have taken over a number of
things here and now they get WBLJ radio station. That is the first station
we ever had, and if they need a radio station, why can't they get a new one
and leave our historic radio station alone?" What her letter and several others of the same ilk failed to note was that the format change was not being
proposed by Hispanics but rather by Anglo station owners who sensed the
format change would bring advertising money seeking new markets.
Meanwhile other letters dismissed the first group of letter writers as racist
and regressive. Thus the temporary controversy became a new forum for
the reiteration of more long-lasting community fracture lines.

Citing Aberle (1962), Gibson (1996) brings up a final concept worth
mentioning here: relative deprivation. According to this idea, happiness or
disaffection with the social order is not a direct product of having more or
having less, but rather of having more or less than one expects to have, particularly in relation to various referent groups. If one has internalized the
idea that one's group identity (e.g., as a white person) is supposed to include
privilege, then falling short of the fully subjective concept of privilege means

feeling relatively deprived and thus unhappy. If, according to an internalized sense of racial or ethnic hierarchy, one's alleged privilege is blatantly jeopardized by the apparent intentional advantaging of another group (e.g., through affirmative action or an effort like the Georgia Project) then resistance to the advantaging effort is predictable.

Populist resistance to immigrants, to Hispanics, and to the Georgia Project may often have been racist, but it is rather facile to be so dismissive. From a structuralist standpoint, low-income whites' failure to find solidarity with the immigrant influx has helped permit the hegemonic reproduction of an unequal social order by supporting the misdirection of resistance. Moreover, if through interventions like the Georgia Project and because of social mobility facilitated by positive, if paternalistic, characterizations like "familial" and "hardworking," some Latinos in Dalton did realize socioeconomic advancement—as a few already had—the privilege of privileged whites still was not really threatened; their materially advantaged starting point mitigated against it, but the more fictive privilege of working-class whites was imperiled. Meanwhile, the success of a few Latinos would obscure Latino claims of being disadvantaged by structural racism.[11]

In Dalton and perhaps everywhere, people look around to gain a sense of the expectations of the groups with which they affiliate (simultaneously contributing to those expectations), to compare how they are faring in relation to those expectations, and to feel confident or uncertain as a result of those comparisons. What it meant to be a Daltonian in the late 1990s was uncertain and contested, with statewide and national trends affecting local sensibilities. Thus the task of school was also complicated. What did kids need to know? What languages were they supposed to speak? Did the linguistic and cultural funds of knowledge that newcomer students brought with them have value or did they somehow threaten extant calculations of what knowledge domains mattered? The Georgia Project leaders profiled in the next two chapters brought different perspectives to these questions and offered different answers to them, referencing different scripts and differently valuing and honoring those that they shared.

# The Georgia Project's Dalton Founders

In a classic piece on revitalization movements that borrows from Weber (1947), Wallace (1956) noted that such efforts are typically begun at the initiative of a charismatic leader. In his typology, such movements grow and flourish with the original leader's continuing investment of energy and vision. However, in many cases, when the original leader dies, becomes elderly, or turns his or her attention elsewhere, the revitalization effort falters. Revitalization efforts that continue to succeed are the less common ones in which there is a successful transition from the initiating personal charismatic leadership model to a more institutionalized bureaucratic form of governance. In the latter scenario, who the leaders are becomes secondary to the quality and functionality of the governance design.

While the comparison of the Georgia Project to Wallace's (1956) model should not be overextended, the tale of the origin and early history of the Georgia Project is the tale first of a charismatic leader initiating a revitalization effort (i.e., renewing the good reputation of Dalton schools in the face of a new demographic reality). Later, according to the model, the Georgia Project would need to become increasingly dependent on its formal design and its institutionalization for its long-term viability. In 2001, the Georgia Project did hire a new executive director, a woman who had previously been a professor of language education at the State University of West Georgia. At the stages focused on in this book, however, the Georgia Project tale was the tale of charismatic leadership abetted by key support from specific individuals and then challenged by some of those same individuals.

The Georgia Project got as far as it did in its first two years because it had powerful backers and implementers. The four people profiled in this chapter and the two in the next played central roles in designing and leading the Georgia Project during my study period, with two or three playing important roles up to the present writing in 2002. Per the framework of "studying up" (Nader 1972), it is the thoughts, understandings, and actions of these six individuals with which these two chapters are most concerned. Collectively the six deserve credit for bringing to fruition a complicated, multifaceted, binational partnership aimed at responding to the many needs of Latino newcomer families and the larger community. This chapter describes the four Dalton-based leaders, the next profiles two from the Universidad de Monterrey, with an additional description of the university context from which they came.

The Dalton business leader and the Mexican business leader who facilitated the original contact between Dalton schools and the Universidad de Monterrey are not profiled here. While their participation was crucial, their involvement was largely one-dimensional as facilitators of communication; ultimately they were not project leaders. For similar reasons, other people important to the project are not profiled here—notably the visiting instructors from Monterrey, some bureaucrats at the Georgia Department of Education, the superintendent's executive assistant, a local bilingual priest, and the City Council member who early on championed the Georgia Project and helped get $750,000 from the city over a three-year period for the nascent project. Important to the project's implementation as these individuals were, they were not crucial to its design and control during my study period. The Universidad de Monterrey professor who coordinated the design of the 1997 Summer Institute is not described here, but his contributions to the Georgia Project and the way those contributions reflected his cosmology and experience are both topics taken up in Chapter 10 on the Summer Institute. Notably, no Latinos who lived in Dalton are included in this profile because none were closely involved in the Georgia Project planning process before or during my period of study. As I finished my field study in mid-1998, this was poised to change, as the Hispanic leadership council initiated by Universidad de Monterrey researchers appeared to have become self-sustaining and ready to assert a local political voice. The preliminary consequences of that initiative are sketched in Chapter 12.

Of the four people profiled here, three worked for Dalton schools and one headed a private law practice, until fully retiring from that in 2000. According to the official structure of the school district, the three Dalton-based educators profiled were related hierarchically, with the superintendent at the top and the curriculum coordinator having authority over the principal (at least regarding curriculum and instruction). One could assert a different hierarchy, however, in relation to savvy regarding Dalton's traditional mores and ways. In this regard, the attorney and the curriculum coordinator were more expert, with the other two identified and self-identifying as outsiders to some extent.

Of these four individuals, all but one (or maybe two) felt exempt from any criticism of Dalton schools that was implicit to the Georgia Project. That criticism, put plainly, stated that Dalton schools were insufficiently meeting the needs of Dalton's Hispanic community (or at least were insufficiently meeting those needs before the project was begun), hence the need for an external impetus. People who were part of the school system when this criticism was first offered were implicated by it, though their responses to this implication varied.

## THE ATTORNEY

The Georgia Project's originator was an established local attorney who continued to devote dozens of hours a week to the Georgia Project through the duration of my field study. As of this writing in 2002, the project remained his main avocation and, if anything, his contribution of time to it had only increased. According to several people at the Universidad de Monterrey who were involved with the Georgia Project, the attorney was the linchpin who held the project together because he had the power and reputation to compel action. After my field study this local power began to fade as some school system leaders "successfully" stopped heeding his desires. This was counterbalanced by his increasing success at attracting external attention, resources, and accolades to the project.

Though there were other leaders involved in the Georgia Project planning process, it was this local attorney, perhaps seeing the Georgia Project as his crowning act of service to Dalton,[1] who was its most obvious and well-known champion. He was a World War II veteran fighter pilot, who from 1957 to 1960 represented Dalton and a large swath of northwestern Georgia for two terms as a Democrat in the U.S. Congress. He left the Congress to successfully run for the Georgia state senate in 1960. He selected Atlanta over Washington because, in those days of Jim Crow, the serious work of desegregation needed even more support at the state level than the federal. In his words, "All the action was happening at the state level. They were seriously thinking of closing the Georgia public school system just to avoid black children going to school with whites. . . . My philosophy has been that if a position is correct, it's never too risky" (Wexler 1999:35). Perhaps because of this gesture (though no doubt he has made hundreds of others) several African American informants in Dalton enthused about what a good man he was.

By the time I first met him in March 1997, the attorney had held a high profile in Dalton for several decades where he and his family had long patrician roots. The attorney's firm was established originally by his father, and for many years included the attorney's brother (until that brother passed away). His firm worked both for the City of Dalton and, on local issues, for several of Dalton's most powerful companies, including the biggest carpet manufacturers. Though a few whispered about his "old boys' network" ways and his tough prosecutorial streak, the attorney was treated deferentially by a wide range of Daltonians.

Nonlocally, the attorney was also treated deferentially, to a point. While he had friendships with several powerful individuals, including some who were leading figures in President Carter's administration, the attorney's locally inculcated, small-town, name-dropping did not initially work well when applied to the beyond-Dalton promotion of the Georgia Project. Yet his success after my study period ended—accruing attention and support from the Center for Applied Linguistics, the National Council of La Raza, Kennesaw State University, and elsewhere—suggests that he was a quick study who got better and better at pitching the Georgia Project (no doubt aided over the time by the project's transformation from an unorthodox conglomeration of strategies to an actual operating multi-component initiative).

I first heard of the attorney who originated the Georgia Project during a visit to the Georgia Department of Education. I was shown a letter he had sent out on law firm letterhead describing the Georgia Project and soliciting support. Confessing my bias and the bias of my conversation partner, we both shook our heads considering the letter. We wondered what kind of hair-brained scheme the project must be. The concept of a small-town attorney championing a major education reform, referencing a small Mexican university we had never heard of, seemed quite odd. In retrospect, I realize how thoroughly I misjudged the situation. (To the credit of my conversation partner, she reacted to the attorney's inquiries by passing along research relevant to the Georgia Project's tentative forays into bilingual education.)

An "old boys' network" style of operating relies on name-dropping, face-to-face encounter, subtlety, and both/all the interlocutors knowing the social position and personal connections that link them and any of the people being discussed. Ironically, this kind of *personalismo* is not substantially different from common Latin American administrative operating patterns (Heath 1988). It may be that, in some senses, the attorney was better positioned to negotiate with Mexican partners than with scholars and bureaucrats closer to home.

*Old boys' network* is also a term that can be applied to how the attorney initially chose to guide the Georgia Project.[2] Under the attorney's leadership and by his informal invitation, approximately a dozen business leaders and the attorney together formed the unofficially named Georgia Project oversight committee. Of this group roughly half were regular participants. Some participated less often because of busy schedules (including business travel), limited interest, and/or because they were only invited to some of the gatherings. There appeared to be a de facto inner circle or executive council. Through my study period all members of the oversight committee were white, but in a 1990s updating of the old boys' network, a few women participated.[3] Following my study period, after the success of the Universidad de Monterrey's Latino leadership development initiative (part of the Parent/Workplace involvement component; see Chapter 10), and after several initially supportive carpet industry executives sold their companies and left the area, the oversight committee did become multiracial as well as more formal.

To be clear, the rationale for explaining the previous information is to be descriptive, not judgmental. The old boys' network form of governance proved highly functional as measured by mobilizing resources and initiating and sustaining the Georgia Project. Moreover, all those who were part of it seemed to know its rules/codes and to accede to them.

For the Georgia Project, the attorney appealed to politicians to hasten the slow moving of bureaucracy (e.g., to help obtain work visas for the visiting instructors from Monterrey); he wrote to local and Atlanta business leaders, inviting them to see the Georgia Project in action and to provide financial contributions (in March 1998 the attorney arranged visits to Dalton by the head of Atlanta's Hispanic Chamber of Commerce, several business leaders, and others); and he appealed, with initially limited success, to university and Georgia Department of Education-based researchers to provide expert assistance. This modus operandi contributed to the fast-growing notoriety of the Georgia Project and it meant the leveraging of countless resources to hasten the project's enactment. However, it also gave the Georgia Project an identity, according to some teachers, as something being created mostly by outsiders, advocated by business leaders and politicians, and imposed upon the schools and the instructors and students there. Goode (2002) suggests that some Dalton educators felt as if the attorney's insistent advocacy painted the district status quo as inadequate, a charge they resented.

Perhaps intentionally, the attorney's initial project leadership left unresolved the tension as to whether the Georgia Project was a school district project or not. Through 1998, most Dalton educators deferred to the attorney's reputation and apparent magnanimity, but that did not necessarily mean they were willing to heed his recommendations for changed school practice. His widespread credibility did not position him as an authority on either school reform or classroom management. In apparent recognition of this fact, on several occasions the attorney spoke publicly of the support by one former Georgia Department of Education administrator for various facets of the Georgia Project. In some circles this provided him additional credibility, but his status as an attorney and not an educator still complicated his task as self-appointed leader of the Georgia Project. After my field study ended, he carefully created a teacher advisory panel for the Georgia Project that had real power (see Chapter 13).

The attorney's mode of operating left intact his respected reputation in many circles. African American and Mexican-immigrant informants noted his fairness and his willingness not only to decry local vestiges of prejudice but to confront them.[4] Dalton's all white (and mostly male) City Council members interacted with him in a deferential manner, as did Dalton school administrators, at least until 1999. The superintendent said of the attorney that "he is dumb like a fox," citing the attorney's ability to have others think of him as a kind, gentle, older man and yet have them do almost exactly as he wished them to. In an article about the Georgia Project in the University of Georgia's alumni magazine, the superintendent later characterized the attorney as "a rainmaker"—that is, one who precipitates action (Wexler 1999:36).[5]

Clearly the attorney's degree of motivation relating to the Georgia Project was high. Though it is a crude way of measuring interest, one day in 1998 a colleague of his and I roughly estimated that the value of service the attorney provided to the Georgia Project was akin to $100,000 per year. We estimated his fee for services at $200/hour (not an uncommon fee for a senior private attorney) and then multiplied that by the ten hours a week he devoted to the project (perhaps an underestimate)[6] times fifty weeks a year. The figure does not include the fees for all of the faxes, phone calls, letters, and so forth, that he initiated on behalf of the Georgia Project that normally would be added to an attorney's billing.

Why was the attorney motivated to be so invested in the Georgia Project? Crucial to the attorney's actions relating to the Georgia Project was his sense of Dalton's present condition and its likely fate without intervention. An informant from the Universidad de Monterrey remembered well the toast offered by the attorney at an elaborate dinner during the Monterrey scholars' first visit to Dalton. To an audience that included school district officials, major carpet industry leaders, some clerical representatives, and the Monterrey visitors, the attorney declared that Dalton had become a border city meaning it was a transnational site, with a transnational and heterogeneous population. Given this new mix and new reality for Dalton, the city and the schools had to become adept at schooling in a different way and had to create a more inclusive vision for the town. Yet as emphatic as these words were regarding the need to be responsive to change, equally salient to the attorney was a proud and traditional affection for his community. Dalton needed to change in order not to change. That is, it needed to be responsive to newcomers so that the demographically more diverse community was still a community, so that the historically preeminent school system in northwest Georgia retained its reputation for excellence.

## THE SUPERINTENDENT

In the draft of the superintendent's resume that was part of his successful application to become Dalton's superintendent in the autumn of 1996, the first line after his name read: "Career Objective: Superintendency of a progressive school system." The goal was vague, but intriguing. From one vantage point, the professed goal was rhetorical cover for a more conservative and traditional operating style. Though the superintendent was Dalton's first external hire in over one hundred years, like all his predecessors he was male and solidly "Georgian." After his encouraged retirement in 2000, informants who contrasted him with his successor—a woman from metro Atlanta—remembered him as the last of the "good old boys." From this view, the superintendent and his hiring process echoed the hiring process Wolcott (1998) documented so piercingly of a committee of male principals ritually convincing each other that they wanted to bring new principals to their district who were committed to change and improvement, yet ended up selecting the candidates who were most like themselves. Their claim to progressiveness was a ritual of joint self-delusion.

An account of the superintendent as a traditionalist is compelling, but it seems incomplete and perhaps even misplaced if we consider how the superintendent initially acted in regards to the Georgia Project. He was outspoken about Dalton's need to accommodate its Hispanic newcomers. He was quoted in both Dalton and Chattanooga newspapers saying that Hispanics had a right to be in Dalton, that many intended to stay permanently, and that it was a responsibility of the schools to be responsive to their needs. Consistently, despite any misgivings he may have had about its external impetus as a project initiated and promoted by a private attorney, the superintendent publicly supported the Georgia Project.

According to several former employees of the Georgia Department of Education who have watched education politics in the state for many years, the superintendent's public position was both rare and daring. When asked privately what he would do if the Georgia Project (or other efforts) successfully kept more Hispanic students in school, thus having a negative impact on district average SAT scores,[7] the superintendent said he was prepared to take any criticism from the community that might occur under such a scenario. Helping students stay in school was the right thing to do.

The superintendent came to Dalton in 1996 from Bulloch County Schools where he had been superintendent since 1988. Bulloch County is in southeastern Georgia about an hour west of Savannah. Its county seat—Statesboro—is a small regional urban center much like Dalton. Like Dalton, Statesboro is a small city located within fifty miles of a medium-sized city. (Dalton is near Chattanooga and Statesboro near Savannah.) Like Dalton, Statesboro had a small cosmopolitan elite whose educational achievement, professional status, power, and worldview differed markedly from many citizens in the county and nearby rural areas. (Dalton elites were largely associated with the carpet industry, while Statesboro elites were associated with agriculture and with Georgia Southern University, the third largest university in Georgia.) In both Dalton and Statesboro, the superintendent's mention of his taste for turkey hunting on his resume would have been considered an asset (at least in traditionally powerful circles). In the same spirit, his identity as a lifelong Georgian would also have enhanced his credibility.

Prior to becoming Bulloch County's superintendent, he had been with that district since 1971, first as a science teacher and later as principal, three times in elementary schools and once in a high school. He was superintendent there for eight years by dint of winning two popular elections for the position. He decided to leave the district when the district converted to an appointed superintendency and he was not guaranteed the appointment.[8]

In one crucial way, Bulloch County offered little needed preparation for the superintendent. There were few Hispanics in Bulloch County. Forty of the 8,325 students enrolled in Bulloch County Schools during the superintendent's last year there (1995–1996) were Hispanic; the Bulloch County system at that point enrolled only two students in English for Speakers of Other Language programs (ESOL) (Georgia Department of Education 1996b). Until coming to Dalton, the superintendent did not know and did not need to know much about Mexican identity or any other Latino cultural identity. Nor did he need to know much about ESOL/bilingual education, multicultural education, and so forth. Thus, he did not readily understand the challenges facing teachers of Mexican newcomer students; he did not know what expertise these instructors employed or needed; he did not know what he did not know (i.e., he seemed unaware other than in a general way of the training he was missing regarding how to successfully lead a demographically fast-changing district); and he had no lieutenants with sufficient topic area expertise to guide him otherwise.[9] It is indicative of the governance of Dalton schools at the time of the superintendent's hiring that his absence of experience in these domains was not viewed as a reason to select another candidate.

His experience with Bulloch County politics likely shaped his considerable political savvy and sensibilities regarding his various constituencies. One does not get elected or reelected in Georgia without political cunning. This political tact was apparent on several occasions, none more spectacular than at a February 1998 meeting of the not formally named Georgia Project oversight committee that included not just the attorney, business leaders, and school district administrators, but also the thirteen visiting instructors from Monterrey, several Whitfield County administrators (who had not participated in the Georgia Project for months), a number of business leaders invited to participate for the first time, and several other interested community members or their representatives.[10]

At that meeting, a bilingual priest who had frequently been cast as advocate for/representative of the local Hispanic community (though he was not Hispanic), declared that Dalton schools were "an incompetent system" in the sense that they appeared not to be competent to the task of educating Hispanic students. After speaking bluntly and provocatively in this manner for two or three minutes the priest ended his comments by challenging the superintendent to explain what he was prepared to do to fix the situation. Though the room was tense, the superintendent responded in a dead pan that his "first step would be to take [the priest] outside and whip [him]." Everyone laughed. The confrontation was over. The superintendent had given no ground, yet parried the challenge. (Of course, parrying the challenge was ultimately different than knowing how to solve the problem that the priest alluded to.)

The superintendent's political sensibility and personal history were important for his relationship with the attorney who instigated the Georgia Project. While not a longtime district employee and thus not one implicitly criticized by the external organization and mobilization for the Georgia Project, the superintendent knew to be responsive to politically powerful locals, particularly those who could mobilize resources. For more than two years he was an ally of the project, even if his experience and training gave him little grounding regarding some of the project's components. Ultimately, however, this instinct put in doubt the superintendent's authority when he backed his staff rather than the local external elites in a 1999 showdown about Direct Instruction. Having previously tolerated the Georgia Project being outside of his close control, when his staff and the attorney (and others on both sides) began to schism he did not know how to keep the loyalty of both and ended up keeping neither.

Still, the superintendent initially succeeded at cultivating a friendly and respectful relation with the attorney and that helped the Georgia Project get started. In late 1997, the superintendent even nominated the attorney to receive recognition in the "Build a Better Georgia" statewide award ceremony because of his Georgia Project leadership. The nomination was successful, and the attorney was one of fifty Georgia residents recognized in February 1998 for their contribution to the quality of life in their communities. Initially the unclear delineation of Georgia Project leadership tasks between the superintendent and the attorney did not harm their working relationship.

In addition to the hazards of the Georgia Project's unclear governance model and the superintendent's lack of experience with Hispanic newcomer students, the superintendent faced a third situational obstacle relevant to his participation in the Georgia Project. Two of his senior administrators had publicly acknowledged superintendency ambitions. Both had applied for the Dalton opening with one, as was broadly announced in the local paper, a finalist. The paper noted that she would have been Dalton's first female superintendent ever, but, as the only Dalton-based finalist, she would have been a continuation of the tradition of hiring superintendents from within the district.

Relations between the superintendent and one of the assistants (the one profiled later in this segment) seemed to be amiable—it was this assistant who the superintendent backed in the struggle with the attorney over Direct

Instruction. However, with the other there seemed to be a kind of political freeze, the origination of which was unclear.[11] As a consequence, this second assistant was largely outside the Georgia Project loop. This was a loss to the Georgia Project if, as this assistant claimed, he really was one of the staunchest advocates within the school district for bilingual education and hiring bilingual teachers. At any rate, the presence of two superintendency-aspiring assistants created a micro-political environment that required careful negotiation by the superintendent from Bulloch County.

Though community realities (i.e., the interests of the powerful and others) recommended that the superintendent support the Georgia Project, his enthusiasm for the project seemed to originate from more than just this consideration. Perhaps, like the attorney and his daughter, the superintendent was motivated by stories from his wife, who was a kindergarten teacher at one of Dalton's most demographically transformed schools. It was the same school where the principal described next was piloting ideas that lent local credibility to the initiatives that the scholars from Monterrey were proposing for Dalton. Whatever his impetus, the superintendent lent the Georgia Project key public support when it was still nascent, hazy, and consequently quite fragile.

## THE INNOVATIVE PRINCIPAL

Given how unprepared Dalton was for the large-scale arrival of Latino students and families, and given how radical a departure a fully developed Georgia Project would be from previous practice, it is easy and valid to wonder what made the Georgia Project ideas palatable to enough Daltonians, especially school personnel, for the project to get up and running. Why were school district leaders willing to engage in this project and champion various elements of it? Part of the answer was that the staff of one Dalton school, led by one particularly innovative administrator, was already convinced of the project's need and had shown a willingness to experiment with several ideas that ultimately were incorporated into the Georgia Project.

The principal of this innovative elementary school played an important bridging role at the beginning of the Georgia Project. She was a bona fide Southerner (albeit from Mississippi, not Dalton), who, as of May 1998, was the district's only administrator with substantial expertise regarding the curricular, school leadership, and school/home relations issues related to the new presence of so many Hispanic students and their families.[12] (See Chapter 7 for details of how this school was piloting a number of project-relevant ideas, including the use of a Mexico-trained teacher as a paraprofessional.) The principal was an expert internal source who could be expected to knowledgeably evaluate the credibility and viability of various Georgia Project initiatives suggested by the Universidad de Monterrey. When I was invited to help with Dalton's Title VII grant proposal, the curriculum coordinator quickly arranged for me to meet with this principal and to read portions of her dissertation.

The principal's dissertation (Beard 1996), including the impulse to research her chosen topic, predated the Georgia Project and was an obvious starting point for her willingness to innovate and her school's later welcome of the Georgia Project. The central question of her dissertation was how schools such as hers needed to adapt in response to their changing student and parent populations. To pursue this idea she solicited elementary school principals from across Georgia to describe professional development needs related to the accommodation of English language learners.

Because they were so central to her school management strategy and to the resultant innovative school climate, a few excerpts from her dissertation are included in Figure 5.1. Manifestations of nearly all of the ideas highlighted in Figure 5.1 could be found at the principal's school at the time the Georgia Project was being planned (see Chapter 7). However, though they were still present at the end of my field study in 1998, by then, district initiatives that were not well articulated with the Georgia Project, notably the importation of the Direct Instruction language arts curriculum, had come to dominate at this school as well as other district elementary schools through the championing of Dalton's curriculum coordinator.

I never heard this principal publicly cross or disagree with the curriculum coordinator despite the way the curriculum coordinator's agenda constrained this school's innovative practices. As the coordinator continued to be marginalized in the Georgia Project's management and to become increasingly questioning of it, this principal seemed unwilling to question the coordinator, a woman she viewed as a friend and mentor, as well perhaps as a superior. (The coordinator had been the principal of this school prior to the innovative principal.) Like the curriculum coordinator, the principal was implicated in the original critique that generated the Georgia Project, as it was at her school that the attorney's daughter had become frustrated as a parapro.

In a school system that ostensibly claimed to support site based management, the principal served as another bridge for the Georgia Project. She was the only major Georgia Project decision maker who was school based. She was the only one who could offer a substantive response to the query "How will this play in your building?" and she was the only major Georgia Project figure positioned to lead the project's adoption at a school. Her two-time participation in Universidad de Monterrey Summer Institute exemplified this leadership.

Shedding light on the taxonomy of local identities, the principal described herself as an outsider. At the time of the study, she lived in Chattanooga, not Dalton. She claimed she was surprised when she was selected to be principal. She thought that not being from or resident in the district would inhibit her application. Perhaps this internalized sense of being an outsider was a motive behind her decision to pursue her doctorate; perhaps she wanted to

**FIGURE 5.1   Dissertation Excerpts (Beard 1996)**

---

(From the Section: *Affirming Language: A Key Component of Culture*)

- In urging the development of English, schools must avoid subtle or blatant criticism of a child's first language. Saville-Troike (1976) note [sic] that language is a key component of culture and is the primary medium for transmitting the culture of a people. They [sic] concluded that language is deeply bound with a person's sense of identity and self-worth. Grundy (1992) urges schools to affirm a student's native language. . . . Altwerger and Ivener (1994) also report that language minority students develop self-esteem when they know their home language and culture are viewed as assets rather than obstacles.

(From the Section: *English as a Second Language (ESL) Program models*)

- Crawford (1991:121) notes that English as a second language is often described as an "alternative method" for teaching language minority children. He concludes that this is somewhat misleading, since ESL is a component of virtually every bilingual program in the United States.
- Ultimately, the program model choice must be made as a local decision.

(From the Section: *Changing Context: Bilingual Education*)

- Garcia (1994) suggests that to prepare the citizenry of the United States for the national and international marketplace of the 21st century, the benefits of bilingualism and multiculturalism must be promoted.
- Garcia (1994) makes two recommendations regarding bilingual education. First, programs should be provided to develop language minority students' first language. Second, Garcia emphasizes that programs are needed to develop a second language for native English speakers.

---

prove her commitment as well as to advance her expertise. That she was committed to the district and to her school and its changes was evidenced by the fact that she enrolled her grandchildren as nondistrict, tuition-paying students at her school.

## THE CURRICULUM COORDINATOR

When the Georgia Project was first being organized, the superintendent was new to Dalton, the attorney was a private citizen not formally involved with the schools, the two Universidad de Monterrey professors knew little if anything about Dalton, and the just-profiled principal was working in a specific school. In that context, the original willingness of the long-serving curriculum coordinator to go along with the attorney's plans lent important credibility to the beginning of the project.

Why this administrator went along with the attorney was never fully clear. Perhaps she agreed with the general assessment that education for Hispanics in Dalton could be improved. Perhaps she was deferring to the attorney's prominent reputation and/or those of his apparent allies. Perhaps she was following the apparent lead of the new superintendent. Perhaps she did not anticipate that she had anything to lose. Perhaps she was sufficiently impressed by her visit to the Universidad de Monterrey as a member of the initial Dalton delegation in December 1996. Perhaps she was motivated by the just-profiled principal and that principal's expertise on staff development needs and other challenges confronted by leaders of schools undergoing significant linguistic and demographic transformation. The curriculum coordinator was particularly disposed to conversing with the principal because of their shared experience.

Like her just-profiled successor, when the curriculum coordinator had been a principal she had the monolingual English-speaking daughter of the attorney on her staff as a paraprofessional. Given its importance for initially motivating the attorney to initiate the Georgia Project, the daughter's testimony about the (poor) quality of schooling and the challensges staff encountered there in trying to communicate with the Hispanic population implicated both this administrator and the just-profiled principal. Relations between the attorney, this administrator, and the principal were all informed by the attorney's daughter's critique of that school and the purported un-responsiveness of the existing curriculum to the "communication barrier."

This brings us to the central emerging role of this administrator in the Georgia Project. She was the leader who by the end of my study appeared most dubious about the project. Her doubt was most conspicuously reflected in her uncertainty about implementing the bilingual education curriculum. She likely spearheaded the unilateral abandonment of this component in 1998. Goode (2002:122) references a letter this administrator sent to the bilingual coordinator in Monterrey that announced, "We have met with teachers, parents, administrators, and community members and have rethought the bilingual curriculum. . . . With this decision we will not pursue the development of a bilingual curriculum." Despite previously making on-the-record comments in favor of bilingual education, her uncertainty stemmed from her relative lack of familiarity with that topic and its various models, the possible threat bilingual education and other curriculum reforms presented to both her status and perceived job performance, and, plausibly, from various political concerns. She told a Georgia Project administrator from the Universidad de Monterrey that she had been told by several Anglo parents that they were not in favor of any district bilingual education efforts. She added her own explanation that bilingual education was not politically correct, highlighting her consciousness that to embrace bilingual education risked being subject to at least some community resentment and criticism. As a longtime middle-class resident, the curriculum coordinator had more ties with Anglo Daltonians and would likely have been more connected to community members who were dubious or unsure of the Georgia Project than were the other leaders profiled in this chapter. As noted in Chapter 4, as an English-only state, Georgia recognized only students' accomplishments on English language assessments, so, to one unsure of bilingual education's favorable effect on all academic achievement, state parameters would have reinforced her caution regarding bilingual education.

Also, because of her long-standing ties to Dalton and the school district, this administrator would have been more steeped in the traditional arrangement of the school district (after all that was the arrangement through which she had charted her own career advancement). According to this arrangement, within the district hierarchy she was the lead curriculum officer with her authority superseded only by the superintendent and the school board members, who collectively seemed little inclined to second guess her decision making. Thus, by position, the curriculum coordinator had a lot of power within the district and a relatively high public profile and a fair amount of public accountability. Apart from the superintendent, the curriculum coordinator was publicly perceived as the district's lead coordinator of academics and thereby she was also held accountable for academic school outcomes like standardized test scores. Given this traditionalist orientation and exposure to public scrutiny, following a risk-averse strategy of endorsing curriculum materials that were traditional and familiar and avoiding politically controversial and/or experimental curricula made sense.

Like the superintendent, this administrator had little formal training in bilingual/ESOL education or with any other pedagogical orientations and methodologies that sought to be culturally responsive to the diverse starting points of immigrant Hispanic students. When she started working for Dalton in 1971, such training was not readily available nor in high demand, given the local absence of Hispanics. Nor had such training or experience mattered through her subsequent promotions, including her move to become a district administrator. Thus, her administrative job description placed her in a position of overseeing at least one curricular challenge that she knew little about.

For the Title VII proposal that she ultimately brought me in on, her lack of expertise compelled her to seek advice from both the dissertation-writing principal and the original bilingual consultant that the Universidad de Monterrey had included in the Georgia Project. From some perspectives, however, depending on such advice appeared to undermine the coordinator's credibility and due status within the district hierarchy. If she was an expert, why did she need expert advice? If she was not an expert, why was she in a position that newly required this expertise?

The adjustments embedded in the Georgia Project's design challenged this administrator's position in additional ways. Both the Summer Institute and the visiting instructor components increased the school site expertise for being responsive to Hispanic newcomers. As such, both were tacit arguments for site-based management, but neither reduced the coordinator's public accountability for the school's performance. In essence, the Georgia Project was asking her to accept a reduction in the power of her position, to subscribe to several strategies built on unfamiliar ideas, and yet to remain accountable for the outcome. Moreover, to the extent the project succeeded, the attorney, the superintendent, and even the principal at the high profile elementary school were more likely to be given credit for the success than was the curriculum coordinator.

As is further explained and clarified in subsequent chapters, as the Georgia Project grew and drew attention, the one component of it that most challenged this administrator's authority and the one that most required her complicity—the bilingual education component—was held in limbo. This resistance was not overt; nor was it exceptional as she was not necessarily the only one in Dalton with doubts about bilingual education or the Georgia Project. But because of her position, her resistance disproportionately complicated and confused portions of the project's development. For example, initially the bilingual visiting instructors brought in from Monterrey were supposed to assist the implementation of the district's new bilingual curriculum, but because that curriculum was not completed when they arrived (nor was it completed subsequently) their task immediately became ambiguous.

The point here is not to be particularly critical of any one person. In fact, this sketch explains why this administrator could have become more dubious of the Georgia Project than the project's other leaders. The other leaders did not find their personal authority challenged by the Georgia Project and, except for the superintendent, they were not as nakedly on the firing line if, simultaneous to the Georgia Project, Dalton test scores dipped (which they did [Goode 2002]). Instead, one of the goals here is to utilize this administrator's position as an archetype of those within the district who had something to lose from the Georgia Project. The very origin of the Georgia Project amounted to a criticism of this administrator, abstractly implicating her along with all other longtime district employees as people who had failed to meet the unprecedented challenge presented by hundreds and then thousands of new Latino students. The Georgia Project's creation also specifically criticized her former leadership (fairly or not) of the school where the attorney's daughter felt instructor/student communication had completely fallen apart. As new components of the project cast new doubts on her tasks and authority, her skepticism was somewhat logical. However, her sense of loyalty or her deference to the formal authority of the superintendent, to the traditional hierarchy of the district, and/or to the proud reputation of the attorney kept her from resisting the project more overtly, though post-1998 changes in the relationship between the district and the Georgia Project likely reflected her disaffection with the project.

Though she ultimately was quite disaffected with the Georgia Project, the curriculum coordinator always appeared constrained in her expression of discontent with the district's status quo. Maybe this reflected an ongoing calculation that she risked more as a critic than as an insider. Certainly it reflected a diagnosis that the traditional structure of the district's management was not problematic and did not need reconfiguring. Perhaps it also reflected a nostalgic impulse or internalization of the dated idea that Dalton was the region's preeminent district. In her diagnosis, to the extent Dalton faced educational challenges, they were of exogenous origin—namely the demographic and socioeconomic change in students served—and they could be solved with a new curriculum purportedly responsive to at-risk students. Hence her championing of Direct Instruction, a rote, phonetics-oriented, fully scripted curriculum that perhaps, as one Dalton informant suggested, was also consistent with her conservative worldview, shaped by being a proud Southern Baptist and growing up in a military family and having two children in successful military careers. Goode notes, "[Direct Instruction] was a good match for the coordinator's own disciplined, linear, personal, instructional style" (2002:122).

In 1998, in a draft version of my dissertation that I shared with a Dalton audience, I wrote "How someone positioned like this administrator within Dalton could be viably included in the Georgia Project over the long term was a challenge that the project's proponents needed to solve. To not do so risked undercutting the project's already limited coherence and its acceptance across the school system" (Hamann 1999a:210). By 2002, this administrator had again been an unsuccessful finalist for the Dalton superintendancy but remained a powerful insider. She referred to her own and the district's involvement with the Georgia Project historically.

# 6

# Mexican University Partners

If, per Wallace (1956), the Dalton-based leaders of the Georgia Project can be viewed, at least in some senses, as participants in a revitalization movement, that characterization has to be shed to explain the formative involvement in the partnership of the scholars and educators from the Universidad de Monterrey. Adjectives like transnational, cosmopolitan, even nomadic, and postmodern, all help clarify who the Mexican leaders were, yet these words should not obscure the salience for these individuals of a Mexican sensibility, informed by Catholicism and tradition and Mexico's eight decade struggle to define a sense of national character. The Mexican participants in the Georgia Project figured centrally in how the project was shaped.

They were the most insistent voice, though increasingly echoed by the attorney, for Latino newcomer schooling in Dalton to emulate the "additive biculturalism" described by Gibson (1997b) that assumes gaining new cultural competencies need not come at the cost of having existing ones atrophy or be discredited. They were opposed to the assimilation by subtraction model decried by Valenzuela (1999), but that was attractive to many in Dalton (e.g., the Dalton school board members quoted in Chapter 4). As one of their thirteen recommendations made after a debrief of the first cohort of visiting instructors (see Chapter 9), they lamented that many Latino students in Dalton were losing their Spanish because of weak Spanish maintenance programs in Dalton. To quote their recommendation as initially recorded in Spanish: "Muchos alumnos hispanos van perdiendo paulatinamente el español debido a una falta de continuidad escolar y a falta de programas fuertes de español." ["Many Hispanic students are slowly losing their Spanish because of discontinuities in their schooling and a lack of strong Spanish programs."]

## TWO SOCIOLOGISTS FROM MONTERREY

While the Georgia Project would not have existed without the impetus and ongoing energy of the attorney who instigated it, and while the Georgia Project would not have been so large and so viable so quickly were it not for the protection and support of it by the superintendent, it was actually two sociologists from Mexico who were most responsible for the project's design and for the very inclusion of three of its four components. Because they had a long-term friendship, a mentor/student relationship, and related tasks in relation to the Georgia Project, I will present both their profiles as a single segment. Because both were scholars and oriented themselves as such, this segment will begin with a review of their training and scholarly experience.

The Georgia Project director at the Universidad de Monterrey began his third stint teaching there in 1996. His first position at the Universidad de Monterrey had been as a professor of sociology from 1977 to 1979, a job he began shortly after earning his Licenciatura en Ciencias de la Educación from there (the equivalent of a bachelor of science degree in the United States). During his first teaching stint at the Universidad de Monterrey, he held two concurrent posts as a professor of public health and a professor of social work at Monterrey's major public university—the Universidad Autónoma de Nuevo León. Given the low wages for higher education positions in Mexico—particularly at the entry level—such a combination of postings was not uncommon.

The Georgia Project director began his second stint at the Universidad de Monterrey in the mid-1980s when he returned to Mexico after having spent several years in Paris, France. In France, he had earned his master's degree in the sociology of education and his doctorate in the sociology of education and culture, both from the Université de Paris VIII–Vincennes. During his time in Paris, he had taught in French and established French as his second tongue. (English was his weaker third language.) The Georgia Project director's various tasks during his second stint at the Universidad de Monterrey included coordinating the university's Center of Health and Development, directing the federally funded (Mexico-funded) study "Culture and Migration in the State of Nuevo León," and working as a professor of adult education.

At the time of the Georgia Project's instigation, his primary job was at the Universidad de Monterrey as a Profesor Titular in the Department of Humanities, but he maintained affiliations and teaching duties at a number of institutions, including the Université de Paris–Versailles Saint-Quentin-en-Yvelines and the Universidad Autónoma de Nuevo León. He also edited the binational journal *Revista Rio Bravo/Journal of International Studies,* which was copublished by the University of Texas–Edinburgh and the Universidad Autónoma de Coahuila. Previously he had been director for several years at the Colegio de la Frontera Norte's Monterrey office and its academic director for the northeast region of Mexico.

It was through his involvement at the Universidad Autónoma de Nuevo León that the Universidad de Monterrey's Georgia Project director first met the student who was to become the Georgia Project's research director. The project director remembered the research director as one of the brightest undergraduates he ever taught. The project director maintained a mentor/student relationship with the research director even while the research director was away in the United States from 1992 through 1996, first as a Fulbright recipient and then as a full-time doctoral student in sociology studying under Robert Bach at the State University of New York–Binghamton. Once he reached the dissertation stage at SUNY–Binghamton, the research director came to the Universidad de Monterrey in 1997 at the invitation of his former professor, the project director. After the rector of the Universidad de Monterrey asked the project director to become involved in the Georgia Project, the project director immediately asked the research director to join the project as well.

Though the mentor/student relationship persisted between the project director and the research director, the hierarchical origins of their relationship were overshadowed by several factors, most notably their collegiality and interdependence. By virtue of his extended studies in the United States and his work with the Center for Immigration Studies at the University of Houston, the research director was more accomplished and more comfortable using English than was his mentor. For communication with English-speaking audiences in Dalton, this linguistic skill frequently cast the research director as spokesperson regarding the Universidad de Monterrey's involvement in the Georgia Project. Similarly, most of the English language texts regarding the Georgia Project that the Universidad de Monterrey produced were drafted and/or translated by the research director, sometimes with the additional assistance of his American wife and/or another Universidad de Monterrey colleague who had earned her master's degree at the University of Texas–PanAmerican.

Further drawing together the project director and the research director were similar research interests, self-conceptions, and cosmologies. Both directors described themselves as "transnational," that is, as individuals whose identity and loyalty were not shaped by one place or even one country. More so than any of the other major players involved with the Georgia Project, the two approached the typology of "cosmopolitan, high-tech, nomadic tribesman" described by Rifkin (1995:1) for whom "where they work is of far less importance than the global network they work in."[1] To the extent the project director felt national loyalties, he was loyal probably first to Mexico and second to France, while the research director's loyalties were yet more complicated.

The research director was born in Bulgaria to a Mexican father and Bulgarian mother. Though they returned to Mexico when he was young, the research director spoke Bulgarian (as well as Spanish, English, Portuguese, and French) and maintained family ties there. His sister and a niece were both named "Sofia," partially in reference to the capital of Bulgaria. The research director was also married to an American citizen (a first generation German from upstate New York who was also multilingual—speaking German, English, Spanish, Catalan, and Vietnamese—and also something of a "nomadic, high-tech tribeswoman"). While the project director and the research director shared an interest and specialty in the migration dynamics that tie together Mexico and the United States—both have studied Mexican sending communities as well as U.S. receiving communities like Dalton—only the research director had long-term personal interests in the United States.

Another characteristic that helped situate and connect the project director and the research director was that neither were Catholic, though their workplace—the Universidad de Monterrey—was a Catholic university. They were not anti-Catholic, but by not being part of the dominant religion of their country they were positioned to be a little more ambivalent about some of the religio-nationalist ideology that was generated in Mexico. They were also positioned to be ambivalent about the bilingual priest in Dalton who was one of the few outspoken voices there championing Hispanic newcomer issues.

According to both the project director and the research director, their ambivalence contributed to their comparatively open attitude toward the United States and to U.S./Mexican relations. Whereas in many Mexican universities students and professors construct the United States as a colonialist, imperious, unwelcome neighbor (see Francis and Ryan [1998] and Pastor and Castañeda [1988]), and whereas in the business community and some other Mexican circles U.S. ways are accorded some veneration, both professors claimed not to be strongly passionate about alleged Mexican victimization, U.S. exploitation, or the ensuing relations that such dynamics generate. This ambivalence about nation states distinguished them from their pro-American Dalton-based collaborators and made their work consistent with an emerging Mexican impulse to see emigration to the United States as not necessarily a disavowal of Mexican sensibilities or loyalties (Jones-Correa n.d.).

Why does it matter to try to intellectually locate these two prior to discussing the Georgia Project? For several reasons: Contributing to the Georgia Project from the perspectives they came from, they suggested the inclusion of the bilingual education curriculum component, the Summer Institute for Dalton teachers in Monterrey, and most importantly (to them) the research projects associated with the Parent and Workplace Involvement component. I say "most importantly" because that component was clearly where their main interests and expertise lay. Though they supported the Georgia Project-related curriculum reforms and teacher training programs, these were not topics that either knew well enough to advocate for or manage without proxies.

In Dalton, the three additional Georgia Project components inserted by these two leaders were accepted to greater or lesser extent by other Georgia Project initiators. However, because they were not originally ideas from the Dalton end, there was considerable variation in how they were understood (or misunderstood) and whether they were tolerated, deeply subscribed to, or ultimately viewed suspiciously by Georgia Project originators and others who were subsequently called into the Georgia Project (e.g., Dalton teachers). One reason for the continuing difference in characterizations of the Georgia Project (see Figures 13.1 and 13.2 in Chapter 13) stemmed from the fact that different pieces of the project had different origins and the motivations and understandings of their originators varied substantially. To these two leaders from the Universidad de Monterrey, Dalton/Whitfield was a type of place, a U.S. locale, like others, being demographically transformed by the play of global economic restructuring and the extension of transnational labor networks. This perspective differed from that of the attorney and the curriculum coordinator, and even the superintendent and principal who were also relative outsiders to Dalton. The perspective also differed from most native Daltonians, white and black, including the leaders of the locally headquartered carpet companies. To these latter people and to a growing number of Dalton Hispanics, Dalton was not like anywhere else; it was not a type of place; it was home.

To this home of others, the two Monterrey sociologists (and their university colleagues and the visiting instructors) brought an institution-based worldview as well as a personal one. In other words, the culture and orientation generated at the Universidad de Monterrey and extant there were ultimately also consequential in Dalton through the Georgia Project. Though they pertain to more than just the biographical sketches of the two Monterrey leaders, the following paragraphs give a glimpse into the institutional world from which most of those on the Mexican side of the Georgia Project partnership came.

Thirty years ago, when its universities were riven by student protest and police repression (see Poniatowska 1971), it would have been hard for most Mexican university administrators to be busy seeking links to U.S. school systems. Certainly, the Universidad de Monterrey would not have been looking to establish such links then; it was too preoccupied with the processes of its own establishment. The Universidad was only created in 1969 (though some of the antecedent Catholic institutions that were consolidated to create the university are much older).

Since 1969, the commercial and demographic links between Mexico and the United States have grown exponentially, recently accelerated by the amnesty provisions of the 1986 Immigration Reform and Control Act and then NAFTA (Suárez-Orozco 1999). Dislocations related to both the changing cultural ecology and political ecology encountered by people of Mexican origin have connected millions of Mexican families to multiple locations on both sides of the international border (Hackenberg 1997).[2]

As a consequence, Mexico's interest in the internal doings of the United States has increased. During the presidency of Carlos Salinas de Gortari (1988–1994), Mexico's political leadership formally recognized how important the activities of Mexican expatriates in the United States were for determining U.S. popular opinion and government policy regarding Mexico (Mendez Lugo 1997). In 1990, the Mexican government established the Programa para las Comunidades Mexicanas en el Extranjero [Program for Mexican Expatriate Communities]. Mexican political parties and the Confederación Nacional Campesina also started formalizing their involvement with networks of Mexican citizens in the United States at that time. Policies were initiated then that since have nebulously permitted Mexican emigrants to maintain their Mexican nationality (though not their citizenship) even if they become citizens of another country—most typically the United States. According to the emergent national political logic, Mexicans in the United States were still part of the Mexican national community (Jones-Correa n.d.).

In the 1990s, Mexico's government leaders also specifically championed the improvement and development of private education in Mexico. While secretary of education in the Salinas de Gortari administration, Mexico's subsequent president, Ernesto Zedillo, publicly questioned the viability and the future of Mexico's public university system and acknowledged the rationale of Mexicans who were newly showing favor to private institutions (Lorey 1995). Previous administrations had largely let be private institutes of higher education. Thus private institutions developed according to the interests of their private sector patrons specifically and of Mexico's upper economic classes generally (Levy 1986).

Within the spirit of Mexico's growing attention to and linkages with its northern neighbor and the growing stature of private education in Mexico, it was logical in 1996 for the rector of the Universidad de Monterrey to jump at a proposed U.S.-sited research project. In a separate effort, though one that was attractive to education planners in Dalton, at the same time as the Georgia Project agreement was being created, Universidad de Monterrey officials were preparing a viable bid to be accredited by the Southern Association of Colleges and Schools, a U.S.-based accreditation agency. (Different informants varied in telling me that this bid had already been approved or that it was still pending.) However, neither the binational context of U.S./Mexico relations nor the bid for accreditation fully explain why the Universidad de Monterrey became a partner in the Georgia Project, nor why the partnership was able to develop so many dimensions so quickly.

At the time of my study, within the mix of Mexican universities generally and within the particular mix of universities around Monterrey (Mexico's third largest city), the Universidad de Monterrey occupied a particular niche that disposed it to being a responsive and viable partner in the Georgia Project. According to Lorey (1993, 1995, and personal communication) and several informants from the Universidad de Monterrey, the following characteristics were particularly important for compelling the Universidad de Monterrey to quickly join the Georgia Project: (1) the dynamics of the Mexican higher education market, (2) the Universidad's private status and related corporate style of governance, (3) the Universidad's Catholicism-originating humanistic orientation, and (4) the individual characteristics of the Universidad de Monterrey leaders who primarily guided the university's side of the Georgia Project partnership.

According to Lorey (1993, 1995), since the late 1950s Mexican universities have been producing more *egresados* (credentialed graduates and school leavers) than the economy has been able to absorb, meaning that Mexico has had more professionals than professional positions, that personal contacts made at university have become increasingly important to landing comparatively rare professional jobs, and that many Mexicans end up with jobs for which their training is unnecessary.[3] This has put different pressures on public universities and private ones. Public universities have been pressured to expand and to maintain low tuitions and minimal entrance standards so the maximum number of potential students can enter a university. At public universities, after admission, there has been a weeding-out process as many students who enter leave without obtaining a degree, but perhaps having obtained advantageous personal ties through university experience.[4] At private universities, the challenge has been to compete with public universities by offering superior future job security or other benefits that are less sure for public university students.

In response to both the larger unequal relation between the United States and Mexico and the specific need for the Universidad de Monterrey to improve the employment prospects of its graduates, participation in the Georgia Project was eminently sensible. The Universidad de Monterrey's stature was raised by the fact that a U.S. school district was coming to it seeking expert advice; this in turn was expected to influence faculty and student recruitment and alumni pride, loyalty, and (hopefully) generosity. (At the time of my research, the Universidad de Monterrey was involved in a substantial fund-raising initiative.) For the Universidad de Monterrey's School of Education graduates who were serving as visiting instructors in Dalton through the Georgia Project, their university linkage had literally translated into jobs in the United States (earning dollars) and experience that would, according to the visiting instructors and other informants, significantly enhance their employability and increase the salaries that they could command at private schools in Monterrey.[5] To promise opportunities like those available through the Georgia Project (though perhaps less exotic than the Georgia Project) was essential for the Universidad de Monterrey's efforts to attract students.

As the Universidad de Monterrey competed locally for students with the Universidad Autónoma de Nuevo León and with three other private universities—Tec de Monterrey, the Universidad del Norte, the Universidad de Regiomontana—it emphasized a humanities orientation (broadly interpreted) to create a niche for itself akin to that of a service-oriented private liberal arts college in the United States (though the Universidad de Monterrey differs from a liberal arts college by offering master's degrees and, like many private Mexican universities, a *preparatoria,* or high school). Within this niche, the Universidad de Monterrey created a sizable School of Education and a large Humanities Department. The latter hosted the applied sociologists who led the Universidad de Monterrey's portion of the Georgia Project. In short, the Universidad de Monterrey's posturing within Mexico's higher education marketplace compelled it to develop programs that made it a good fit for partnership with Dalton's schools.

The Universidad de Monterrey's School of Education differs from such entities at U.S. universities in that more of its graduates will go on to teach in private schools and in the context of its bilingual education program. In the city of Monterrey, bilingual education (with rare exception) means dual instruction in Spanish and English. Though at the university level in Mexico the association of English with the imperiousness of the United States sometimes means that English is viewed ambivalently (Francis and Ryan 1998), both languages are taught because both are deemed useful. This contrasts with much bilingual education in the United States where cultivation of the first language is often thought of only as a useful bridging step for the important process of teaching English (Rippberger 1993). Foreign language instruction in U.S. schools is not usually thought of as bilingual education. The importance of this different perspective regarding bilingual education at the Universidad de Monterrey and in Dalton is considered in Chapter 11.

As a private institution, the Universidad de Monterrey had a much smaller constituency that it had to answer to than did, say, the much larger nearby public university—the Universidad Autónoma de Nuevo León. Unlike the public Mexican universities with their leftist orientations related first to their agreement with the federal government brokered in 1929 to be self-controlled as long as they contributed to the government's revolutionary aims and second to their history of public conscience and protest, Mexico's private universities have traditionally responded to the upper-middle class and elite families whose children they seek to enroll and to the interests of business leaders and others who function as their directors and patrons (Levy 1986). The Universidad de Monterrey was not as beholden to or limited by the governmental bureaucracy and complicated public politics that were manifest at Mexican public universities.

Thus the Universidad de Monterrey could act quickly when presented with a promising opportunity. First faced with a phone call from a favored patron then another from a Georgia attorney (both in September 1996), just months later the Universidad de Monterrey had signed on to a four-component agreement worth hundreds of thousands of dollars. Whatever the merits of deliberations by faculty committees and the checks and balances that characterize higher education administration at Mexican public and U.S. public and private universities, none of these latter types of institutions could have mobilized as easily and quickly the wide range of resources that the Universidad de Monterrey summoned for the Georgia Project. The Universidad de Monterrey's willingness to extend a line of credit to its own scholars while they negotiated the accord and started getting funding from Dalton was also crucial to the Universidad's fast response and something that would likely have required more deliberation in other institutional environments. Given the tenuousness and unorthodoxy of the Georgia Project's earliest phases, time for more deliberation might well have let the enthusiasm peter out and kill the project altogether. At a minimum, given the impatience of the Georgia Project's private sector promoters in Dalton, delay would likely have meant the exclusion of the Universidad de Monterrey.

Finally, one of the Universidad's founding tenets stated that service to others was humane and integral to personal development.[6] Students were required to perform approved service to others. Though, as of May 1998, the Georgia Project had not yet been used as a means for Universidad de Monterrey students to satisfy their service requirements, assisting the Georgia Project's general premises and helping a needy Mexican community in the *extranjero* were firmly consistent with the Universidad de Monterrey's general philosophy of operation.

Perhaps the imprint of this orientation was most visible in the spirit that the visiting instructors brought to their task. Goode (2002:151–152) quotes a Dalton teacher who contrasted the visiting instructors with the bilingual paraprofessionals Dalton subsequently recruited locally:

These girls who came from Monterrey were well educated. They had almost a missionary zeal about helping the Mexicans in this town. I find they've sort of a different attitude than with our homegrown help. . . . We have a few bilingual parapros who have come from Mexico who are good, but they don't have the education and for whatever reason there is not that . . . sense of awe when one of these folks goes with me on home visits that there was with those Monterrey teachers. I think the Monterrey teachers, because of their training and because of the fall back on that spirit of benevolence, that zeal . . . these girls had to be here because they wanted to be here. They wanted to help. That's it. They wanted to help. . . . If I'm remembering right, part of their training is like a segment of social work. Something that's lacking from teacher training programs here. And they were better prepared to be representatives of the school system.

# Part Three

# A Novel Binational Partnership: From Launch to Consolidation

# The Complaints of a "Parapro," Action, and One School Pointing the Way

> In the domain of education, when we perceive that children or schools
> are not performing as we imagine they should, we seek or construct
> stories to explain why, and to orient our efforts at addressing perceived
> problems. Education policy is implicated in these myth-making
> processes: any plan of action, recommendation for change, or statement
> of goals involves (either explicitly or implicitly) an account of purported
> conditions and a set of recommendations for addressing them.
>
> —*Rosen 2001:299*

In 1993, before there was a Georgia Project, Dalton's daily newspaper subtitled a feature story with the byline: "Schools key to assimilating Hispanics" (V. Hoffman 1993). In the article, school leaders were quoted as saying that limited English proficient immigrant students needed from one year up to three years to learn adequate English to be successfully mainstreamed (a claim contrary to most second language acquisition research [e.g., Collier 1987, 1995; Cummins 1981; Hakuta, Butler, and Witt 2000; Mitchell, Destino, and Karam 1997]).[1] The extra challenges such students encountered in mainstream schools were reduced to issues of language difference. In the article, "Hispanic" families were distinguished from "American" families.

At that time, the small but expanding English to Students of Other Languages (ESOL) program was Dalton schools' only major curricular accommodation to the newcomers.[2] Additionally, a few schools feeling the greatest demographic impact were hosting "cultural appreciation days" for which students were encouraged to bring to school traditional foods and artwork from their native lands. The idea of a coordinated district-wide (or countywide) response to the schools' new Hispanic population was not yet on the table, nor had any business leaders come forward to instigate such an effort. That would take another two and a half years. In the meantime, Dalton would undergo accelerated immigration and louder formal and informal responses to it in the public sphere. Responses included INS raids at local plants (Rehyansky 1995a, 1995b) and bitter reactionary letters to the editor in the local newspaper.

The point of this chapter is to highlight how fast moving and unorthodox the creation of the Georgia Project was by describing how fast Dalton's demographic transformation occurred and the conventional wisdom that preceded it. In particular, the chapter lays out the particular "cocktail"— frustrated well-meaning teachers, earnest steps taken at one highly impacted elementary school, a new superintendent, the serendipity of particular binational contacts, and the perseverance of the attorney—that led to the creation of the Georgia Project. Though the ideas encompassed in the 1993 newspaper article referenced earlier were still extant when I first became acquainted with Dalton, they are discussed here mostly for purposes of juxtaposition. Four years later these ideas were awkwardly paired with very different ones to provide the impetus for the Georgia Project.

## AN ATTORNEY'S INQUIRY

Just before the end of the 1995–1996 school year at the invitation of the attorney's daughter, the attorney and three other local leaders observed classes at the East Side elementary school where the attorney's daughter had been working as a parapro. According to school district data, that school's Hispanic enrollment had risen from 54 in 1989 (13.7 percent) to 384 (57.7 percent) in the spring of 1996 (concurrent with an overall expansion of the school from 395 to 665 students). During their visit, a frustrated teacher complained about the fact that she was about to pass Hispanic students on to the next grade level, even though she had only just, in her mind, gotten them ready to begin the grade level they were finishing.

How accurate the teacher's assessment was or whether the teacher intended it to generate any reaction beyond sympathy did not matter; that conversation and others like it between the attorney and her colleagues were precipitous.[3] The school district needed to be queried and its plans for educating Latino newcomers made clear. The attorney quickly arranged various meetings at his office with district leaders to discover how the district was responding to the ongoing influx of Hispanics. To his surprise and frustration, he heard from the retiring superintendent that there was no district-wide plan. The retiring superintendent did note, however, that the district was open to suggestions.

Working openly with the school system but according to his own dictates, the attorney sent out a blizzard of letters seeking to locate ideas or any possible support for the not-yet-named Georgia Project from dozens of sources. People who were not particularly involved with the Georgia Project from the Mexican consulate in Atlanta, the University of Georgia, Georgia State University, and the Georgia Department of Education have shown me letters from the attorney requesting various forms of support. The first communication from the attorney that bore real fruit, however, was a conversation he had with a family friend, the CEO of one of Dalton's largest carpet manufacturers. That conversation and the response it generated are discussed momentarily, after a short statistical portrait of the school district at the time of the attorney's initial visit.

## A STATISTICAL PORTRAIT

Quantitative data show clearly how sudden and dramatic Dalton and Whitfield County's ongoing newcomer influx had been at the time the Georgia Project was created and how, within the Dalton system, the impact of this influx was much more pronounced for the poorer East Side catchment area than the wealthier West Side. Yet test data, at least SAT scores, give some explanation for the apparent relative complacency of the retiring superintendent. In the spring of 1996, at the time the attorney visited the school where his daughter worked, the school district's enrollment tally counted 1,243 Hispanic students, a number almost equal to the 1990 Census count of 1,422 for all Hispanics in the city. The spring 1996 count of 1,243 Hispanic students was more than five times greater than the total 1980 Dalton count of 237 "people of Spanish origin."

According to school district data, Dalton's 1989 school enrollment was 4 percent Hispanic; by the spring of 1996 that proportion had grown to 28 percent and by the fall of 2001 to 55 percent. (see Table 7.1). While white enrollment did decline in Dalton between the fall of 1989 and the spring of 1996 (3,131 to 2,526), as black enrollment stayed steady (527 to 532), when the attorney first visited Dalton schools, the bulk of the increase in Hispanic school enrollment meant for growth in the district's overall enrollment, not replacement. The number of Hispanic students enrolled in Dalton in September 1989 was 151; in the spring of 1996 it was 1,243 and in the fall of 2001 it was 2,987 (see Table 7.2).

Despite the Hispanic influx, as the Georgia Project was getting started, Dalton schools' longtime record of high quality still seemed to be intact, at least as measured by the district's average SAT scores of 1063 combined in 1997, which were frequently cited. This score was the second highest average in the state and well ahead of both the national average of 1016 and the Georgia average of 960 (Georgia Department of Education 1998).[4] (Georgia's state average for SAT scores ranked forty-ninth in the country that year [Deck 1997].) The high SAT average may have been a misleading indicator of district quality and health, however, not just because of the

TABLE 7.1   Dalton's Proportional Enrollment by Race/Ethnicity, 1989–2001

| Year, measured in Sept. | Hispanic | Black, non-H | White, non-H | All others, non-H* |
|---|---|---|---|---|
| 1989–1990 | 3.89 | 13.60 | 80.78 | 1.72 |
| 1990–1991 | 5.71 | 13.45 | 78.99 | 1.83 |
| 1991–1992 | 7.60 | 14.01 | 76.40 | 1.97 |
| 1992–1993 | 9.86 | 13.72 | 74.35 | 2.03 |
| 1993–1994 | 14.94 | 13.50 | 69.25 | 2.29 |
| 1994–1995 | 21.26 | 13.13 | 63.03 | 2.56 |
| 1995–1996 | 26.77 | 11.88 | 58.63 | 2.70 |
| 1996–1997 | 33.04 | 11.23 | 52.88 | 2.83 |
| 1997–1998 | 36.73 | 11.49 | 48.83 | 2.96 |
| 1998–1999 | 41.55 | 10.58 | 44.56 | 3.32 |
| 1999–2000 | 45.44 | 10.18 | 40.67 | 3.71 |
| 2000–2001 | 51.50 | 9.13 | 35.21 | 4.20 |
| 2001–2002 | 55.40 | 8.10 | 32.20 | 4.20 |

*Includes Asian/Pacific Islander, American Indian/Alaskan Native, and Multiracial.

TABLE 7.2   Dalton's Enrollments by Race/Ethnicity, 1989–2001

| Year, measured in Sept. | Hispanic | Black, non-H | White, non-H | All others, non-H* | Totals |
|---|---|---|---|---|---|
| 1989–1990 | 151 | 527 | 3,131 | 67 | 3,876 |
| 1990–1991 | 220 | 518 | 3,042 | 71 | 3,851 |
| 1991–1992 | 296 | 545 | 2,972 | 77 | 3,890 |
| 1992–1993 | 380 | 529 | 2,865 | 79 | 3,853 |
| 1993–1994 | 591 | 534 | 2,739 | 91 | 3,955 |
| 1994–1995 | 902 | 557 | 2,674 | 109 | 4,242 |
| 1995–1996 | 1,178 | 523 | 2,580 | 119 | 4,400 |
| 1996–1997 | 1,512 | 514 | 2,420 | 130 | 4,576 |
| 1997–1998 | 1,688 | 528 | 2,244 | 136 | 4,596 |
| 1998–1999 | 1,992 | 507 | 2,136 | 159 | 4,794 |
| 1999–2000 | 2,280 | 511 | 2,041 | 186 | 5,018 |
| 2000–2001 | 2,707 | 480 | 1,852 | 221 | 5,260 |
| 2001–2002 | 2,987 | 439 | 1,738 | 229 | 5,393 |

*Includes Asian/Pacific Islander, American Indian/Alaskan Native, and Multiracial.

intrinsic limits in any standardized outcome measurement of this type, but also because graduation data—particularly Hispanic graduation data—suggested a sizable portion of Dalton's potential SAT-taking population was not taking the test because they were not staying in school. According to district data, in September 1996, the Hispanic proportion of the ninth grade enrollment was 30.5 percent (113 out of 371) and tenth grade

30.0 percent (82 out of 273), but eleventh grade was only 17.3 percent (46 out of 266) and twelfth grade 11.8 percent (27 out of 229). Those eleventh and twelfth grades would have been the SAT-takers that generated the scores noted previously.

## THE ATTORNEY PRESSES INTO ACTION

Because of his daughter's tales and what he had learned directly from his first school visits, the attorney was convinced that the school district's status quo was inadequate and that it was time to communicate and mobilize. Among the people the attorney contacted was his client, longtime family friend, and fellow Daltonian, the wealthy CEO of one of Dalton's large carpet manufacturers. Shortly after the attorney had shared his concerns, the CEO intervened in a crucial way on behalf of the emergent project, linking it to Mexico and highlighting the significance of personal, business-related, transnational linkages for shaping the experience of thousands in Dalton. This particular linkage was the result of a 1994 partnering between the CEO's company and a Mexican company that had been articulated shortly after the passage of NAFTA. According to sources at the Universidad de Monterrey, the Dalton CEO three times called a powerful Mexican business partner asking that partner how Dalton could be assisted in its efforts to accommodate its influx of Mexicans. After the third call, the Mexican business leader was convinced of the CEO's seriousness and he agreed to contact the rector of the Universidad de Monterrey to discuss creating a partnership between Dalton schools and the university.

Though the Mexican business leader had no official affiliation with the university, he was from one of the most eminent (and wealthiest) families in Monterrey, his grandfather had played an instrumental role in the founding and the development of the Universidad de Monterrey, and several executives in the corporation he headed were on the Universidad de Monterrey's two tiers of trustees and directors. A request from this leader was bound to generate activity at the university. As the rector of the Universidad de Monterrey subsequently confirmed, "when this business leader calls we respond."

Though what was being proposed was pretty nebulous during this first period of binational contact—nebulous because of the number of people between instigator and respondent, as well as the still fuzzy sense at the Dalton end of what challenges were faced there—the rector of the Universidad de Monterrey did ask one of his sociology professors if he would be willing to head up a collaborative project in Georgia. Making the whole proposition seem slightly more real, in September 1996 the monolingual instigating attorney back in Dalton decided to call the designated professor at the Universidad de Monterrey who, fortunately, was trilingual, though English was the weakest of his three languages.

## THE NEW SUPERINTENDENT'S LETTER

In September 1996, the attorney also successfully petitioned Dalton's new superintendent to draft a letter (Figure 7.1) in support of the nascent project that would clarify some of the district's wishes and needs. The superintendent's letter marks the first substantive communication between Dalton schools and the Universidad de Monterrey; thus it was disproportionately important for the shaping of Universidad de Monterrey leaders' conceptualizations of the school district's wishes, understandings, and expectations. The superintendent sent a copy of the letter to the attorney.

Several facets of this letter merit specific attention. Foremost is the school district's expression of need for bilingual teachers. The number suggested in this letter—sixty-eight—well exceeds both the six who were supposed to pilot the program in the spring of 1997 (but did not because of visa problems) and the fourteen who did come in October 1997. Given this first suggested number, it is striking that the Dalton superintendent successfully reduced the proposed number of visiting instructors for 1998–1999 from twenty-five, the figure suggested by the attorney to Universidad de Monterrey officials, to the sixteen that were ultimately agreed upon. (See Chapter 9 for a fuller review of this project component.)

Also important, this letter suggested district leaders' understanding of and commitment to bilingual education as an appropriate pedagogy. The letter clearly expresses the district's interest in being able to provide first language support to native Spanish speakers in various academic content areas with the goal of literate, bilingual graduates. Unlike the common and ultimately assimilationist bilingual education strategy known as transitional bilingual education, in which native language support lasts only as long as it takes for a student to gain sufficient mastery of English, a long-term valuing of native language is suggested here, with a continued valuing of newcomer students' culture and heritage readily inferable. As is subsequently shown (in Chapter 11), most Dalton officials' understanding of bilingual education was superficial and their support for it was neither nuanced nor deep. To Universidad de Monterrey educators it appeared that Dalton leaders were asking for something that they knew more about than they actually did. This discrepancy subsequently caused confusion and misunderstanding.

In his letter, the superintendent asked Universidad de Monterrey officials to direct further questions and communication to the Georgia Project's instigating attorney. In hindsight, this referral contributed to the question at the Universidad de Monterrey end as to who at the Dalton end was actually in charge of the Georgia Project. Was it the school district's chief executive or the private attorney? It also illustrated a different relationship at this stage between the attorney and the Dalton school district than what subsequently developed.

**FIGURE 7.1  The First Letter from Dalton Schools to the Universidad de Monterrey**

Dear [Monterrey Georgia Project Director],

As the Superintendent of the Dalton Public Schools, I send you greetings on behalf of our students, faculty and Board of Education. I truly look forward to this excellent opportunity to work with you to provide the needed educational opportunity our students deserve.

You have already received information regarding our eight schools. I am extremely proud of these schools and the work being done to provide an outstanding education for our students.

I have now met with our eight school principals on two occasions to discuss the possibilities of assistance from Universidad de Monterrey. They are very excited about the assistance you may offer.

We have discussed many strategies which could assist us. We have a high percent of Spanish speaking students at three of our schools and this number increases each year. All of us agree that adult bilingual assistance in the classes would be of great benefit to all concerned.

By providing instruction in the native language, these students could increase their skill levels in academic subjects. Also, we could provide intensive English instruction with the ultimate goal being that of a literate bilingual student.

I am unclear of the training your teachers receive. In the University System of Georgia, a student in training to be a teacher must spend three months in a school in an experience called "student teaching." This person is under the supervision of the University and the classroom teacher. If you have such an experience for those in training to be a teacher, we could provide this experience in our schools. If your teacher training does not contain this requirement, perhaps the "Georgia Experience" with Dalton Schools could serve in the place of some of your courses in education training.

Additionally, if there is training for school administrators, we would welcome these students. I am certain there are many positive experiences anyone would receive by working in our schools.

Also, if nurses or school counselors are available or in training, we would certainly welcome them.

Perhaps this program could lead to an exchange of educators. We could possibly send some of our teachers for training in Mexico. Other ideas

**(continued)**

include: instructing our teachers in the Spanish language, creating Saturday classes for children and adults (families), summer school, obtaining textbooks in Spanish and many others.

It is my desire and I have the approval of our Board of Education to hire someone to coordinate all these activities. I am certain this person should be extremely organized and willing to work hard to implement this program.

I have listed the schools below and the number of your teachers/students they have requested. I asked the principals to state their needs, perhaps these numbers are too high, but I believe they confirm our needs.

Fort Hill—13, Brookwood—2, City Park—2, Roan—20, Morris—10, Westwood—4, Dalton Jr. High School—5, Dalton High School—12.

This is a total of sixty-eight (68) people! Perhaps an unrealistic number at the beginning of this project. But please remember, I did ask for the needs. One-half of the number would be wonderful. As you analyze our needs it will be obvious that we will appreciate any assistance you provide.

We would do all we could to provide housing and substance [sic] for these individuals. I am certain our community would welcome your students/faculty with open arms.

Please consider this proposal and contact [the attorney] with your thoughts regarding this request.

Again, I truly look forward to working with you as we develop this program.

Sincerely,

DALTON PUBLIC SCHOOLS SUPERINTENDENT

The letter promised Dalton would hire a coordinator for the Georgia Project. This step was never enacted in the way initially implied; the superintendent's executive secretary was designated coordinator, but none of her other duties were eliminated and no new allocation was made. Clearly committed to the Georgia Project's success, the executive secretary supported its development by working extra hours and during weekends, even drafting an application nominating the Georgia Project for the Innovations in American Government Award offered by Harvard's Kennedy School of Government.

This laudable dedication, however, permitted Dalton to avoid an administrative reconfiguration to support the Georgia Project. Through the four years of Dalton's most substantive involvement with the Georgia Project (1997–2001), execution of the project's administrative tasks depended on the extra energy and goodwill of an employee who had substantial unrelated responsibilities and no formal expertise in bilingual/multicultural education, nor any regarding immigration issues. When the personal relationship between the attorney and secretary-cum-coordinator deteriorated, the secretary's lack of expertise in immigrant education reduced the chances of her and the attorney finding topic-area common ground. In other words, there was no basis for a reconciling conversation that would begin with words such as: "Here is what we both know needs to happen."

Before writing the letter, the superintendent consulted with principals in each Dalton school to survey their wishes and needs. With the partial exception, however, of the profiled innovative principal, Dalton principals (and other school-based personnel) were not systematically included in the continued Georgia Project planning process that led to and guided the project's formal enactment. In 1997–1998, the principals were consulted regarding the performance of the visiting instructors from Monterrey and there appeared to be open channels of communication between the schools and the superintendent. Still, the point remains that from this letter Universidad de Monterrey officials could surmise more and more systematic site-based input than subsequently occurred and could presume more site-based knowledge and support than actually existed.

As the Georgia Project was getting started, Dalton officials were unsure of all that was potentially on offer—hence the questions about bilingual nurses, administrators, and so forth—and they were depending, not surprisingly, on familiar models (e.g., the University System of Georgia) as a building block upon which to base their requests. School districts in Georgia are accustomed to relying on state institutions of higher education as sources for teachers and other personnel. This was their starting point in terms of what they sought from the Universidad de Monterrey. At the Universidad de Monterrey end, where the initial understanding of Dalton was also trusting but limited, the superintendent's letter was read with enthusiasm.

## FACE-TO-FACE

After the first attorney/Dalton schools/Universidad de Monterrey contacts in September, continued phone, letter, and fax communication culminated in the first face-to-face meeting between Dalton and Universidad de Monterrey representatives in December 1996. A week later than originally intended to accommodate a personal concern of the Dalton attorney, the first meeting between Dalton and Universidad de Monterrey officials took place on December 12, the holiday for the Virgin of Guadalupe (Mexico's patron saint), on the campus of the Universidad de Monterrey.[5]

The attorney, with his conviction that a communication gap needed to be remedied, the principal, with her research and firsthand experience arguing for better responsiveness to Latino newcomers, and the new superintendent, with his willingness to entertain many possibilities regarding what a partnership with a Mexican university might bring, all flew together on a commercial flight. Joining them were the district's curriculum coordinator and the chairman of its school board. The school district covered the costs of its three employees (the two others paid their own way). This detail is worth noting because it shows that Dalton, perhaps in deference to the enthusiasm and/or persistence of the attorney, was already willing to commit $2,000 to a still fuzzy and unorthodox plan to partner with a Mexican university.

The hosts at the Universidad de Monterrey included the two profiled sociologists, the coordinator of its master's program in education science (who later directed the first Summer Institute), the original bilingual education consultant (further described in Chapter 11), the then-director of the Division of Education Sciences and the Humanities (who was later involved with the recruitment and oversight of the visiting instructor component), and a representative of the Department of Languages. That the Department of Languages professor was invited to participate and that he subsequently was not involved in the Georgia Project at all indicates that, at this stage, the Universidad de Monterrey project leaders were not quite sure of what would transpire either. They were not sure what the Georgia Project would become or whose involvement would be helpful.

Though Dalton leaders and the attorney had various vague ideas of what a partnership with the Universidad de Monterrey might bring—as the superintendent's original letter to the Universidad de Monterrey Georgia Project leader demonstrates—Universidad de Monterrey participants felt that the central and only solid item on the Daltonians' agenda was to ask for the Universidad de Monterrey's help bringing bilingual teachers to Dalton. Perhaps phone communication between the attorney and Monterrey representatives had also contributed to this impression.[6] Moreover, Monterrey leaders felt Dalton's one-dimensional proposal, on its own, was not something they were particularly interested in. They responded with two offers. First, humorously, they offered to help Dalton place a help-wanted advertisement in a Monterrey newspaper if it was just recruiting assistance that Dalton was seeking. Their more serious suggestion was to help Dalton find bilingual instructors if the school district and attorney would also welcome additional components for the project.

The night of December 12, after a day of hearing Dalton leaders describe their school district and community, the two Universidad de Monterrey's sociologists profiled in Chapter 6 put together the basic four-component framework for the Georgia Project that was ultimately accepted. They first presented this framework the morning of December 13. It was embraced enthusiastically by the Dalton representatives, though not with full comprehension. In March 1997, the attorney requested the Monterrey sociologists clarify what the Parent and Industry/Workplace Involvement component entailed (see Chapter 12). More seriously, the subsequent confusion regarding the bilingual curriculum component also indicated that the understanding of all that was on offer may not have been very deep (see Chapter 11).

Another detail from the meeting not yet noted also mattered subsequently. The Universidad de Monterrey personnel's recollections of events (the primary source for the previous paragraphs) excludes remembrance of a two-page outline prepared by Dalton's curriculum coordinator, distributed at the meeting in Monterrey, and kept in the sociologists' files. That outline raised the prospect of staff development for Dalton educators in Spanish, cultural awareness, and (the only detailed item on the list) clarifying the phonetic differences between English and Spanish languages so as to help teachers better understand reading difficulties of Hispanic students and to facilitate a quicker transfer to English. It also raised the prospect of summer programs for kindergartners (presumably Hispanic) "who are to be retained or placed for the next year with the goal being that all first graders are on grade level" and also for "graduation remediation" (again presumably for Hispanics). The outline mentioned parent education programs, specifically family literacy and take-home material for learning English. Then it outlined more than a dozen specific tasks under the caption "University of Monterey" [sic]. The task list was divided into two parts "resource for" and "recruitment of bilingual teachers." "Resource for" tasks included "psychological testing personnel, books and tests, and assistance obtaining the Mexican school records for Dalton staff with degrees from Mexican colleges." It is unclear when during the meeting this outline was presented or why it was not remembered. It would not be the last time, however, that a suggestion from the curriculum coordinator was overlooked.

Four additional details from the December 1996 encounter merit description. First, because of the assistance of English speakers from the Universidad de Monterrey, both sides were able to communicate with each other, become enthused about the project, and recognize that they enjoyed each other's company. Second, despite the enthused communication, Universidad de Monterrey officials came away from the meeting thinking that the Dalton carpet executive who had initiated the Monterrey link was also ready to provide the bulk of its financial support.[7] Third, even with a detailed update about Dalton, Universidad de Monterrey officials mistakenly referred to Dalton in their meeting notes as Dalton County. The familiarity of each side with the other was still quite limited. Finally, demonstrating both conviction and impatience,[8] the attorney clearly indicated his desire to have the first Monterrey visiting instructors in Dalton by the end of January 1997, a time line that soon proved not to be viable.

## A PILOT SCHOOL

Another reason that this unlikely partnership was viewed as palatable at the Dalton end was one elementary school where changes were an important antecedent for the Georgia Project. That school—the one most frequently showcased to visitors once the Georgia Project started—had been slowly developing a partially bilingual curriculum, assembling bilingual staff, and using a Mexico-trained educator during the two years prior to the Georgia Project's start. That school's experiences were a primary reason that the ideas being considered for the Georgia Project seemed palatable and practical. In some sense, the Georgia Project could be construed as an effort to take this school's initiatives to scale district-wide.

The innovative principal there, who completed her dissertation in 1996 on the staff-development needs of schools with large language minority populations, encouraged her staff's professional study of how to better understand and meet the needs of the building's Hispanic majority and its other students. This study included staff members' attendance at the National Association for Bilingual Education (NABE) meetings and, later, high participation in various Georgia Project-related opportunities.

At this school, extensive efforts were made to assure all parents were included through the use of adult interpreters (as necessary) in teacher conferences and the open invitation for parents to join their children for lunch at school. (With many parents working double shifts, this popular accommodation often was the only means for parents and children to spend waking time together during the working week.) During my study period, greater than 90 percent of enrolled students' parent(s) had attended a parent/teacher conference and more than 90 percent had signed an agreement of understanding with the school that outlined *school* responsibilities/tasks, *shared* responsibilities/tasks, and *family* responsibilities/tasks vis à vis the education of students. The turnout at the school's five annual family activity nights averaged 400 participants (the school enrolled 700 students).

Regarding curriculum and organization, the principal supported her school's experiments with multi-age and two-way bilingual classrooms. Moreover, all children in this school studied forty minutes of Spanish four times a week. There were signs in two languages throughout the school and welcome Spanish chatter in the halls. (As recently as four years earlier, student chatter in Spanish was corrected with a stern "We speak English here.")

A few years before the Georgia Project, the principal had brought back from the NABE meetings a Spanish language curriculum—"Estrellitas" (or "Little Stars"). During 1997–1998, every student at this school, including first language Spanish speakers, used this mostly phonetics-oriented curriculum to study Spanish oral and literacy skills. Some students studied more Spanish than this in dual language classrooms.[9] The school operated according to the assumptions (backed by research cited in the principal's dissertation) that (1) developing Spanish language literacy skills aids the acquisition of academic

English for the majority of this school's students who come from Spanish-speaking households and that (2) for students who speak English as a first language the acquisition of Spanish represents an important opportunity and a way of bridging communication gaps with their peers. As the principal acknowledged in her dissertation, having English speakers study Spanish also counters the stigma frequently attached to Spanish and Spanish speakers in the United States. (See Snow [1992] and Francis and Ryan [1998] for further discussion of language stigmas and their implications for learning.)

This school led the district in hiring bilingual instructors and staff. English monolingual administrators and other educators pursued opportunities to study Spanish. While school leaders emphasized the importance of English language acquisition, they challenged the notion that to learn English requires rejecting one's first language and rejecting the various tie-ins between that language and these students' emergent cultural identities. In other words, there was an incipient and in-use understanding of "additive biculturalism" (Gibson 1997a) in this school.

Most important, the leaders in this building were not afraid to admit what they did not know. Instead, be it at conferences or through continuing education opportunities—such as the principal's successful bid to get her doctorate—staff at this school showed an eagerness to seek answers for the various challenges they confronted. Staff development for all staff was a priority in this building; consider the participation of a parapro and two administrators in the inaugural 1997 Universidad de Monterrey Summer Institute. This building was not dominated by an assumption that "We know exactly what we are doing." Rather, the operational ethos seemed more closely to sound like, "We know we have to prioritize the learning of all children and we are willing to learn and do whatever is necessary to that end."

In one other way this school made the ideas of the Georgia Project seem less far-fetched. As another illustration of corporate benevolence in play in Dalton prior to the Georgia Project, beginning in the mid-1990s this school successfully hosted a Mexico-born and trained instructor whose services were donated to the school by a carpet company that had originally hired him as a line worker. (Recall the endnote in Chapter 6 that 20,000 members of Mexico's teachers union had left Mexico to become immigrant laborers in the United States [Mendez Lugo 1997].) This teacher, who served officially as a parapro, made palatable and tangible for district leaders and some community members the idea of hiring Mexican-trained educators. Given how little educators in Dalton, Georgia, knew about schooling in Mexico prior to the Georgia Project, validation of the quality of Mexican instructors, even if just a single instance, provided important credibility to what was to become a key program of the Georgia Project, the importation of visiting instructors from Mexico.

Just as this Mexican teacher's pioneering efforts enabled, they also constrained. His Mexican credentials were welcome in Dalton, but only partially. He was welcome as a parapro, not as a teacher. Also, Dalton was quite willing to accept his contributions, but was not allocating resources to pay for them. In microcosm this dynamic was similar to the early reception to the whole Georgia Project; it was welcome as an addition, but not seen as an indicator that existing structures and resource allocations needed to be reallocated.[10] The nationality-marked hierarchy placing Anglo-Georgians ahead of Mexicans was not deeply questioned.

Still, with its various efforts and innovations, this school more than any other anticipated the Georgia Project and embraced it. More staff from this school participated in the Universidad de Monterrey's first two Summer Institutes than from all seven other Dalton schools combined. Two of the three administrators who participated in the first Summer Institute were from this school, including the principal. When the visiting instructors from Monterrey arrived, this school requested and received a greater number of them than any other school. Through mid-1998 this school best embodied what the Georgia Project and Georgia Project-like efforts could look like in Dalton schools. However, there were a number of factors that inhibited it from becoming a model to be imitated by other Dalton schools.

Many of the understandings and habits in place at this elementary school matched scholars' recommendations for ways more advanced grades could be structured to meet the needs of a diverse student body (see, for example, Lucas et al. 1990). Nonetheless, by virtue of the age of its students (Pre-K through Grade 2) and its East Side location (i.e., the poor side of town), this school started at the bottom of the status hierarchy within Dalton. In fact, the low-status starting point for this school may explain why it was able to be so innovative. Appropriately or not, schools that enroll middle- and upper-class students and schools that enroll students at higher grade levels (e.g., secondary schools) have higher status and more political interference with their activity. A local newspaper reporter worried about the consequences of Dalton's Mexican influx on the district's high school sports, particularly football (Green 1996); such a concern was irrelevant in this school because of the age level of students. To paraphrase one Dalton teacher (not from this school): "Parents think it is cute when elementary school students learn a couple words in Spanish, but when the curriculum gets more advanced, when kids start studying division and multiplication in the third and fourth grade, when reading gets harder at that level and higher, parents and others worry that Spanish gets in the way of *more important* studies. At that level parents start resisting changes in the traditional curriculum." At that level, too, equal support for all students continues to be espoused, but there is increasing pressure for differentiation and segmentation. However, on December 12 and 13, 1996, when five Daltonians visited the Universidad de Monterrey, the mood was optimistic; the concerns noted here were not on the table.

# Designing a Partnership: Three Meetings, a Grant Proposal, and a Challenge

Not waiting for the January arrival of the Universidad de Monterrey visitors, Dalton's daily newspaper published several articles favorably describing the promise and prospect of the Georgia Project in December 1996 (e.g., Hamilton 1996b, 1996c). I am not sure that these articles were the result of a coordinated campaign by the Georgia Project's powerful initiators, though that seems probable, but I am sure that the articles were intended to lay a favorable foundation for popular acceptance of the Georgia Project.

The first article (Hamilton 1996b) was published the day the Dalton delegation left for its first visit to Monterrey. The article began with the question: "How do you teach someone you cannot communicate with?" and the answer: "You can't." The article—entitled "Educators seek ways to reach Hispanics"—identified Hispanics' problem in Dalton as a communication problem, presented the Georgia Project as a solution to the problem, described the project one-dimensionally (referring only to the prospect of bilingual teachers coming), and repeated the attorney's story about how his daughter's frustration with language barriers impeding the learning environment at a Dalton elementary school had been his original motivation for action.

The second article (Hamilton 1996c), also a front-page piece, was printed shortly after the Dalton contingent returned from Monterrey. It outlined the four proposed components,[1] included enthusiastic quotations from each of the travelers, except the Dalton school board chair (who was not quoted at all), and mentioned the pending January visit by Universidad de Monterrey project coordinators, noting that the carpet executive who had initiated the

Monterrey contact would pay for the Monterrey contingent's transportation and lodging during their January visit. According to this article, however, the plan was to have student teachers, not certified graduates, come from Monterrey.

Shortly thereafter, there was a third article (*The Daily Citizen-News* 1996), an editorial celebrating the attorney who had initiated the Georgia Project as "Citizen of the Week." Perhaps seeking a metaphor that would be broadly appealing in a town as religious as Dalton, the article compared the attorney to the Good Samaritan described by Jesus in the New Testament. The attorney was lending a helping hand while other Daltonians were remaining silent. The moral of the Bible story is that those who lend a helping hand are blessed and holy, while the silent are not so virtuous.

Dalton's daily newspaper printed another flurry of favorable articles at the end of January 1997 during the four days representatives from Monterrey were visiting. Headlines for those articles include: "Communication revolution arrives in Dalton today" (Hamilton 1997a), "Visiting professors shocked by size of communication problem" (Hamilton 1997b), and "Business involvement aids Georgia Project" (*The Daily Citizen-News* 1997a). Reiterating the ideas that Hispanic students and Anglo teachers in Dalton faced a communication gap and that the Georgia Project would bridge that gap thus resolving Hispanic students' problems, the "Visiting Professors Shocked" story began with a description of a lengthy conversation (presumably in Spanish) between one of the Monterrey visitors and a young Hispanic student. The student's teacher claimed shock at the exchange because she had never seen the girl particularly expressive; in fact, the teacher had previously worried that the girl had a speech or learning problem. The article's intended conclusions were easy to draw. If only somebody could communicate with these Spanish-speaking students, the students' general talent could be displayed and cultivated.

## FOUR DAYS AND ONE POWER DINNER: THE SECOND DALTON/UNIVERSIDAD DE MONTERREY MEETING

The favorable newspaper stories were not the only efforts to sell the Georgia Project in January 1997. Though the ostensible reason for the visit by five Universidad de Monterrey-affiliated researchers was for them to gain familiarity with Dalton and thus to be able to fine-tune the proposed Georgia Project components, the visit was also used as an occasion for sophisticated political maneuvering by the attorney and his business community allies to advance the Georgia Project.

As a minor example of this maneuvering, the previously mentioned bilingual Anglo priest flew to Monterrey on the carpet industry executive's donated corporate jet as it went to pick up four of the five researchers from Monterrey. According to Universidad de Monterrey informants, this gesture was politically astute as it demonstrated to the Catholic leaders of the Universidad de Monterrey that there were non-Hispanic Catholics in Dalton excited by the Georgia Project and willing to facilitate its advancement.

When the plane returned to Georgia it brought the priest plus Monterrey's project director, research director, the then-director of the Division of Educational Sciences and Humanities, and the coordinator of the Teaching of Educational Sciences (who was also already identified as the coordinator-to-be of the proposed Summer Institute). The Monterrey visitors immediately embarked on a busy agenda coordinated at the Dalton end with significant input from the Universidad de Monterrey visitors. Joining the Monterrey contingent was Monterrey's designated bilingual curriculum coordinator, an alumnus who had flown in from Texas at the invitation of the Universidad de Monterrey leaders.

The first day included the morning flight, the motel check-in, a light lunch at the school district central office, a tour of two carpet mills, a 5:00 PM reception at Dalton High School (after the school day was finished), and a dinner hosted at the Dalton Country Club. One of the carpet mills toured belonged to the company of the carpet executive who had initiated the Monterrey contact and who had donated the services of his corporate jet. The other tour, however, went to a mill operated by a different major Dalton carpet producer. The owner of that mill was also the coordinator of the Country Club dinner and the host of another dinner—the final night's "power dinner" that is described shortly. Following a strategy that public words compel public action, the agenda coordinators were publicly display-ing that the Georgia Project was supported by more than one person or com-pany. Having the leaders of two of Dalton's largest carpet mills take a pub-lic role in the visit supported and promoted the claim that the business community favored the nascent project. The audience of this gesture included the Universidad de Monterrey researchers. However, not-yet-involved Dalton business leaders (who would hopefully feel compelled to participate) and Dalton educational leaders were its more likely main tar-gets. Remember that, despite the willing participation of Dalton school lead-ers in the fall of 1996, the attorney's original diagnosis was that Dalton lead-ers felt little compulsion to be responsive in any intentional way to the influx of Hispanic newcomers. Allying with a constituency he was close to, he thought leadership by business would compel Dalton schools' action.

The second day of the visit was given over to the tour of four schools— all three majority Hispanic East Side elementary schools, plus the high school. This was followed by a debriefing with school district leaders, a tour of Mexican neighborhoods (coordinated by the bilingual priest), and a meeting and dinner with Mexican leaders and parents (also overseen by the priest). The exact description of the final part of the January visit agenda read, "Dinner with Father [X] and others from Mexican community." Though the priest did speak Spanish and offer mass and various sacraments in that language, neither he nor members of the Mexican community identified him as one of their number. That the priest was identified as part of the Mexican community by Dalton's Georgia Project planners is indicative of how little interpersonal connection Dalton's business and school leaders had at the time with the growing Hispanic population. This helps explain the ironic specter embedded in the Georgia Project of Dalton leaders going to a Mexican university to facilitate contact with people who occupied Dalton workplaces and attended Dalton schools.

The third day of the visit included a morning workshop coordinated by the attorney and attended by, among others, reporters from the daily newspaper. Later, at Dalton College, the Mexican visitors met college leaders, the mayor, industry and Chamber of Commerce representatives, and staff from the Carpet and Rug Institute—a Dalton-based consortium that promotes the carpet industry. Dinner that night was at the home of the primary owners of one of Dalton's largest carpet mills.

Though the Monterrey visitors did know the dinner was on the agenda, they were surprised by its formality and impressed by the attorney's performance at it. More than a year later, they remembered it more clearly than any other part of their visit. It was the signature event of their first encounter with Dalton. Their surprise at the formality suggests both that they were unaware of the codes/internal understandings used by the Dalton elite to indicate the tone of the occasion and that the Dalton hosts were unaware (or unconcerned) that expectations regarding the tone of the dinner were not self-evident or transparent to the visitors.

The meal was hosted in a large room. In deference to the hosts' Jewish background, the Catholic priest included a prayer in Hebrew with the before-meal blessing. Of the thirty or so people present, the only African Americans there were servers and the only Hispanics were the five Mexicans from the Universidad de Monterrey and one local editor of a Spanish-language weekly newspaper published by *The Daily Citizen-News*.[2] There was a large main table and two smaller side tables. The meal was served in several courses, with diners sitting at assigned seats. Universidad de Monterrey informants remember all of the school district officials present were crammed together at a side table, while the superintendent remembers being the only district official present. According to either of these renditions, however, power and status were asserted with school district personnel not at the top of the decision-making hierarchy. The message was clear; resisting the Georgia Project meant differing with several of Dalton's most powerful individuals.

During a toast before dessert, the attorney made enthusiastic comments about the project and challenged anyone present to make public his or her doubts, so they could be responded to. Whatever an individual's private thoughts may have been, the silence that met the attorney's challenge publicly signaled and abetted the emerging project's momentum. A mandate without dissenters was a powerful mandate indeed. Sixteen months later, no Dalton business leader had made public any strong objections to the Georgia Project.

The attorney continued his toast by declaring Dalton to have been inexorably changed by its Hispanic influx, that it was now a "border city" requiring different and more inclusive leadership than that which had previously sufficed. Though in other instances he had characterized the presence of Hispanics in Dalton as a problem necessitating solutions (to be sure, solutions quite different from some of the reactionary ones in public circulation), this time he emphasized the opportunity the presence of Hispanics in Dalton meant for the city and, as emphatically, the opportunity of the prospect of collaborating with the Universidad de Monterrey. Added to the list of virtues brought about through the Georgia Project was the appealing story line that Dalton was doing something novel, something innovative, progressive, and necessary. Those in support of the project, he implied, demonstrated those virtues as well.

## THE FEBRUARY 28, 1997, GEORGIA PROJECT OVERSIGHT COMMITTEE MEETING

When the five Monterrey visitors left Dalton on January 25, there were two immediate tasks before the Georgia Project's instigators: (1) Prepare for the March 1997 ceremony in Dalton at which a document would be signed that formalized the partnership between Dalton schools and the Universidad de Monterrey and that outlined the four component structures of the Georgia Project, and (2) Work to bring a pilot group of six Universidad de Monterrey alumni to begin teaching in Dalton classrooms. Pursuit of these two tasks led to some alteration and supplementation of the January 1997 verbal agreement. The Whitfield County school system was unilaterally added to the partnership at some point in late January. (The Universidad de Monterrey Georgia Project people were not so much upset at this as surprised by it.) Additional Mexican partnerships, apart from the emergent one with the Universidad de Monterrey, were briefly considered. The not-officially-constituted Georgia Project advisory group made up of Dalton business leaders met formally in Dalton at the end of February. And significant energy was spent trying to arrange visas for the proposed pilot group of Monterrey instructors. As part of this latter campaign, Dalton-based Georgia Project instigators, particularly the attorney, generated a lot of correspondence trying to convince the INS to accelerate approval of the necessary visas. This in turn forced the project leaders to articulate more clearly what the Georgia Project was supposed to be.

In a January 29 letter to David Poythress, the Commissioner of the Georgia Department of Labor, the attorney asked for the state government's assistance in acquiring the visas necessary to bring the proposed pilot group of instructors from Monterrey. The letter is the first written record I have encountered that mentions the possible participation of Whitfield County schools. Characterizing the challenge that the new presence of Hispanic students put before the schools as a "problem," the attorney declared, "The immediate solution is the engagement of bilingual teachers who have knowledge of various Hispanic cultures." The attorney's word choice was telling. Like Oboler (1995), he recognized the plurality of culture types uncomfortably lumped together under the label "Hispanic," and he recognized that successful communication with Hispanic students would be made more likely not just by finding instructors who knew the students' first language but by finding instructors who also were familiar with the students' cultural orientations/backgrounds.

If the first letter indicated that the attorney's understanding of the challenges before Dalton was more nuanced than the understanding of many in Dalton schools and the broader public, a second letter to David Poythress written just two days later revealed some of the limitations in the attorney's perspective. With his trademark enthusiasm, he exulted, "David, I have been involved in both public and private undertakings for a long, long time. I cannot recall an effort that involves such a homogenous support group. The quality of those supporting the project gives testimony to the importance of the undertaking." I presume that the double meaning of the term "homogenous" was unintentional, that the attorney meant to emphasize the unanimity of support by the project's backers. However, in a May 1998 e-mail to me, a middle-management-level Dalton carpet executive volunteered that, "[The attorney] is part of a community within a community and sometimes forgets that the vast majority of folks in this area do not possess the same interests and enthusiasm for new programs as he does."

The homogenous group that the attorney was referring to were the dozen or so business and industry leaders whom he had personally invited, cajoled, pressured, or otherwise welcomed to help oversee the Georgia Project. As he had done in person at the recent private dinner for the Monterrey visitors, the attorney was trying to mobilize resources and compel action by noting how distinguished and powerful the supporters of the Georgia Project were. In many ways the strategy was expedient, but assembling such a homogenous group of project supporters also had its drawbacks, drawbacks that only slowly manifested themselves, but that lingered through the end of my research period.[3] A number of the parties who would be affected by the Georgia Project and/or who would be relied upon to enact and support it were excluded from its governance. That the structure and membership requirements of the oversight committee were unwritten and unspecified also facilitated those excluded from the process to view it with doubt and suspicion.

One advantage of the small size, informality, and homogeneity of what in a March 5 memo by the attorney was referred to as the "Georgia Project Planning Committee" was that it could act quickly.[4] That memorandum describing the group's February 28 meeting shows multiple tasks being tackled at once and the use of a planned division of labor (i.e., organizing into subcommittees). The meeting included a report from a group seeking project funding from industry and community groups, an update on the logistics and likely cost of having visiting Monterrey instructors engage in coursework at Dalton College, mention of both school systems' willingness to pinpoint sources of public and private grant money, review of the planning for the impending March 1997 Georgia Project agreement signing ceremony, and the approval of a tentative budget.

According to that budget, the Dalton school system would contribute $101,170, including the entire $61,420 to be designated for the visiting instructors, three-fourths of the $13,200 designated for curriculum design, and 37.5 percent (or $29,580) of the expected Summer Institute costs. Whitfield County Schools were to contribute $13,250, including one-fourth of the curriculum design cost and 12.5 percent (or $9,950) of the Summer Institute costs. Local industry and community partners were to contribute $108,450, including all of the $68,650 designated for the Parent and Workplace component and half of the total cost of the Summer Institute.

While the whole budgeting exercise was speculative because funding was not in hand, the initial failure of the industry and community fund-raising initiative later meant that Whitfield County Schools were presented with an unexpected bill of over $20,000 for the cost of the Summer Institute. This alienated Whitfield County Schools (a tentative partner to begin with) and explained much of the reluctance of that district's leaders to be involved in the Georgia Project in 1997–1998. Dalton schools avoided the bite of a stiff bill by obtaining $250,000 from Dalton municipal coffers in April. These monies covered the cost of the parent and industry research piece and meant the higher-than-expected expense of the Summer Institute could be handled without resentment inducing penny-pinching elsewhere.

Three other items on the February 1997 meeting agenda also merit mention. According to the text of the March memo describing the meeting, the Mexican immigrant editor of one of Dalton's new Spanish-language weekly newspapers "also is working to give us a list of additional colleges [as sources of potential bilingual instructors] from his home *village* of Guadalajara, Mexico" [italics mine]. That the second largest city in Mexico was mischaracterized as a village, however inadvertently, again indicates how little decision makers in Dalton knew about Mexico. It is unclear whether the assembly of a list of other Mexican institutions represented doubts about the Universidad de Monterrey partnership by at least some Dalton Georgia Project planners or whether instead it was indicative of their hubris—expecting the Georgia Project to expand quickly and outstrip the support capacity of the Universidad de Monterrey.

Mentioned casually on the memo's first page was an offer by one of Dalton's carpet executives (an executive on the planning committee) to make his guest house available in late spring to the Universidad de Monterrey personnel planning a one-month visit. This note probably referred to the scheduled visit by a team of applied sociologists from the Universidad de Monterrey who intended to conduct a needs assessment of the Hispanic community. Though the needs assessment was conducted, this housing offer was never taken up. The executive who made it did quietly contribute thirteen frequent-flier vouchers to the Summer Institute effort, reducing the airfare costs paid by both Dalton and Whitfield County Schools for the travel of their instructors to and from Mexico during the summer of 1997. The same executive also absorbed the rental cost for the never-used apartment that was to house the pilot group of visiting instructors from Monterrey during the spring of 1997. The apartment was rented from February through May.

Finally, the March memo identified a Dalton district administrator as helping with the visa application process (an administrator who subsequently was not involved with the Georgia Project). Only during the summer of 1997, after being unsuccessful at bringing any of the proposed first group of Monterrey instructors to Dalton, did project leaders finally decide to hire an Atlanta-based immigration attorney to take over the visa application process. The second-to-last notation in the three-page memo cited an INS official as feeling confident that the pilot group of Monterrey instructors would receive their visas and be in Dalton before the March 19 signing ceremony. As just noted, this optimistic appraisal was unfounded.

## RAISING FUNDS: DALTON'S TITLE VII PROPOSAL

At the same time that the Georgia Project planning committee and several school district administrators were getting ready for the March 19 signing ceremony and the hoped-for arrival of a pilot group of visiting instructors, Dalton's curriculum coordinator was busy trying to enact one part of that March memo, namely Dalton schools' promise(s) to seek funding for the Georgia Project. On the advice of an administrator in another district, she decided to seek federal *Title VII—Systemwide Bilingual Education* funding. Obtaining the complicated Request for Proposal she began drafting the proposal in mid-February. It was due April 4, 1997.

On February 27, she faxed a six-page draft to the Georgia Department of Education's coordinator of ESOL and Migrant Education programs. This Georgia Department of Education administrator had communicated with the Georgia Project's instigating attorney on a few previous occasions and had worked with ESOL teachers in the district, so she was modestly aware of Dalton's ongoing demographic change and the nascent Georgia Project.[5] In her comments on the Dalton coordinator's draft, in the section "Meeting the Purposes of the Authorizing Statute," the Department of Education employee scribbled "Add GA Project."

During an earlier telephone conversation on February 20 between the Georgia Department of Education administrator and Dalton's curriculum coordinator, the state administrator mentioned that I might be able to assist the grant writing effort.[6] The state administrator then called me at the end of her phone call to Dalton. Minutes later, I called the Dalton curriculum coordinator and, before the end of the day, I was hired to assist the grant writing. Three weeks later it was apparent that I would be the lead author of Dalton's application. The curriculum coordinator made it clear that as the grant writer I was to seek funding specifically for the Georgia Project. Thus that orientation was reflected in the successful grant proposal (Dalton Public Schools 1997).

This was the start of my involvement with Dalton schools. Two and a half months after Dalton officials and the attorney first traveled to Monterrey, I was asking questions about why the district wanted a system-wide bilingual program, what the Georgia Project was supposed to be, and who I needed to talk to in order to gather sufficient information for the assembly of a viable proposal. I was not directed to the members of the oversight committee, but I was directed to the bilingual priest as a spokesperson for the Hispanic community. (In our first conversation he protested that designation.) At my own instigation, I later talked with the then-director of Centro Latino, Dalton's only Hispanic-oriented organization, which was established and funded by local (predominantly Anglo) churches.[7] Centro Latino's director, a Puerto Rican Baptist somewhat new to Dalton, seemed only passingly aware of what the Georgia Project was or proposed to be. After the curriculum coordinator shared with me copies of the literature review and conclusion in the principal's dissertation, I was directed to the principal of the innovative elementary school. I obtained copies of both the curriculum coordinator's and the principal's resumes. They listed each other as references. Neither listed the new superintendent.

In the initial Title VII text prepared by the curriculum coordinator there were several paragraphs regarding current bilingual education research that are worth highlighting because they contrast sharply with the policy statements and strategies pursued by this administrator later. After characterizing Dalton as a "pro-active school system unwilling to compromise excellence," noting the existence of ESOL classes at all Dalton schools, noting the use of Integrated Learning Systems (ILS) computer technology "to diagnose individual academic and language needs" to guide both Spanish and English instruction, claiming "Bilingual personnel have been hired whenever possible," and mentioning Dalton's two pilot, two-way bilingual classrooms (both at the innovative elementary school), the administrator insisted that Dalton's efforts to serve limited English proficient (LEP) students to that point had been insufficient. She wrote:[8]

> Despite the mentioned additions to the curriculum, the needs of the limited English speaking student were not being met. As more bilingual personnel were added the benefit of native language instruction, explanation, direction, clarification, and translation to the learner became glaring. The goal to assist nonEnglish speakers to learn and use the English language remained stable, but the method to achieve the goal was changed. Immersion alone was not adequate.
>
> Language minority students in the two-way bilingual classes were exceeding both the language and academic achievement of their peers in the traditional single language classes. Likewise, the English speakers in the two-way class were advancing academically in two languages. With the addition of Spanish instruction at the elementary level even more gains among all students in the bilingual classes have been noted.

This text was followed by four paragraphs describing Thomas and Collier's research findings and the claim that action-research by Dalton educators had come up with similar findings.[9] The discrepancy between Dalton's pilot efforts and the use of fully functioning program models by Thomas and Collier (1997) was not acknowledged and perhaps not understood.

As I took over the bulk of the proposal authoring task, the reference to Thomas and Collier remained part of the text as did a reference to the vaguely described bilingual holistic model that the original Monterrey bilingual education coordinator had recommended during the January visit by the Universidad de Monterrey team. I added references to educational research by (in alphabetical order) Beard, Cummins, Garcia, Grant, Meier and Stewart, Muncey and McQuillan, Ramirez, Saville-Troike, and Valdés. I used Beard's (1996) dissertation to note the existence of a local expert on bilingual education and staff development challenges related to managing multilingual schools with high LEP populations and also to corroborate several points.[10] For an example of the latter, Beard's citation of Cummins, Garcia, and Saville-Troike's work pointed out the need to avoid stigmatizing a student's first language.[11] This point rationalized why Dalton was insistent on creating two-way bilingual models (a claim made in the Title VII application, but not enacted as of fourteen months later except in the original two pilot classrooms). The references to Grant (1988) and Muncey and McQuillan (1996) made the point that program innovations that ignored teacher input did so at their own peril. This was to echo the Title VII Request for Proposal's emphasis on seeking practitioner input for both planning and implementation phases.[12] Ironically, this claim in the grant proposal also was not closely honored as first-year Title VII funds were expended.

I used Meier and Stewart's (1991) criteria to support an easy claim that Hispanics in Dalton had acquired little political power, leaving them vulnerable to the possibly sympathetic but not empathetic understandings and attentions of others. Ramirez' research comparing varying pedagogical models for LEP students further substantiated the claim made already in the curriculum coordinator's draft text that English immersion was an insufficient means for LEP students to make the academic gains that the school district sought for all its students.[13]

Research added to the grant proposal made Dalton school officials seem versed in education research and aware of several potential problems that the Title VII grant's implementation might encounter. Presuming that they read and reviewed the grant proposal (some of which, to establish need, was quite critical of Dalton's responsiveness to that date), I figured that the additional research represented supplementation to Dalton administrators' understanding of the challenges before them. In retrospect, having watched much of the Title VII plan of operation not be enacted and several of the errors that I used research to warn about instead be committed (e.g., the perils of excluding teacher input), my original presumption was, at best, naïve. As an outside grant writer working for a district with no professed experience with competitive grant writing, I helped Dalton administrators submit a viable Title VII proposal to the U.S. Department of Education without those administrators necessarily having a deep understanding of what they were promising nor a compulsion to enact the grant as promised.

Perhaps, reflecting the fact that the Georgia Project was still thought of both expansively and rather fuzzily, the curriculum coordinator who oversaw my writing (and who, at my insistence, prepared the budget) allowed me to characterize the Georgia Project as an eight-component rather than a four-component model. To be able to list those overseeing the Georgia Project as the Title VII Coordinating Committee (the existence of such a committee was required in the funding authorization) and to be able to list them as key personnel, I characterized what I thought was the existing oversight group as a fifth component of the project. In fact, the nine members named as already part of the coordinating committee included all five Daltonians who had traveled to Monterrey in December 1996 and four individuals affiliated with the Universidad de Monterrey. The Monterrey group included the two profiled sociologists, plus the original bilingual curriculum component coordinator and the former director of the Universidad de Monterrey's School of Education (who was identified nonetheless as the director even though, three weeks before the grant was submitted, her replacement had come to the Georgia Project accord signing). Unwittingly, I excluded from the coordinating committee all the participants in the February 28, 1997, Georgia Project planning meeting that was described in the previous segment, except for the attorney.

Components six, seven, and eight of the Title VII grant proposal more obviously departed from the nascent Georgia Project's existing structure and agenda. The sixth component, a conversion of Dalton's existing Grant-in-Aid staff development program, promised that the district's generous policy of paying for Dalton educators' professionally related higher education costs would be used to promote the bilingual competence of all staff, to work toward the ESOL credentialing of all certified staff, and to encourage existing Spanish-speaking paraprofessionals to earn a Georgia teaching certificate. The seventh component fit the planned summer 1997 "Survival Spanish" class for Dalton staff (which was to be partially funded by a large local carpet company that had otherwise not been involved in the Georgia Project) within the Georgia Project rubric. Finally, the eighth component was a proposed Dalton Summer Academy that would consolidate and expand some existing summer programs (the bilingual and Kindergarten-orienting Little Bloomers program, the Migrant Summer program, the Challenge Camp for "gifted" fourth- to sixth-graders, the Scholars Camp for highly motivated third- to sixth-grade students, and the Friendship University orientation for incoming language minority students). These programs were to be placed within the rubric of the Georgia Project and were to be overseen by the mandated Title VII Coordinating Committee. In turn, the committee could also add new programs to these offerings.

Perhaps reflecting the tension regarding whether the Georgia Project was a school district initiative or an externally directed initiative that required outsiders to keep the educators to task, components six, seven, and eight, all of which were existing programs controlled by the school district, were never made part of the Georgia Project structure. In fact, it was not clear that any non-school district personnel involved with the Georgia Project have ever known that these components were promised to be added to the Georgia Project. This suggests that Dalton education administrators were willing to accept the Georgia Project and its accompanying external oversight as a supplemental program, but they did not think of it as an initiative that should change existing practices or as a reason to have those existing programs be subject to another tier of external review and control.

As the second example of how practice deviated from Title VII script, the coordinating committee specified in the grant proposal was never actually called together, nor was an advisory committee composed of parents and other representatives of children and youth that, according to Section 7116(g)(2)(B)(ii) of the Title VII authorizing Bilingual Education Act, was to report to the coordinating committee. Instead, the attorney's unnamed, quasi-official Georgia Project oversight committee continued to function, sometimes in conflict with the will and intent of Dalton administrators, and always without immediate jurisdiction over the Title VII funds.

According to the grant proposal, the coordinating committee was to include not just the nine people mentioned several paragraphs back—the Dalton five and Universidad de Monterrey four—but also was to be expanded by four to include a Dalton teacher, a representative from Dalton College, and two parents from the Hispanic community (Dalton Public Schools 1997:29). The intents of this expansion were to add previously excluded voices to the Georgia Project planning circle and to solidify the linkage with Dalton College. The college was a more appropriate operator of possible future Georgia Project adult education endeavors than was the Dalton school system.

However, through the end of my research period inclusion of excluded voices mostly did not come to pass (though as the relationship between the Georgia Project and the school district subsequently fractured, at the attorney's impetus the Georgia Project formally included the voices of teachers and local Latinos and African Americans). Dalton College continued to pledge support for the Georgia Project, but had not substantively contributed to it through June of 1998. No Dalton teachers were formally involved in Georgia Project planning or oversight. Instead, some Dalton teachers (excluding those who participated in the Summer Institute) voiced their confusion about the Georgia Project and their suspicion of it. In contrast, while local Hispanics also remained excluded from formal Georgia Project governance mechanisms during this period, the Georgia Project did create an alternative means for their input—a Latino leadership council that was part of the Parent and Workplace Involvement framework.

Three other points about the Title VII proposal should be considered before the March 19 accord signing is described—one concerning its contribution to enthusiasm regarding the Georgia Project, one concerning the role of Direct Instruction according to the grant proposal text, and one concerning which Hispanics were prioritized for program activities and which were not explicitly considered. First, even though the Title VII plan of implementation was not closely followed, the grant proposal's approval during the summer of 1997 did add momentum to the Georgia Project cause.

Second, though Dalton used Title VII funds for the implementation of the Direct Instruction reading model, it should be clarified here that the grant proposal text itself made only one reference to that model and did not describe Direct Instruction as a program that would be funded through Title VII. The text read, "A few mainstream efforts (i.e., programs used with all children) like the Direct Instruction reading model have proven surprisingly effective with LEP students and will be continued" (Dalton Public Schools 1997:53). The curriculum coordinator mentioned her interest in the Direct Instruction model and had me read some promotional literature about it (see Adams and Engelmann 1997). Setting aside my personal reservations about this DISTAR-derived rote instruction model (though I had many reservations at the time), I still largely left Direct Instruction out of the proposal because, whatever its merits (and there are some), it was not a model consistent with the framework specified by the U.S. Department of Education for a *Title VII—Systemwide Bilingual Education* grant.

As the third point, after my involvement with the Title VII proposal's development was over, a state government official who reviewed it suggested that an abstract be attached to its front (in addition to the introduction). In the abstract, which was written by Dalton's curriculum coordinator, there was a clarification at the end of the first paragraph stating that the Hispanic families who had recently come to Dalton intended to stay permanently; they were not transient. This was a claim that other Georgia Project creators, notably the attorney and those from the Universidad de Monterrey, also made. While this claim had much truth—many Hispanic Daltonians did and do intend to live in Dalton permanently—it was only partially accurate. As any school-based Dalton administrator would readily explain, at the time of the Title VII application, a portion of Dalton's Hispanic population remained highly mobile. This portion of the population was unsettled rather than settled, with the forces of the global economy, family and other sending community ties, and household survival strategies all intertwining to make their decisions to live in Dalton tentative and provisional, not necessarily permanent choices (Hamann 2001a).

The accuracy of the original permanent residency claim, however, is not the main concern; rather there is the question of its rationale. Embedded in the idea that the Hispanic population intended permanent residency was the belief that such an intent mattered. In other words, the school system needed to act, not necessarily because there are so many Hispanics in Dalton per se, but because at least some of those Hispanics intended to become part of the community. The converse of this idea was that if Dalton continued to attract a constantly turning-over Hispanic population pool it would not necessarily need to act.

This was a troubling example of a theory in use (Argyris and Schön 1975) because it suggests first that Dalton may have felt less an obligation to respond to students and families who were in the district for an indeterminate or cyclic period of time (which clearly many were). Second, if the twin forces of the global market and a local reactionary response combined to keep some Hispanics in Dalton unsettled, there was not necessarily an obligation on the part of schools, or other institutions, to act on behalf of those unsettled individuals or families. This theory in use hardly marks Dalton as unique; calculating how schooling needs to be recalibrated and how community needs to be redefined to accommodate the displacement and high mobility that marks the end of the century are both substantial and largely incomplete projects (Hamann 2001a). Nonetheless, this theory in use was unreconciled with the espoused theory that ended the grant proposal abstract; it claimed that the Georgia Project "is the vision of an existing school system in the northwest corner of Georgia determined to be successful on behalf of *all* students" (Dalton Public Schools 1997:i—italics added).

## SIGNING THE ACCORD: THE THIRD DALTON/UNIVERSIDAD DE MONTERREY MEETING MARCH 1997

In early March 1997, such abstract concerns were clearly not the ones predominating as Universidad de Monterrey officials prepared to return to Dalton and Georgia Project personnel in Dalton arranged to be their hosts.

School district officials were busy crossing their fingers in hopes that a March 18 local sales tax increase referendum would pass, bringing in millions of needed dollars to build two new schools and to renovate two others. That a bond referendum to fund the same construction had failed in 1994 made educators nervous. Fortunately (from a school system perspective), the front-page headline in the March 19 *Daily Citizen-News* reported: "Voters Buy Sales Tax." A smaller headline on the same front page reported: "Georgia Project Agreement to be Signed Today."

The signing ceremony held at Dalton High School that day was historic and contradictory, representing both the culmination of the attorney's and others' dogged efforts to that point and the paradoxical indifference (or unawareness) of much of Dalton to the Georgia Project. The combined wealth of the eighty or so people who assembled in the spacious auditorium may well have exceeded a billion dollars. Joining most of Dalton's leading business executives were the rector of the Universidad de Monterrey whose family owns a large Mexican supermarket chain, the head of one of Mexico's largest business conglomerates, and an executive who led one of that conglomerate's largest subsidiaries. The head of the conglomerate was the one who, on behalf of his Dalton-based business partner, had set up the original link to the Universidad de Monterrey.

Yet even at the apex of the ceremony, four-fifths of the auditorium was empty. After a hasty song and dance presentation of the mid-eighties pop song "Footloose" by a largely Anglo student group and a second song sung by a slightly larger and more mixed group, both at the beginning of the ceremony, there were no more students to be seen. More than a thousand of them were outside the auditorium in the hallways and classrooms of the high school, going about the business of a regular school day. There did not appear to be any Dalton teachers present either (though there may have been a handful). One of the Universidad de Monterrey contacts later pointed out that he, too, had thought it odd that political dignitaries (e.g., the Mexican Consul General from Atlanta), Mexican guests, and wealthy/powerful Mexicans and Daltonians were all present, but that among the absent were local Mexican parents and the students and educators for whom the Georgia Project was supposedly meant. The historic signing of a binational accord was not a reason for adjusting students' school day to be witnesses.

Earlier that morning in Monterrey, five people had boarded the Mexican industrialist's corporate jet to head to the ceremony. The five heading to Dalton included the industrialist, the rector of the Universidad de Monterrey, the new director of the Universidad de Monterrey's School of Education (who had taken the position since the January visit by Universidad de Monterrey scholars), the Georgia Project research director, and a second executive who was not subsequently involved in the Georgia Project. The Georgia Project director was absent; instead he was tending to a long-standing obligation in Paris. The visitors were in Dalton for less than a full day, attending the ceremony, meeting quickly with school district officials, the attorney, and several local business leaders, and then reboarding the jet to head back to Monterrey.

Apart from the incongruous production of "Footloose," the ceremony proceeded as one would expect. A second student group (which included several Hispanic students) joined the first on the stage and both groups were quickly introduced in Spanish. They sang a second song and asked in English for the audience to join in with the chorus. After bowing, they departed both the stage and the ceremony. The attorney stepped to the podium and announced that it was an "historic day." The Georgia Project would "utilize the many talents of those who've just moved here."

Then, perhaps with an eye to the ongoing political shenanigans at the Georgia Department of Education and likely with the intent of enhancing the Georgia Project's credibility, he looked out to the audience, singled out the one Department of Education employee who had been responsive to the Georgia Project (and the only one who was in the audience), thanked her, and announced to all that she "really knows what bilingual education is all about." Perhaps some could doubt the attorney's knowledge of education and thus the educational agenda he was promoting, but the support of a state education agency employee who spoke Spanish and whose expertise and job description related to the schooling of language minority students was intended to show that the attorney's ideas were on the mark.

Dalton's superintendent spoke next, characterizing the Georgia Project as "a partnership of opportunity." The Whitfield County superintendent made a brief address, claiming he felt honored to be included in the Georgia Project. The final presenter was the rector of the Universidad de Monterrey. Speaking English that he may have perfected while earning his MBA at Harvard University, the rector briefly described the Universidad de Monterrey, specifying that respect for human beings, truth, and service to others were its three basic values. He said that he was impressed by Dalton's and Whitfield's apparent willing embrace of its newcomers and ended by identifying the Georgia Project within the larger context of NAFTA.[14]

As all four speakers gathered to sign several copies of the Georgia Project agreement, the attorney, who was performing double duty as moderator, put a final spin on the ceremony's meaning: "Today is not a victory, it is the beginning of a project that will improve the schooling for all our children." With four of the other five most important architects of the Georgia Project in attendance, as well as several others who had played important, if one-dimensional roles, the attorney was not the first to declare that the Georgia Project was for *all* students, nor was he the last—the editorial and other coverage in the next day's local newspaper declaring support for the Georgia Project repeated the theme (*The Daily Citizen-News* 1997b;

Hamilton 1997c). Like the idea that Hispanics had come to stay in Dalton, that the Georgia Project was for all became one of the espoused theories of Georgia Project promoters.

At this stage, how it would be "for all" was nebulous, as was the question of how the project would be paid for. Important ground had been covered in the three months since the attorney and school district and Universidad de Monterrey officials had first met in Monterrey, but, with the ongoing blockage of visas for the pilot group of bilingual instructors from Monterrey, the Georgia Project was not anything tangible yet. Nonetheless, it was about to confront its first Janus-faced ideological challenge almost at the same time that it secured its most important early funding. The ideological challenge had a populist face and a pseudo-intellectual one; both problematized what "for all" was intended to mean.

## CONTESTING THE GEORGIA PROJECT'S PURPOSE

In mid-April, less than a month after the signing ceremony, one of Dalton's city councilors succeeded in getting his fellow councilors to commit $250,000 a year for each of the next three years to the nascent Georgia Project. The money each year would come from a budget windfall that was the result of a complicated city utility bond agreement through which Dalton was due any savings over a three-year period that resulted from a change in interest rates. When the first Georgia Project money was approved, it came from that year's $12 million windfall. As this was city money, however, it could not be used to cover the costs of any portion of the Georgia Project that Whitfield County chose to participate in.

According to The Daily Citizen-News (1997c) editorial published two days after the public funds for the Georgia Project had been approved, there had been a demonstration against Georgia Project funding outside of the City Council meeting. Using the Georgia Project as a new excuse for protesting the presence of immigrants in Dalton, one of the demonstrators asked, "Will the last person to leave Whitfield County please take the American flag with them?" Though the comment was illogical (people were coming not going), it was intended to be hostile and, on those grounds, it was dismissed by editorial writers as unfounded racist fear. Other demonstrators complained aloud about foreigners stealing American jobs and the country being overrun with immigrants. The newspaper called this the "usual litany of complaints." Suárez-Orozco (1998) would have called it a performance of the "anti-immigrant script." Several code words in the editorial clarified that the demonstration was populist not bourgeois; this was a working-class demonstration and class issues informed the newspaper's dismissal of it.

Instead of supplementing its dismissal of the anti-immigrant script with an account of the "pro-immigrant script" (Suárez-Orozco 1998) as the paper had in earlier editorials, this time it made a clarification that the Georgia Project really was about teaching English. To quote from the middle of the editorial (*The Daily Citizen-News* 1997c:4A):

Again, the goal of the Georgia Project is teaching English. There may be reasonable arguments against the Georgia Project. Maybe it costs too much money, or maybe there are simpler ways to teach English to these students. Even its director, [the attorney], admits that the Georgia Project is an experiment that may be changed or refined in the future. These reservations need to be considered. But we don't need to listen to the sort of argument offered at the City Council meeting Monday night. It was ignorant and it has no place in the public dialogue.

The pseudo-intellectual face of resistance to immigrants and opposition to the Georgia Project was manifested differently. In a public thank-you note to the City Council for the Georgia Project funds in which the attorney made no reference to the protesters outside the City Council meeting, the attorney did choose to counter a related emergent assault on the Georgia Project's bilingual education emphasis. As one can see in the partial reproduction of that letter in Figure 8.1, a city councilor had handed over to the attorney a copy of one of Linda Chavez' (1995) assaults on bilingual education that had appeared in a recent *Readers Digest*. That

FIGURE 8.1   The Attorney's Thank-You Note Challenge

Dear [first name of City Council member],

Thanks for your fax of [Linda Chavez's] 1995 article on language problems within schools.

The writing is a skillful blend of half truths, blarney and prejudice.
The author obviously is unfamiliar with bilingual education and ESOL programs—and the differences between them.

The writer's method is similar to articles telling us that a black man's brain is smaller than ours and that the Holocaust never happened.

I am curious to know who sent this two-year-old article to you. If you know, please tell me.

[attorney's first name signature and typed first name only]

Linda Chavez was a virulent, outspoken conservative but not much of a scholar presumably did not matter to the Daltonian(s) who had forwarded the article to the City Council member. The appeal to the councilor and the use of research (however dubious its quality) was a middle-class strategy of resistance.

Though it was challenged as adamantly by Georgia Project proponents as the demonstrators had been, the article left more of a mark. It compelled the attorney and the newspaper to defend the Georgia Project on the grounds that it would teach English quickly. The Georgia Project's research grounding—Thomas and Collier's (1997) study of pedagogies that best contributed to English language learners' overall academic achievement (rather than just English acquisition)—was ignored, as was the idea that there was valuable cultural capital that Mexican immigrants brought to Dalton's mainstream. Instead the Georgia Project's multiple facets were subsumed under the alleged goal of teaching the host society's language. The point here is neither to question the value of teaching English, nor to protest its inclusion in the Georgia Project, but rather to identify how the project was being constructed by one of its most public proponents (the newspaper editors) according to a single assimilationist dimension of it. (Was this indeed education "for all?") This unwitting tactical move by Georgia Project proponents made the whole project vulnerable to questions about whether it was the best or fastest way to teach English. In turn, this further opened the space for alternative pedagogical strategies, like Direct Instruction, which would compete with the Georgia Project's attempt to make Dalton classrooms bilingual.

Two worries raised by the local bilingual priest during a March 1997 interview also remained unreconciled as the Georgia Project was poised to transition from a plan to a collection of programs. First, the Georgia Project would be weakened if it identified the Mexican presence as a problem and the Georgia Project as the solution to that problem. While espoused theories that the Georgia Project was for all and that it represented an enrichment opportunity for all in the community ostensibly countered this concern, reductionist assimilationist theories in use regarding the Georgia Project (e.g., that its main goal was to teach English to immigrants) suggested that the Georgia Project was being proposed as a one-directional tool to "remedy" the most tangible "problem" of the Mexican newcomer presence in Dalton. Second, the priest noted that a bilingual-education agenda competed with an ESOL-remediation orientation. Bilingual education can accommodate ESOL (by definition ESOL is part of a bilingual program for English language learners). However, without a conscious attempt at reconciling the bilingual and ESOL perspectives, the ESOL agenda can remain assimilationist rather than additive and remain in competition with bilingual education. Both of the priest's concerns proved prescient.

Still, the attorney's impatient enthusiasm and the securing of city funds meant the Georgia Project was moving forward. Within six months, three of the four promised project components would be in full operation. All four components are described, one at a time, over the next four chapters in the order of their prominence in the Dalton public sphere, starting with the most prominent—the visiting instructor program—with the Summer Institute, the bilingual education initiative, and the parent/workplace components following.

# Visiting Instructors:
# Experts or Parapros?

The rationale for importing trained bilingual educators from Mexico can alternatively be interpreted as creative, crass, enlightened, exploitive, simplistic, and ingenious. Perhaps there was a grain of truth to each of these interpretations, as bringing in Mexican teachers and paying them paraprofessional wages highlights a paradox. So too does the fact that the Georgia Project enlisted an immigration lawyer to help them obtain H1-B visas, reserved for skilled workers in labor categories where the domestic supply is too low, yet Georgia education law did not formally recognize their Mexican training—that is, their skill. Was it their skills that were prized, their low cost, their immediate availability, and/or their cultural kinship with the bulk of Dalton's newcomer students? Perhaps because of these contradictory understandings rationalizing the visiting instructors' presence, there were differing interpretations regarding how to view them, how to work with them, and how to adjust other project strategies to take advantage of their presence.

By one more progressive interpretation, recruiting bilingual teachers from Mexico started to remedy a problem identified by Meier and Stewart (1991) who found that under-representation of Hispanics in professional education positions (i.e., as teachers and administrators) and educationally relevant political positions (e.g., school board seats) corresponded with inferior educational opportunity for Hispanic students in those locales they studied.[1] Their argument, which was derived from their empirical correlation data, was not per se that Latino students need Latino teachers from a standpoint that non-Latinos cannot teach Latinos well. Rather they claimed that an absence of Latino educators was symptomatic of an absence of Latino political power within the community and that it was this absence of power and the forces that sustained this absence that likely were more directly responsible for Latinos' struggles at school.[2]

Taking this point literally, it would follow that in districts where the ratio of Hispanic students to Hispanic educators and politicians is much higher than the similar ratio for other groups, Hispanic educational opportunity is reduced.[3] At least partially reflecting the recentness of its demographic transformation, Dalton had very few Latino educators at the beginning of my study and, excluding the visiting instructors, few when it ended. One can also infer from Meier and Stewart (1991), that the value of bringing in Latino educators might be reduced if those educators are politically marginalized and not allowed full status as teachers.

## THE RACE/ETHNICITY OF DPS CERTIFIED STAFF

Reyes and Valencia (1995:305) refer to the "shocking discrepancy" nationwide between the proportion of Latino teachers and the proportion of Latino students. Dalton was an acute example of this discrepancy. In 1995–1996, only one of the 301 certified Dalton teachers that year was Hispanic;[4] none of the certified administrators or support personnel were Hispanic (Georgia Department of Education 1996b), though some uncertified staff were. In 1996–1997, four certified K–12 teachers in Dalton were Hispanic; again there were no certified Hispanic administrators or support staff (Georgia Department of Education 1998).[5] In 1997–1998 the tally was up to seven Hispanic teachers (of 321). Again the number and percentage of Hispanic certified instructors, support personnel, and administrators appeared to be tiny in comparison to Hispanic students—7:321 or 2.1 percent versus 1,622:4,496 or 36.1 percent (Georgia Department of Education 1999).

Yet these official statistics did not clearly reveal Dalton students' access to Hispanic instructors nor their parents' access to Hispanic adults in Dalton buildings, because Hispanic parapros and other Hispanics who served as mediators and interpreters in the various schools' administrative offices would not be included in a tally of certified employees. In 1997–1998, the thirteen visiting instructors from Monterrey who had an obvious instructional role would not have been included in the tally, because these instructors' Mexican teaching certifications were not recognized in the official count of the *Georgia Public Education Report Card* (Georgia Department of Education 1999). Officially the visiting instructors from Monterrey were classified as uncertified parapros. What the official statistics did show was that before and during the time of my study Hispanic and other Dalton students had little access to professionally recognized, Georgia-certified, Hispanic instructors and administrators. Counting the Monterrey instructors as teachers would improve the ratio noted previously to 20:321 or 6.2 percent (still a 1:6 ratio in relation to the proportion of Hispanic enrollment).

Less empowered groups generally have less school success because they have less access to resources, because the district receives less pressure to accommodate them, and/or because they tend to be at higher risk of creating an oppositional culture (i.e., one that draws its coherence from opposition to the perceived-as-unattainable mainstream; see Ogbu [1987] and Gibson [1997b]). This review of school district's employment patterns is one indicator of the fact that Hispanics in Dalton did not have much representation within the district nor much political power in the larger community. Whether the paucity of Latino instructors indicated an absence of readily available candidates and/or a past or current reluctance to hire Latinos was unclear.[6] From the perspective of "espoused theories" (Argyris 1998; Argyris and Schön 1975), no Dalton administrator indicated an unwillingness to hire Hispanic educators; several alleged a scarcity of candidates. More often, however, the idea of hiring or not hiring a Hispanic teacher was sidelined in favor of an emphasis on hiring an instructor who knew Spanish. After all, bridging the originally diagnosed "communication gap" seemed more like a linguistic than culture-matching task.

Thus a key rationale for the hiring of the visiting instructors from Monterrey was to help increase the numbers of Spanish-speaking educators in the district. A fall 1996 tally, which atypically counted only certified instructors, counted twenty-five in Dalton who spoke Spanish, with thirteen at the high school, five at the innovative East Side elementary school, and the remaining seven scattered between four other schools. Two of the West Side elementary schools had no certified instructors on staff who spoke Spanish (Dalton Public Schools 1997:39). While this paucity was broadly recognized and the idea was widespread that more Spanish speakers were needed to staff Dalton's schools, the problem diagnosis of many who favored this component was only as deep as a desire for Spanish speakers. They did not need to come from Monterrey, nor even be Latino.

## THE VISITING INSTRUCTORS FINALLY ARRIVE

Finally in October 1997, more than six months after the Georgia Project accord signing at Dalton High School and after two other Georgia Project components had already begun (see Chapters 10 and 12), fourteen unmarried young women from Monterrey arrived to teach in Dalton schools. This gave the Georgia Project an obvious and sustained presence not just in the schools but also the larger community for the remainder of the school year. The visiting instructors were present at high school football, soccer, and basketball games. As featured guests, they attended meetings of the City Council, the (all-white) Intercultural Inclusion Committee, and the Georgia Project oversight committee. They engaged in multiple school tasks, predominantly instruction and counseling, but also interpretation/translation, clerical work, and home visits. They were initially quite active in several outreach programs of the local Catholic church, but, at the suggestion of Universidad de Monterrey Georgia Project leaders who noted Dalton Hispanics' multiple religious affiliations, that activity subsequently became more muted. Because of their sustained presence (which contrasts with the intermittent presence of various Georgia Project leaders based at the Universidad de Monterrey), the visiting instructors were frequently cast as spokeswomen for the Georgia Project, though their knowledge of the project's other components was limited.

The local reaction to the Monterrey instructors was variously welcoming, accommodating, flirtatious, trusting, skeptical, and distant, but never directly hostile, according to the instructors themselves. The Georgia Project's complicated management structure, along with this being the visiting instructor program's first year, meant that roles and responsibilities of the visiting instructors were at times improvisational, confused, and contradictory. According to the questionnaire answers of the visiting Monterrey instructors and my ethnographic observation—including observation of and conversations with the visiting instructors, with certified Dalton teachers, and with various administrators—the Monterrey instructors frequently were informally relied upon by teachers and administrators as information sources and were welcomed by Hispanic students. Their contribution to their certified Dalton colleagues' professional development was haphazard and neither systematic nor coordinated. Their status as colleagues versus subordinates of Dalton teachers was contested.

The initial confusion regarding the visiting instructors' task had three primary points of origin. First, practically until the moment the visiting instructors made it to Dalton in early October 1997, their arrival date was uncertain. Dalton school leaders had to simultaneously plan for their presence and absence. Second, this double planning was further complicated by the uncertainty regarding what particular skills these visiting instructors would actually have. Though their selection process at the Universidad de Monterrey was multifaceted and quite rigorous, no Dalton administrator had ever seen them teach and, except for the principal and assistant principal from the innovative elementary school who had both attended the 1997 Summer Institute in Mexico, Dalton administrators had little idea of what skills and orientations were implied by a Mexican teaching certificate. Third, the visiting instructors' and the Universidad de Monterrey's leaders' original understanding of the visiting instructors' task was quietly undermined by the delays and blockages of the Georgia Project Bilingual Curriculum Component (see Chapter 12). The visiting instructors originally understood their task to be the enactment of this curriculum, but with it incomplete when they arrived that role was not viable.

The tasks the visiting instructors quickly were assigned or which they took on varied from school to school. In most of the elementary schools, the visiting instructors were taught how to deliver the newly installed Direct Instruction program, which requires breaking classes into smaller groups. Direct Instruction is a strictly scripted, all-English-language, supposedly "teacher proof," phonetics-based curriculum (Adams and Engelmann 1997). In practice, the visiting instructors' delivery of Direct Instruction was like that by Dalton teachers and paraprofessionals, except often a higher portion of the visiting instructors' students were native Spanish speakers, the instructors' best phonetic efforts were often still deeply accented, and several would improvisationally respond in Spanish to students' confusion or restlessness with explanations, discipline, or humor. If students' observable engagement was an indicator of effectiveness, the lessons actually became more effective with these departures from script and Spanish-language forays.

At the high school, the visiting instructors were put under the supervision of the district's ESOL coordinator (who also had a large teaching load at the high school). The visiting instructors were assigned tasks there ranging from teaching ESOL classes (though always with another instructor in the room because without a Georgia teaching certificate they were required to work under a certified instructor's supervision), to assisting with a Spanish-for-Spanish speakers class, acting as bilingual tutors and assistants in sheltered English science classes,[7] and serving as the Spanish-speaking assistants in shop class. This last duty was surprisingly important as almost all the directions and warning signs regarding safe operation of the heavy machinery in the shop room were in English. Furthermore, the shop teacher knew less than a hundred words of Spanish so the assistance of the visiting instructor literally made the shop safe and accessible to newcomers with limited English proficiency (whether a less-trained bilingual parapro could have played the exact same role, however, is a different matter). Except for those students that the high school visiting instructors encountered by taking on additional roles (e.g., de facto counselor and soccer coach), all the students the visiting instructors worked with at the high school were part of the overburdened ESOL program.

The high school effort was the only formal connection between the ESOL program and the visiting instructors. In many schools visiting instructors and ESOL instructors were not even sure of each other's names. Several factors worked against collaboration between the visiting instructors and the ESOL teachers: (1) There were perceived contradictions between ESOL and bilingual education philosophies;[8] (2) Though initially invited to be part of the Georgia Project by the attorney, Dalton's ESOL coordinator was not actually part of the Georgia Project development process until she was appointed at the last minute by the high school principal to oversee the duties of the two visiting instructors in that building; and (3) None of the six profiled Georgia Project leaders (or any other district leader) tried to coordinate or at least harmonize the efforts of the two programs during my study period.

Though ESOL can be enacted different ways, when the Georgia Project was created pullout tutorials were the dominant, if flawed, method at the elementary level in Dalton, whereas whole ESOL classes were created at the secondary level.[9] As its name implies, the goal of ESOL is to teach English to students whose background in that language is limited. The immediate point of ESOL is to help such students gain access to the mainstream curriculum, while the broader one is to teach a language necessary for the negotiation of U.S. society. However benevolently intended, ESOL in and of itself is by definition assimilationist, teaching the language system of the mainstream. In work in Kansas and Rhode Island, as well as in Atlanta and Dalton, I have found that ESOL thus often attracts assimilation-oriented individuals to teach it. When the Universidad de Monterrey's new coordinator for the Bilingual Curriculum Component asked a Dalton ESOL teacher if she knew any Spanish (a different question than whether she used Spanish in her instruction), the instructor dismissed the question saying "I don't need to" (i.e., "That kind of cultural capital is not of value").

The philosophical orientation of at least some Dalton ESOL teachers differed from that of the visiting instructors. Both saw Dalton's English-language-learning Hispanic students as their main student population,[10] but many ESOL teachers envisioned an assimilationist rather than acculturative task.[11] In contrast, the visiting instructors, as Mexican nationals, claimed that knowledge of Spanish and pride in Mexican heritage should not be forfeited as part of the task of making the whole curriculum accessible, including English—that is, theirs was an "additive biculturalism" perspective (Gibson 1997a).[12] Further distinguishing the visiting instructors' perspective from that of mainstream ESOL teachers, several of the instructors also admitted to becoming somewhat politicized by what they saw and learned regarding the aggregate disadvantage of Hispanics in the United States. At risk of being simplistic, ESOL teachers saw their main task as teaching English language learners who happened to be Hispanic, while visiting instructors saw their task as teaching fellow Hispanic students who happened to be English language learners.

Further complicating the relationship between visiting instructors and ESOL teachers, was ESOL teachers' fears that the visiting instructors were hired not as their complements but as their replacements and that ESOL was being discarded in favor of bilingual education (ignoring that ESOL should be part of bilingual education). Without the incorporation of ESOL instructors into the Georgia Project planning structure and without the intervention of a district administrator to respond to this fear, the fear and its entailing suspicion lingered. With the cost of deploying visiting instructors substantially less than that of an ESOL teacher with a Georgia-recognized credential, a plausible motive for replacement was easy to identify.

The most important factor complicating the relationship between the visiting instructors and Dalton staff (both certified and paraprofessional) during my study, however, and the factor upon which this component ultimately foundered was the visiting instructors' ambiguous status. Were the visitors from Monterrey teachers or were they parapros? Though those were the two existing categories, neither fit very well. The visiting instructors conceived of themselves as professionals and several mentioned in their survey responses that they were frustrated at not always being treated as such. The visiting instructors were certified teachers with extensive university training and, in most cases, a year or more of teaching experience (typically in Mexican private schools). None of them were certified in Georgia, however. This meant that they could not lead their own classrooms and they were not supposed to function without at least the nominal oversight of a Georgia certified instructor (even what that certified instructor was much less adequately prepared). Their functional authority—for example, visibly high credibility with Mexican immigrant and other Hispanic students—was not matched with formal authority.[13] Weighing in on behalf of the visiting instructors and the Georgia Project, a *Daily Citizen-News* article (Schleter 1997) emphasized that the instructors were trained and credentialed educators.

The visiting instructors also could not be compensated like certified staff. According to district policy and Georgia law, the visiting instructors' wage matched the compensation given a paraprofessional who had a four-year college degree with no seniority. To recognize that the visiting instructors were intended to be more than paraprofessionals, the school district, as part of the Georgia Project agreement, rented both housing and transportation for them.[14] This extra compensation frustrated some locally based parapros who felt this extra compensation was unfair. Ironically, some of the discomfort that certified Dalton instructors had with the presence of the Monterrey instructors was that the Monterrey instructors were paid too little, thus for reasons of economy making them attractive to Dalton leaders and allegedly jeopardizing the job security of certified instructors. Contributing to this interpretation was the already noted idea that the visiting instructors had been hired as a kind of replacement worker—an interpretation consistent with the common idea in the Dalton public sphere that local jobs were heading to Mexico and/or being lost to Mexicans. The superintendent's comments on several occasions that the visiting instructors were, even with housing and transportation, still significantly cheaper than a Georgia certified instructor also contributed to this fear. (His comments were intended to defend the Georgia Project from questions regarding its cost; which were broached by a different group of stakeholders—cost-conscious community members.) Meanwhile, some Dalton teachers and administrators were emphatic that however welcome the visiting instructors were, they were not peers.[15]

Though reproduction and contestation of status hierarchies clearly informed the reception of the visiting instructors by both parapros and Dalton's certified instructors, it did not always do so in conflictive or distancing ways. One factor that reduced fellow educators' suspicion of the visiting instructors was the instructors' temporary status. The fact that the visiting instructors initially professed to only wanting to stay a year or two, combined with their discussion of long-term job prospects in Mexico and the reality that obtaining indefinite visas would be difficult, all worked to counter the idea that the visiting instructors were intended to be replacements. The uncertainty that several demonstrated as they adapted to their new environs probably also made them seem less suspicious.

Despite the ambiguity and suspicion noted earlier, all of the visiting instructors claimed that they felt welcomed and useful in their different schools. This perspective was largely echoed by Georgia Project leaders, school administrators, and many teachers. Three factors in particular seem to explain why this was so: the visiting instructors' skill, the visiting instructors' ironic autonomy, and Dalton's still powerful sense of Southern hospitality and good graces.

During a March 1998 visit to the Universidad de Monterrey, I witnessed part of the selection process for new visiting instructors for 1998–1999. It was rigorous—including multiple interviews, several evaluations of English proficiency and teaching performance, psychological profiles, and more. One consequence of this selection process (in which both profiled Georgia Project leaders from Monterrey and others were centrally involved), was that only highly competitive candidates were sent to Dalton. Dalton got the best that Monterrey had to offer. The instructors' skill combined with the obvious dearth of sufficient numbers of bicultural/bilingual instructors in Dalton meant that their talents were prized and used frequently, despite any misgivings that Dalton staff may have had in private.

That there was a dearth of existing teachers and parapros with the skill sets brought by the visiting instructors can be demonstrated by the way some Dalton instructors relied on the Monterrey teachers. As Dalton teachers tried to communicate with and effectively educate Mexican immigrant students, they sometimes asked the visiting instructor about how school was organized and conducted in Mexico and what Mexican students' or parents' experience with schools may have been. Dalton teachers used the Monterrey instructors as interpreters and translators, getting in-class interpretations of Spanish and English, having interpreters for communication with Spanish-speaking parents, and getting translating assistance to send written Spanish-language messages home. Classroom and school/home communication were regularly characterized by Dalton educators as tangibly improved because of the visiting instructors' efforts.

The ambiguity of the visiting instructors' task that existed for all the reasons already reviewed had the ironic consequence of allowing the visiting instructors to define much of what they actually did. As Weiss (1994) and Hamann (1995) noted for paraprofessionals, as Dentler and Hafner (1997) noted regarding the merits of site-based management, and as Miramontes et al. (1997) noted specifically in relation to school responsiveness to language minority students, instructor autonomy allows instructors to customize or supplement an externally assigned program to account for its weaknesses and oversights. By identifying needs in the environment before them—for example, secondary-level Hispanic students' desire for a Spanish-speaking, culturally empathetic counselor to whom they could confide the struggles of adolescence and relocation—visiting instructors could take on tasks like de facto counselor and demonstrate to administrators and peers the value of their unanticipated contribution. Given the success of one visiting instructor at the high school in becoming a confidant of Hispanic students there, school personnel assisted that visiting instructor's attempt to enroll in a counseling graduate program at nearby University of Tennessee-Chattanooga so she could gain the credential to formally become a school counselor. In an environment where district and Georgia Project leaders were uncertain of all that was needed to help the school district adjust to its new demography, the visiting instructors' improvisations, permitted by their autonomy, were particularly instructive.

The visiting instructors' autonomy had a second implication for the Georgia Project leadership. Trained as bilingual instructors, recruited to enact the bilingual program that Universidad de Monterrey Georgia Project leaders thought was so needed that it was one of the four components of the project included in the March 1997 accord, the Monterrey instructors were able to use some of the confusion regarding their role to actually be bilingual instructors adapting the curriculum on a case-by-case basis. Without shirking the tasks given to them by Dalton colleagues and often with their tacit or explicit support, the visiting instructors still had the time and opportunity to use their Spanish and cultural familiarity to help Spanish-speaking Mexican students make academic progress in other topic areas apart from English. Aiding this last effort was the visiting instructors' familiarity with schooling in Mexico and thus with ways various concepts (e.g., arithmetic) had been presented to those Dalton students who were once enrolled in Mexican schools.

Though I was not in a position to gauge the full importance of the final dynamic that contributed to the welcome of the visiting instructors by Dalton staff—the display of Southern hospitality—it was still clear that a reason the visiting instructors were welcomed to Dalton schools was that the welcomers would have thought it rude to act differently. There was a nucleus of seventeen Dalton teachers and administrators who had been treated deferentially while attending the 1997 Summer Institute in Monterrey who may have felt a particular compulsion to offer as bright a reception as possible to the visiting instructors; but even for those who did not participate in the Summer Institute and who had doubts regarding the Georgia Project and/or Dalton's demographic transformation, the fact remained that the visiting instructors had been invited to Dalton (unlike, perhaps, many of the Hispanic workers in Dalton) and etiquette dictated that hosts treat guests well.

Before looking further at Dalton teachers' beliefs and at the ultimate fate of this component in Dalton, some additional topics should be considered: the cultural (mis)match between Hispanic students in Dalton and the visiting instructors, the missed opportunities of the visiting instructors' presence, and a structuralist critique of Dalton's deployment of visiting instructors. One might ask how culturally similar the visiting instructors actually were to Dalton's Latino newcomers. The Monterrey instructors were all professionals with university degrees. Most Dalton Hispanics had much less schooling than that and even those with significant school experience were nonetheless in Dalton almost always as laborers and not professionals. Moreover, all but two of the instructors were from Monterrey, and Monterrey was not a major sending community exporting laborers to the United States and certainly not to Dalton.[16] During their June 1997 needs assessment of the Dalton/Whitfield Hispanic community, the Universidad de Monterrey research team did find about twenty immigrants from Monterrey living in the "Little Mexico" trailer park, but that was beyond the Dalton city limits and thus outside the Dalton schools' jurisdiction. Twenty was also not a large number considering the city's and county's combined Mexican-origin population probably exceeded 20,000 at that time.

Trying to identify the exact degree of (dis)similarity between the visiting instructors and the students they work with, however, misses Erickson's (1987) point that of primary inportance in the instructor/student relationship is credibility; similarity is only a factor that often facilitates that end. According to the visiting instructors, to Dalton educators, and direct observation, the visiting instructors had a high degree of credibility with Hispanic students and were viewed as culturally similar by the Hispanic students. Their credibility with other student groups was not clear and usually not highly important because they did not work at great length with many non-Hispanic students, except at the school presided over by the profiled innovative principal.

The effort to bring in visiting instructors who were viewed as peers by school district staff was not as successful, but it may have fallen apart altogether if the visiting instructors had more closely matched the Hispanic students' socioeconomic profile. That the visiting instructors had grown up in professional families (all had fathers who worked in white-collar jobs and several had mothers who were professionals as well), had attended university, were trained as teachers, and were competent in English, together made the visiting instructors more accessible to Dalton teachers than were, for example, the Mexican immigrant, limited English proficient, working-class parents with whom Dalton educators sometimes had to interact.

The assumption that Dalton needed bilingual teachers from Mexico drew the ire of some Dalton teachers and paraprofessionals. Presumably, these angry instructors were either unaware of or unconvinced by national and regional data showing a shortage of bilingual educators (American Association for Employment in Education 1997; Schaerer et al. 1996;

Varisco de García and Garcia 1996) and the district's alleged longtime frustration with its efforts to find and hire bilingual teachers.[17] Several bilingual Anglo teachers were angry enough to write a letter to the editor of the school district's newsletter—*Chalktalk*—after a November 1997 article about the Georgia Project highlighted a quote by one of the visiting instructors who claimed that: "Even though the school has teachers who speak Spanish to the children, it's different when the kids know we are from their homeland." The angry Dalton teachers felt that the visiting instructor was questioning their classroom efficacy and perhaps even threatening their job security.

Using a Likert-scale survey instrument to conduct research on Dalton's teachers' attitudes regarding Spanish, bilingual education, multicultural education, and other mostly language-related factors, John Keyes conducted research in Dalton simultaneous to mine.[18] He found that 72 percent of the respondents from the school of the visiting Monterrey instructor quoted earlier "agreed" or "strongly agreed" with the statement, "In our school system a bilingual education program is/would be worth its cost—in time, energy, and money"; just 8 percent "disagreed" or "strongly disagreed." However, from the same school only 21 percent of respondents "agreed" or "strongly agreed" with the statement, "Hiring educators to come to our school system from a country such as Mexico is/would be one of the most effective ways to meet our school's language needs." Fifty-two percent "disagreed" or "strongly disagreed."

At the remaining schools in the district, general support of bilingual education was more measured, 44 percent agreeing that it was worthwhile and 25 percent disagreeing.[19] However, resistance to educators from Mexico was also more measured, 31 percent favoring it as a solution to district needs, with 38 percent opposing it and the remaining portion claiming neutrality. A key implication of this data is that Georgia Project and related initiatives were more strongly supported in the abstract than in practice. There was also the suggestion that bilingual instructors were viewed as needed, but not necessarily instructors who were either Mexican or bicultural.

That the visiting instructors were not *more* credible to Dalton educators (and thus treated in a more collegial fashion—as noted they were treated respectfully), represented a missed opportunity that could have improved the palatability of the Georgia Project among the school district's rank and file. Dalton teachers who collaborated with the visiting instructors seemed to be impressed by their competence. One Dalton teacher who had attended the Summer Institute told me that she had more respect for the professional competence of the visiting instructor she was working with than for most of her other colleagues. Most Dalton teachers, however, had little sustained contact with the visiting instructors, which permitted some to be suspicious (as previously noted) and most to be indifferent to their presence. What was lost through this indifference was the chance for these

Dalton instructors to learn about schooling in Mexico and thus to gain knowledge that would have assisted their attempt to be credible to their own Hispanic students and to those students' parents.[20] Thus, school district–based Georgia Project leaders missed a staff development opportunity that would have enhanced the project and contributed to the district at large.

Finally, a different structural criticism can be raised regarding the visiting instructor program, but ultimately it should be rejected. One might ask if through the visiting instructor program Dalton was trying to get a cheap fix for the educational challenge brought by rapid growth in its Hispanic population. Many Dalton teachers, as well as scholars from the University of Georgia and other locales distant from Dalton, asked why Dalton was not recruiting bilingual educators from within the United States. The first answer to this question was that Dalton had been looking for bilingual staff from within the United States for several years, but the supply of such educators was small relative to demand and most such educators lived far away from Dalton so there were additional recruitment challenges. The latter was because of the dearth of bilingual training programs in the Southeast (except South Florida). If there was free play of supply and demand pricing in this arena, what the hypothetical price, per bilingual teacher, that Dalton would have needed to pay to attract a domestic bilingual force is an intriguing question, but the political reality was that the campaigning that would have been required to get the general public (as well as nonbilingual Dalton teachers) to accept such a price likely would have made the Georgia Project mobilization seem easy by comparison.

Such a logistics-based response, however, ignores two additional factors that rationalized the Georgia Project leaders' existing course of action. Dalton's new needs caused by the growth in its Hispanic newcomer enrollment were more complicated than those that could be solved just by getting instructors who spoke Spanish. In addition to the linguistic skills that the visiting instructors brought with them from Monterrey, the thirteen also brought important cultural capital, much of which was relevant to Dalton's particular Hispanic student population and some of which facilitated the instructors' ability to negotiate both Dalton and the larger community. The visiting instructors were culture brokers (Wolf 1956) or, more accurately, interpreters (McFee 1968), who were able to explain curriculum, understand problems, act empathetically, and advocate for newcomer students to a degree that required knowledge more complex and culturally embedded than just skills in two languages.

A concern that the visiting instructor program did not resolve was whether Dalton hurt itself by bringing in talent that was likely to be present only temporarily. In the short term, it did not seem to have better alternatives. In the long term, perhaps Dalton leaders (and Georgia Project leaders external to the school system) needed to be developing strategies to get the visiting instructors to permanently relocate to Dalton. Or perhaps they needed to use the time they gained by using visiting instructors to insist that state institutes of higher education develop programs that attract and/or create bilingual/bicultural educators who would be willing to work in Dalton. As of January 2002, Monterrey-based leaders reported that five former visiting instructors had taken permanent positions in Dalton or Whitfield County schools.

There was one more advantage to Dalton's use of visiting instructors. Given the recentness of Dalton's Hispanic influx and the concentration of Hispanic adults in Dalton in nonprofessional job categories, it was easy for students and teachers of all ethnic identities to absorb messages linking ethnic identity and job prospect parameters. This included a notion that school was less important for Hispanics because school success was not clearly linked to qualifying for the job categories most Hispanics then occupied, that is, Mexican-typed jobs (Tienda and Fielding 1987). (During my study period, very few local Hispanics worked in the primary sector [Piore 1979] of the Dalton/Whitfield economy.) By their very presence, the Monterrey instructors served as counterexamples, challenging such an easy but mistaken belief. For those who viewed them as professionals, the Monterrey teachers were role models. The Monterrey teachers' professionalism and professional credentials challenged anyone's notion that Hispanics could not or did not become professionals. Whether any Dalton Hispanic students actually did emulate the visiting instructors was not a question the time horizon of my research permitted me to answer. That some wanted to is hinted at in the comments of the first six winners of the Georgia Project's Cleland/Coverdell Scholarships awarded in August 2001 (see Chapter 13).

## GUIDANCE AND OPINION FROM THE UNIVERSIDAD DE MONTERREY

As the visiting instructor program was getting underway and through the course of its operation, its coordinators at the Universidad de Monterrey end remained closely involved and, as warranted, advocated in pointed but professional ways on the visiting instructors' behalf. Though much of the tale of this advocacy is reserved for Chapter 11 and the description of the bilingual education component, one portion is included here.

On December 19, 1997, in Monterrey, Universidad de Monterrey Georgia Project leaders organized a combined celebration/retreat/debrief with the original fourteen visiting instructors who had just returned for Christmas in Mexico after their first two-month stint in Dalton. From that meeting, these leaders drafted an internal document listing thirteen proposals and suggestions for the work with Dalton. Most of these proposals were repeated in the February 1998 report of Monterrey's new bilingual component coordinator that generated so much controversy (see Chapter 11). Several are worth highlighting, in part because they illustrate how early the Monterrey leaders recognized some of the points with which this project component would permanently struggle. The first one also illustrates the

Monterrey leaders' dawning recognition of how thinly versed Dalton's educational leaders were regarding bilingual education issues.

The first observation on their list said bluntly, "The [Dalton] principals do not have a clear idea of the Georgia Project, nor of the role of the bilingual teachers from Monterrey. This explains why the teachers lack sufficient time and do not have a defined workspace. There needs to be a workshop for the principals to define the work place roles of the bilingual teachers." The proposed workshop for principals never happened.

The second suggested remedy of a presumed oversight: The Monterrey teachers had never been told which Latino students needed the most support. The seventh suggested the ESOL system needed to be overhauled as some students were finishing their studies in Dalton still lacking basic knowledge and skills. The eighth noted that the Spanish then taught in Dalton was not Mexican Spanish and seemed humorous and unfamiliar to Dalton's Mexican newcomer students.

The two that were most salient (in my mind), however, were the fourth and fifth. The fourth noted that it was impossible for the visiting instructors to plan satisfactory lessons when they were constantly pulled into doing supplementary activities that were discontinuous and even illogical one day to the next. The fifth suggestion questioned the logic of having the visiting instructors teach English phonics (i.e., Direct Instruction) as counterintuitive, adding that a Mexican instructor was never going to be able to pronounce American English like someone from the United States.

## AFTER MY FIELD STUDY

In late-1998, during a visit to report some of my learnings and after I had finished my field work, I learned of an incident that, though appropriately handled, took some of the innocence and even lustre away from the visiting instructor component. One of the visiting instructors preparing to return home after two years of work in Dalton packed and attempted to mail a box full of curricular materials and other supplies for her future work in Mexico. Bluntly, she tried to steal property of the school district and would have succeeded had she not asked colleagues to help ship the box. Two possible "accomplices" did not try to impede her but other colleagues became suspicious and revealed the attempt to Dalton district personnel who then communicated the story to deeply embarrassed leaders at Monterrey. Exacerbating this incident was the fact this particular instructor had previously gotten in trouble drinking on weekends and having unexcused absences from school that, though forgiven by her Dalton principal, had raised the ire of others in the district.

According to the same Monterrey informant from whom I obtained the information and the permission to retell it, this incident permanently damaged the trust and enthusiasm of the Dalton administrator who had most enthusiastically advocated for this program, the woman who in the spring of 1998 had taken the initiative to nominate the Georgia Project for Harvard's prestigious Innovations in American Government Award. (It was one of 100 semifinalists from an applicant pool of more than 1,500.)

Because of this incident, the Universidad de Monterrey publicized the story within educational circles in Monterrey impeding both the instigator and possible accomplices in their attempts to find work back in Mexico. The three involved visiting instructors were not invited to a reunion in Monterrey in 2001 that celebrated all of Georgia Project efforts and that was attended by the founding attorney from Dalton.

In 1999, with relations between the attorney and school district becoming increasingly uncomfortable (for reasons touched on in the next three chapters), the superintendent and school board moved to substantially reduce the number of visiting instructors. That bid was ultimately unsuccessful, but the matter was not resolved before a young teacher at the innovative elementary school took what others have characterized as a substantial professional risk by writing a letter in favor of the continuation of the visiting instructors' program. The Universidad de Monterrey also drafted and shared two reports with the school district at that time that, in addition to their obvious purpose of making recommendations about how to improve the visiting instructors' program, may have also had the goal of reiterating the competence that the visiting instructors and their Mexican coordinators brought to the table.

In the teacher's letter, which the attorney publicly shared at the deciding school board meeting and thereafter, the teacher began, "As a Dalton educator who has worked closely with Monterrey Teaching Assistants, I would like to comment on the possible reduction in the number of teachers next year." Though more substantive parts of that letter are noted momentarily, two terms from that initial sentence illustrate how the visiting instructors' status remained ambiguous. In the terminology used by the district, the author refered to the "Monterrey Teaching Assistants," but later in the same sentence she calls them "teachers," the latter as acknowledgment of their professional competence.

In the letter's second paragraph, the author goes on to note that while her school has done comparatively well at assembling bilingual staff who "are crucial to the functioning of [her] school in relation to translation and communication," these same staff mostly do not have "training and certification in early childhood education." She was challenging the district's common equating of sufficient interpreter services with adequate responsiveness to Dalton's Latino newcomers. As her punchline she offers, "In my experience, Monterrey Teaching Assistants at the primary and elementary levels are knowledgeable of issues in early childhood education. They also are trained in bilingual education and language acquisition. From this perspective, Monterrey Teaching Assistants are irreplaceable." Though I lack the perspective to credit this letter with the program's preservation, the visiting instructors' program in Dalton was continued at the same level in 1999–2000 as in 1998–1999.

As importantly, however, the challenge to the number of visiting instructors by the district marked the continuation of a pattern; the previous year the district had shaved back the attorney's suggestion to the Universidad de Monterrey that they supply twenty-five visiting instructors to a tally of sixteen. The idea of bringing in sixty-eight teachers, as the superintendent had initially suggested back in 1996 (see Figure 7.1), seemed long forgotten.

In March 1999 before the school board showdown, program leaders from the Universidad de Monterrey had shared with the school district a document entitled, "Maximizing the Human Resources of the Teacher Aid Program," that, as its title hints, both presumed maximizing such resources was sought at the Dalton end and argued for that same maximization. The document sought to answer three questions: "(1) What are the Monterrey teachers doing now in their schools? (2) What do they recommend to do next year? (3) How can they offer their best to Dalton?" The answers were thorough and brought up some unfortunately familiar themes—for example, that the visiting instructors did not want to have to use the cafeteria and other marginal spaces as sites for formal instruction and that they did not want to teach Direct Instruction.

The Georgia Project's director at the Universidad de Monterrey did not think that document or a companion one entitled "The Crucial Question: Is Our Project Becoming Transformative" had much effect in Dalton, however. To paraphrase his recollections as offered in January 2002 (more than two and a half years after the fact), he said the documents had not led to any changes in the schools' curriculum, but they did gain the visiting instructors a little more autonomy to pursue some of the goals and objectives of the Georgia Project.

In 2000, a second dissertation (Haynes 2000) regarding the Georgia Project was finished that examined closely one facet of the visiting instructor program and that may have, unwittingly, supported Dalton's discontinuation of that program two years later. Haynes, a first grade teacher at the innovative elementary school, looked comparatively at the verbal discourse style and its relation to culturally congruent teaching during instruction of four groups of teachers—the visiting instructors from Monterrey, Dalton teachers with an ESOL certificate, Dalton teachers who had attended the Georgia Project Summer Institute in Monterrey, and a control group of Dalton teachers who had not gone to the Summer Institute and who were not ESOL-endorsed. With twelve teachers in each group, Haynes found few statistically significant differences between groups in most of the several domains of verbal discourse that she examined using Amidon, Flanders, and Casper (1985) as her source of recommended patterns. Though Haynes was careful with her caveats regarding the specificity and narrowness of her research questions, it is not difficult to imagine that an unsophisticated reading of her study could lead one to conclude that the Monterrey instructors brought nothing special to the table.[21]

Crucially, her study by the very way it was designed did not attend to several potentially salient factors germane to weighing the worth of the visiting instructors' program. First, she looked at what teachers did, rather than at how what they did was received and was consequential. This matters because it asks us to bypass the students' response to assume that what teachers did would have a reliable effect on students. This proposition was untested by looking at student learning and achievement with each of the four teacher groups. Yet we know teaching and learning is more complicated than a straightforward relationship between teacher action and student outcome.[22] This is the crux of a constructivist understanding of learning (Howe and Berv 2000): The relationship, the teacher's credibility to their students, also matters (Erickson 1987). Foley (1990) noted that students engaged in the same behavior, in that instance joking, received different and consequential responses to that behavior by their teachers. So too is it with teachers, the same actions are differently received and differently consequential with students. The context of the interaction matters, which leads to one final point.

Haynes (2000) did not broach how the teaching by the visiting instructors was shaped and at least sometimes compromised by their formal status as paraprofessionals, ostensibly teaching according to the dictates of another instructor with whom they were not closely interacting and who may not have understood well the needs and proclivities of Latino newcomer students. Thus, the research design allows the visiting instructors (and the other teacher groups) to appear singularly responsible for what they did in the classroom, unwittingly exempting those administrators and others whose decisions helped shape those actions.

Though I have no direct measure of who read her dissertation or how it was understood by those readers, it is important to note here that those inclined to be skeptical of the visiting instructor component and of the larger Georgia Project would not have found their skepticisms challenged by this dissertation. Indeed those disposed this way already could claim this study confirmed their doubts. Ironically, Haynes (personal communication) was clearly an advocate for the visiting instructors and impressed by them.

The visiting instructors' program faced a more public and thus more difficult challenge a year later when Dalton's superintendent since 1996 chose to retire (under some pressure). Though his advocacy for the visiting instructors' program had been functionally intermittent (as exemplified by the yo-yo-ing number of instructors he sought), he had always welcomed the program and safeguarded the unorthodox allocation of housing and transportation support to the visitors in acknowledgment that whatever their formal classification they were more than just parapros. Two years after the superintendent left, the attorney reminisced how the superintendent had frequently said publicly that Dalton's investment in the visiting instructors was "the best money he had ever spent."

In the spring of 2001, a year after a Georgia Project-sponsored needs assessment by the well-regarded Center for Applied Linguistics (2000) had recommended maintaining and improving the visiting instructors' program and as the number of visiting instructors' serving in Whitfield County schools was starting to take off with other nearby systems also expressing interest, Dalton's new superintendent sent a letter to the Universidad de Monterrey saying Dalton was no longer willing to cover the transportation and housing costs for visiting instructors in 2001–2002, but that the district was willing to still hire some compensating them like other paraprofessionals. The Universidad de Monterrey Georgia Project leaders, who had been frustrated for years at Dalton's ongoing subordination of the visiting instructors (see the bilingual coordinator's visit described in Chapter 12), found this offer untenable. The e-mail from Monterrey to Dalton's new superintendent rejecting her offer was pointed, "Please be informed that the Monterrey Teachers will not be available to [Dalton] under the conditions outlined in your e-mail. As you know, we are talking about certified teachers in Mexico, not paraprofessionals, and the special benefits offered to them were established and agreed to in order to compensate for that difference."

In August 2002, a prominent *New York Times* newspaper article (Zhao 2002) cited federal educational statistics and quoted Harvard professor Marcelo Suárez-Orozco to assert that the national shortage of teachers qualified to teach English language learners had become even more acute.

# Summer Training in Mexico and Its Challenge to Traditional Governance

Though the visiting instructors' program was clearly the most consistently high profile of the Georgia Project's initiatives, it was not the first to become operational. That honor, depending on one's criteria of calculation, belongs to either the Parent/Workplace Involvement component (Chapter 12) or the Summer Institute component described here. Both got underway in June 1997. The first Summer Institute saw seventeen intrepid Dalton educators—fourteen teachers, two school-level administrators, and one paraprofessional—join seven Whitfield County teachers for an exhausting four-week seminar in Monterrey, Mexico, led by professors from the Universidad. Ten of the Daltonians were from the innovative elementary school, including the principal profiled in Chapter 5 and her assistant principal. The Dalton contingent represented about 5 percent of the district's professional staff.

Upon their return in July to local television news crews and short-lived interest from the print media (e.g., C. Quinn 1997), they all hailed their experience as formative and a great success. Many enthusiastically described their month-long opportunity studying Spanish, Mexican history and culture, and bilingual education as a "life-changing experience." Yet despite several accommodations by Universidad de Monterrey staff to make the 1998 Summer Institute less exhausting—the 1997 version regularly featured twelve-hour days, homework assignments, and a few overnight bus journeys—both Whitfield County and Dalton enrollments for the 1998 Summer Institute were well below the inaugural year's levels. Among the reduced number of 1998 enrollees were several 1997 "repeaters."

This chapter describes the 1997 Summer Institute and some of its apparent effects and consequences, then tries to explain why in 1998 participation was reduced. The presence and absence of district leadership factors significantly in the Summer Institute story. The principal of the innovative elementary school provided important leadership—albeit at one building—while, based on the enrollment decline and what might have been, the superintendent's and the curriculum coordinator's records relating to this component were mixed. The chapter ends with a discussion of the format change in 1999 and the success of two Dalton teachers at writing another Title VII grant to support the district's continued participation in this component.

## THE 1997 SUMMER INSTITUTE

Dalton schools benefited in several tangible ways as a result of the 1997 Summer Institute and its four-week, four-course curriculum. Participants learned about Mexico and Mexican culture, improved their Spanish-language skills, studied bilingual education, and reviewed (in their least favorite class) the philosophy of communication in a multilingual classroom. They made several visits to private and public schools in urban Monterrey and, during a short eye-opening trip, in rural Zacatecas.

Visits to proud but resource-poor rural public schools were a priority for Monterrey's Summer Institute director who, early in his career, before his involvement with the Universidad de Monterrey, had been a rural school teacher for four years in Guanajuato, Mexico. By his own account, that experience had been formative. Aside from his interests, visiting rural schools, however briefly, was appropriate because so many Mexican immigrants in Dalton/Whitfield hailed from rural Mexico. The Summer Institute participants, however, did not see these schools with the same proud lens as the Summer Institute director; rather their overwhelming impression was that these schools and their hosting communities were so poor that they doubted much viable education could take place there.

Cumulatively, the Summer Institute program improved participants' ability to understand, teach, and be friendly to their many Mexican-origin students. Participants said they gained empathy for students who were trying to learn English and accumulated ideas for additional means to cross language barriers. For most, the Summer Institute was the first time in their lives that they had had to negotiate in an environment where they did not know the dominant language very well. Only three had ever been to Mexico, and one of these—the innovative principal—only as part of the two-day visit to the Universidad de Monterrey that initiated the Georgia Project (see Chapter 7). The participants came to value those who were patient with their fumbling Spanish and their pantomime. Participants returned home vowing to be more patient with the fumbling English of some

Hispanic parents and students. Though I do not have a "before" sample for a more versus less comparison, in my observation of the 1997 Summer Institute veterans during 1997–1998, this patience was manifest.

Figure 10.1 shares some of the written impressions of Summer Institute participants. The quotations were culled from the "after" questionnaires that, with the curriculum coordinator's support, I had them fill out upon returning to Dalton. Most responses were written before the start of the

FIGURE 10.1    Summer Institute "After" Questionnaire

---

1. Now that the trip is over, what are your impressions of Mexico (or at least Monterrey)?

- I have great memories. I would not care to live in Mexico but the experience has made me more aware of the needs of our students. The poverty was depressing and the fact that the poor do not receive an equal education [is] not fair and I understand now why our students face so many difficulties.

2. How, if at all, do you think the Summer Institute will change the way you interact with students (Hispanic or otherwise) and their parents back in Dalton and Whitfield?

- I will be more sensitive to the difficulties of the language barrier—I want to emphasize heritage more: Hispanic, African-American, and Anglo. We are going to have festivals!
                              —this respondent led a multigrade-level classroom
                                                    of students ages 5 to 7

- The Summer Institute changed my life! I feel more confident when speaking to non-English-speaking students. I learned key words that help me communicate with the students in my classroom. It also makes the students try harder when they realize that I am trying to learn their language too.

3. Do you think the Summer Institute will change the way you interact with any of your colleagues? Why? Why not? How might it change your interactions?

- Yes! I have already had teachers ask for help when dealing with students.
- I feel more confident. This experience will allow me to speak up more on the students' behalf.
- Yes. I think my colleagues will not understand what I saw, what I experienced. They will not be as fired-up as I am and they will not be unless they experience Mexico for themselves. They may think I am being over-zealous in my Spanish-speaking/maybe a show-off. They just won't understand.

---

(continued)

I will try to explain but will come nowhere close to capturing the awesomeness of my Mexico experience. It was truly life-changing.

- I hope I can convey the incredible inequalities in educational opportunities between the different socioeconomic levels in Mexico.

- We need to spread the word about such simple things like why we find toilet paper on the floor behind the toilet. They cannot put it in the sewer system so big trash cans are provided. No one told them they could drop it in the toilet here. Looking an adult in the eye is a sign of disrespect for them. After seeing how some of them live, I understand why they think what we call slums are palaces.

- I hope so! I feel like we need to be more aware of one another's heritages and try to learn from each other rather than have students adapt to the "teacher." Integrate the heritage of all people with openmindedness and acceptance.

4. What were the most positive elements of the Summer Institute? Why?

- The most positive elements of the Summer Institute to me were found in the <u>loyalty</u> and <u>dedication</u> of the <u>professors in Monterrey and in the comfort of knowing that Dr. [the innovative principal] was always there being the strong and dedicated leader that she is.</u>

  —(underlining in original)

- Being a part of the culture and talking with principals/directors and teachers at many different schools gave us a better understanding of what these children are used to and expected to do.

5. What components of the Summer Institute did you least like? Why?

- The non-stop schedule; the instructors and coordinators at UDEM planned great activities for us, but on top of our daily class schedule it was exhausting. I would have enjoyed at least one free afternoon/weekend to rest, study, or go into the downtown area for shopping, eating, and exploring in small groups.

6. Do you think Dalton, Whitfield, and the Universidad de Monterrey should collaborate for another Summer Institute in 1998? If not, why not? If yes, should there be any changes for next year's program?

- Yes, definitely. It was a very positive learning and cultural experience and I will always remember my time in Mexico. I believe it would be valuable for any teacher who wants to learn more about Mexican students and culture in order to better help them in the classroom.

- Yes. I would encourage an on-going collaborative effort. Our percentage of Hispanic students dictates this need. Many students learn and more will be able to if we can overcome the language barrier. In addition, American

(continued)

children will benefit as they are the next generation and our country is already multicultural.

- I think another Summer Institute is a must. If we are to educate our teachers on how best to work with the Hispanic population, then other Institutes must be conducted. Some changes should occur—Living with a family would be a great way to learn more about the culture, language, and way of life in a practical setting. The Summer Institute was a success, and I am proud to have gotten the opportunity to be a part. I would definitely go back if given the chance.

- Definitely, every place we went we said, "Everyone at home should see this."

- Yes! Yes! Teachers gain a multitude of knowledge: History, culture, language.

1997–1998 school year, but a few were made after participants were back at their schools, with their colleagues and students. Several comments supported the old anthropology axiom that only when the familiar (e.g., poverty, inequality) becomes strange (e.g., poverty or inequality in a different society) does one see it. Many comments, only a few of which are included here, illustrate that language differences were perceived by the teachers as the most important difference between the instructors and their Mexican students. Perhaps this was because language differences were so tangible and readily identified and/or because such a diagnosis was part of Georgia Project leaders' discourse and thus part of the discourse in Dalton's public sphere.

Without reviewing each of the comments individually, it is worth highlighting one teacher's comment about the importance of the presence of her principal and another indicating her fear that colleagues who did not attend the Summer Institute would be further estranged from her—understanding even less her use of Spanish with students and her enthusiasm. That participants uniformly were impressed by the Universidad de Monterrey operators' organization and seriousness of purpose should also be noted.

The participants in the 1997 Summer Institute were unanimous in their claims that the Institute had been worthwhile. However, they were not unanimous regarding why it was so fulfilling, nor about which of their needs it addressed. Participants from the innovative elementary school reported a "been there, done that" response to the portions of the Summer Institute that focused on the grounding philosophies of multicultural education. Their answers also suggested that, more than some other participants, they had internalized many of the tenets of multicultural education— for example, teachers need to be adaptive to students' cultures, as well as students being adaptive to that of the teachers. Several participants wondered whether other participants should have been better prepared or screened.[1] Behind these comments may have been allusions to a tearful confrontation between educators not from the innovative elementary school and those who did work there. Those who did not work there complained about all the attention and suspected extra resources that the innovative school received, while teachers from that school felt their task was hardly easy or unfairly supported.

## AND THEN WHAT?

After the summer of 1997, at the innovative elementary school, where a "critical mass" of teachers plus the principal and assistant principal all had the chance to attend the Summer Institute, there was a visible continuation of the Summer Institute's energy. Other staff in this building learned from the learning of the Summer Institute participants. Curriculum materials picked up during the Summer Institute were used in this school's classrooms in 1997–1998. The involvement rate of Hispanic parents at the school was high. In 1998, this school again sent the most participants for the 1998 Summer Institute, eight of Dalton's total contingent of ten, including four repeaters. It is instructive to remember that the principal noted in her dissertation research by Ambert (1991) and Carter and Chatfield (1986) that highlighted the importance of a principal's leadership in determining staff attitudes toward language minority students and the related issues of staff development and practice.

As readers might already have inferred, the response at other Dalton schools to the Summer Institute was scattershot and limited. Because of the bonds built among participants in their month-long intense cross-cultural experience, there were several Summer Institute veterans' reunions back in Dalton, a pattern that gradually petered out. But none of Dalton's seven other schools made sustained efforts to have participants share their new insights, learnings, and resources with colleagues. Nor were there any professional development efforts intended to help participants continue their learning or to figure out how to apply their impressions and ideas from Mexico into Dalton practices.

Perhaps the seven attendees from the other seven Dalton schools should be called mavericks. As that word implies, they often viewed the educational tasks of their school in quite different terms than most of their colleagues, including their schools' leaders. A catalyzing experience such as the Summer Institute could paradoxically make these educators even less like their colleagues (as one of the respondents quoted in Figure 10.1 suggested).

In their study of school-within-a-school pilot projects related to the Coalition of Essential Schools initiative, Muncey and McQuillan (1996) noted that voluntary reform initiatives and professional opportunities attract a particular kind of educator and that these educators who attend special trainings and publicly promote new structures and ways of teaching are often viewed suspiciously, jealously, and/or dismissively by their colleagues who have not participated in the reform-related training activities. They further noted that those participating in the change process could be as dismissive of their hesitant colleagues. The 1997 mavericks felt that they had an amazing career development experience but also found their colleagues wanting to hear only short answers to their polite queries of "How was it?" and "What did you do?"

In February 1998, fresh from reading Dentler and Hafner's (1997) study illustrating the importance of administrator expertise on immigrant education issues if immigrant students were to fare well, I recommended to district leaders that they seek the concentrated participation of administrators and a substantial number of individuals from another Dalton building, but such an outcome did not ensue. I even suggested to the superintendent that it might be an extraordinarily valuable experience for him, but he demurred, guessing aloud that the school board would not be excited by that proposition and the absence from Dalton that it would entail. A month before the scheduled departure for the 1998 Summer Institute, the innovative principal who had participated in 1997 was the only administrator intending to participate. The experience of the innovative school had not been persuasive to those in other Dalton school environments.[2] Elsewhere, the explanation that a month away from family and home during the summer was too much of a sacrifice was persuasive enough that only another handful of mavericks were willing to participate.

There clearly was validity to the charge that a month away from home, family, and perhaps from a second job did make the Summer Institute not viable for many Dalton educators. For that reason, in March 1998 Dalton and Universidad de Monterrey officials began giving some thought to a 1999 Summer Institute that would be a two-week retreat in Dalton and a two-week stint in Mexico, an idea they subsequently enacted. Nonetheless, that in the four-week format more than 10 percent of the staff at the innovative elementary school figured out a way to participate with the more rigorous schedule in place suggests that the same yield of participants would have been possible from other Dalton schools if there had been leadership from school-based personnel or district officials. That this leadership did not materialize before the second Summer Institute showed that from a theory in use perspective this portion of the Georgia Project and its related ideals were less of a priority than was espoused.[3]

The Universidad de Monterrey Georgia Project leaders are not targeted by this criticism. Based on the substantial positive feedback they received from the first program's participants, it made sense for them to arrange a similar program for the second summer. They also were not responsible for the funding misunderstanding that curtailed Whitfield County's involvement in the 1998 program (see Chapter 8). The tentative 1998 Summer Institute syllabus that was unveiled in Dalton in early March 1998 did show that, in response to the few complaints and suggestions for change by 1997 participants, the 1998 organizers were willing to adjust the program. For example, the second Summer Institute's agenda made accommodations for first-week culture shock, reduced the first program's twelve-hour-per-day agenda by shortening it slightly and interspersing it with free time, and added more school visits and interactive activities with Mexican public school children participating in the Universidad de Monterrey's community outreach summer program.

In the questionnaires that 1997 participants filled out after the first Summer Institute, most indicated that they expected to keep meeting as a group and expected to share their learning with colleagues during the 1997–1998 school year. Both activities ensued only informally and haphazardly. There was no systematic district-coordinated attempt to build on or extend the gains of the first Summer Institute. Given the enthusiasm upon return of the first Summer Institute participants and the reality that family and economic logistics meant that a number of interested Dalton instructors could not participate in the Summer Institute directly, those championing the Georgia Project in Dalton missed a significant opportunity to reap more benefits from the Summer Institute by not organizing a formal follow-up with Summer Institute participants; not continuing staff development activity that would allow Summer Institute participants to reflect upon how the summer's learning had and could change their classroom or (in the case of administrators) school management practices; and not creating a formal opportunity for those unable to participate in the Summer Institute to attend a day, weekend, or even after-school workshop led by Summer Institute graduates at which the lessons of the summer could be disseminated and reflected upon.

Such missing efforts at dissemination might have, at little cost, expanded the impact of the Summer Institute, helped ensure that participants' learning validated or changed their practice in a way that supported newcomer students, and reduced the gap between those who had gone and those who had not by creating an intermediate category of those who had consciously learned from the experiences of the Summer Institute veterans.[4] It also might have induced wavering potential participants to enroll for the 1998 Summer Institute.

The 1997 Summer Institute participants claimed their experience made them feel quite validated and valued as professionals. Having been so enthralled with their Summer Institute experiences, several participants returned to Dalton saying that the institute was proof that the school district cared deeply about their professional development. Though it is an imperfect proxy for validation, it is telling that only three of the seventeen Dalton participants turned in expense reports for reimbursement for the limited incidental expenses they incurred during the Summer Institute (e.g., weekend meals). Many of those who did not submit reports explained that they felt uncomfortable seeking reimbursement when they had personally gained so much from the experience and the district had made such a large investment on their behalf. Such attitudes appeared to have increased participants' engagement in task and their loyalty to the school district. That such enthusiasm was not aggressively built upon by Dalton-based Georgia Project leaders, however, was not necessarily indicative of a lack of support for the Summer Institute per se.

The three Georgia Project leaders who were positioned to encourage further activities building off of the Summer Institute—the attorney, the superintendent, and curriculum coordinator—were not well positioned to recognize their opportunity.[5] Unlike the innovative principal who because of her dissertation research knew the importance of administrative leadership regarding adaptiveness to the needs of language minority students and who did make sure the staff in her building took significant advantage of the Summer Institute, the other three lacked action-motivating conviction regarding this finding. Without being deeply versed in the challenges of serving language minority and Hispanic students, they lacked the compulsion to act. As an advocate based outside the schools, the attorney's role could have been to pressure district officials to make specific plans (albeit perhaps jeopardizing an already fraying relationship). The superintendent and curriculum coordinator could have planned staff development sessions or coaxed school-based administrators to do the same, in either case perhaps inviting Universidad de Monterrey Summer Institute personnel to participate and perhaps taking a lead in identifying themselves as ones seeking to learn from the Summer Institute participants' experience.

However, given their own lack of familiarity with the lessons imparted during the Summer Institute (i.e., Spanish, Mexican culture, and multicultural education), none knew that they should do this. They did not know what they did not know. With the explicit acknowledgment that it may not have been in the professional interest of either the superintendent or the curriculum coordinator to assume a socially critical posture, Murtadha-Watts' observation pertains: "Without socially critical leadership, educators may interpret accountability measures and multicultural education policies as conflicting policy purposes that may in turn lead to nonaction in implementing a multicultural curriculum that engages children . . ." (Murtadha-Watts 2001:119). Also pertinent is Huberman's and Miles (1984) finding that if users of an educational innovation perceive little support, then the innovation tends ultimately to be foiled.

Several Summer Institute participants commented on how important it was to them that they were able to volunteer to attend the Summer Institute, rather than be forced to do so. Given the feeling by many Dalton residents (teachers included) that the ongoing demographic change had been forced upon them, compulsory participation in the Summer Institute could easily have felt more disempowering and could have bred resentment. The leadership dilemma then for the Georgia Project leaders regarding the Summer Institute was how to compel greater participation rates without making participation feel forced. The ecstatic testimony of the first cohort of participants, however, was insufficient to make this happen absent administrative leadership.

## CENTRALIZED VERSUS DECENTRALIZED AUTHORITY

If ignorance regarding the value of the Summer Institute's content is one explanation for Dalton's district leadership to not do more to promote the institute or to coordinate other professional development aligned with it, there is also a more political explanation—to maintain the traditional hierarchy of school and district management, ideas that challenged that authority had to be dismissed. Summer Institute participants were bringing back new curricula and new ideas about how to interact with their students. By the institute's very design, they were gaining expertise, expertise that subtly challenged the expertise and cosmology of those (i.e., school and district administrators) who ostensibly were to manage them. Though I never heard such a challenge so bluntly raised, hypothetically Summer Institute participants could, after their summer of learning, reject the admonitions of their coordinators using the logic that the admonitions were inaccurate. In other words, participants could protest "I now know what these students need and what you are recommending is not it."

As the next chapter discusses more fully, in 1997–1998 Dalton schools were in transition as the curriculum coordinator and others were success-fully championing the district-wide adoption of Direct Instruction after its popular piloting at one elementary school. Direct Instruction (Adams and Engelmann 1997) is a rote, phonetics-based, fully scripted curriculum. At a statewide event promoting Direct Instruction, that it was "teacher-proof" was cited as one of its virtues. The model's promoters also noted that their claims that research demonstrated Direct Instruction's effectiveness only pertained to those sites that implemented it with fidelity. Improvisations and adaptations were inappropriate.

Thus there was a contradiction in logic and worldview between the operative philosophy of the Summer Institute and that of Dalton's new cur-riculum model, Direct Instruction. The former assumed a high degree of instructor autonomy regarding how teachers should manage their class-room. Thus it was bent on offering teachers linguistic and cultural tools (i.e., curricula and diagnostic and pedagogical strategies) that enhanced their repertoire in the face of Dalton's demographic change. In contrast, Direct Instruction saw instructor autonomy and discretion as problematic. It follows that the implementation of Direct Instruction limited the application of Summer Institute participants' learning. It also follows that Direct

Instruction champions had little philosophical basis for supporting any professional development follow-up to the Summer Institute.

Resistance to the Summer Institute was not overt, however, just as resistance to the Georgia Project was not overt (at least until much later). Rather, those who little understood the philosophical and epistemological bases for the Georgia Project but who championed traditional initiatives such as Direct Instruction created an environment where the ideas and practices of the Summer Institute were given little quarter. The daily operation and politics of managing a fast-changing district undercut the Summer Institute.

At a meeting in March 1998 between Monterrey leaders and school district officials (with the ubiquitous attorney also present), the pertinent question arose asking what the total was for the minimum number of participants necessary to operate the Summer Institute (at higher per participant costs); the idea also arose to seek participants from other Georgia districts that were also confronting demographic changes. A few weeks later, the superintendent's executive secretary was able to report that she had found three additional participants from Gainesville, Georgia, making a second Summer Institute viable.

For the first time, the Georgia Project included new partners from beyond Dalton, Whitfield County, and Monterrey. Moreover, the Georgia Project may have helped precipitate some Latino-responsive teacher training elsewhere in the state. Though the Gainesville participants in 1998 were said to have found their experience highly valuable, no one from that district returned for the 1999 Summer Institute. Rather in 1999, several Gainesville educators participated in the inaugural operation of another teacher training institute in Mexico that was the product of collaboration between the University of Georgia's College of Education and a public university in Xalapa, Veracruz. Project leaders at the University of Georgia (who were my colleagues for the year I spent teaching there in 1998–1999), were well aware of the Georgia Project and suggested that its success had made their ideas seem less far-fetched and perhaps hastened their approval and implementation.

The last overt Dalton schools' action in favor of the Georgia Project supports the idea that Dalton leaders' undercutting of the Summer Institute was unwitting. In 1999, two Dalton teachers who were both part of the Georgia Project's newly created teacher advisory committee wrote a successful Title VII grant proposal that obtained funding to allow Dalton to continue supporting Dalton educators' participation in the Summer Institutes. Starting in 1999 the format of the institutes was changed, with the first two weeks hosted at Dalton State College and only the second half in Monterrey. As of the summer of 2002, the only way Dalton schools remained involved in the Georgia Project was by supporting the participation of a modest number of their educators in the Summer Institute.

# 11

# We Want Bilingual Education Except We Don't

Given the national uproar regarding bilingual education that was growing louder at the end of my research phase as California voted on Proposition 227 to ban bilingual education, it should not be surprising that the Georgia Project's embrace of bilingual curriculum development became its most problematic component. When I first became involved with Dalton schools, however, it did not look like this component would be so controversial.

Even before bilingual education had been agreed upon as a part of the Georgia Project, bilingualism had been recommended as an integral part of how Dalton would meet the local Chamber of Commerce's *Target Tomorrow* goal of preparing students to be competitive in a global economy. Also before the Georgia Project, Dalton had committed to gradually adding Spanish as a foreign language to each grade level's curriculum until it was available through grade 8. (In high school it was already available both as a foreign language and through the newer course Spanish for Spanish Speakers.)

In the superintendent's September 1996 first letter to the Universidad de Monterrey (Figure 7.1); at the subsequent face-to-face meetings between Dalton officials, the attorney, and Universidad de Monterrey officials in December 1996 and January 1997; and also as part of my Title VII grant-writing consultant orientation in March 1997, Dalton officials were surprisingly clear that bilingual education was one of their priorities. Included in each of these detailings of intent was the promise of bilingual instruction (i.e., including native language support) in the various academic content areas. As part of its favorable introduction of the Georgia Project to its readers, the local daily newspaper editorialized in January 1997 that, "Teaching Spanish-speaking students in their native language, while at the same time teaching them English, is absolutely necessary. To insist, as some cynics do, that Spanish-speaking students be taught only in English is both cruel and a disservice to society" (*The Daily Citizen-News* 1997a).

However, as of May 1998, it was still unclear what the bilingual curriculum component was supposed to accomplish or whether it would be allowed to accomplish anything at all. This was partly due to a change in Monterrey's advisors for the component, but it also reflected the general ambivalence and confusion by some Georgia Project leaders about what bilingual education supposedly was. When Dalton released its 1998 annual report in the summer of 1998, the glowing segment on the Georgia Project excluded mention of this component even existing. That fall the attorney was insisting the component was still alive, while Dalton said it had ended (unimplemented). Even as late as April 2000, Monterrey officials chose to describe this component as "suspended" rather than terminated.

That Monterrey should favor this component more than those in Dalton (excepting ultimately the attorney) should not be surprising, though they thought it was something Dalton also wanted. Not only where they the component's original champions, they came from professional backgrounds where their multilingualism was a key asset to their scholarly inquiry and career advancement. However, because they were trained as sociologists rather than education specialists, the Universidad de Monterrey Georgia Project leaders' main strategy for supporting the bilingual approach was to use the support of Universidad de Monterrey-affiliated consultants whom they knew well.

The original bilingual consultant, a professor at Texas Wesleyan University who had previously been at the Universidad de Monterrey (and who had remained affiliated), gave up his task of advising Dalton in the fall of 1997 when his busy schedule became overwhelming. Whether he had begun to witness resistance to the bilingual education component and this assisted his decision was unclear. It was clear that he was the one who suggested Dalton's adoption of a "bilingual holistic model" (described subsequently). Dalton-based Georgia Project leaders initially accepted this recommendation, though their familiarity with what they were agreeing to was limited and though the curriculum coordinator would later resist it as part of what seemed to be a larger effort to reassert her authority over curriculum matters.

When the original bilingual coordinator from Texas Wesleyan University left that position, the Monterrey team selected another Universidad de Monterrey graduate to take over the role. The new coordinator, a graduate of the Universidad de Monterrey who grew up living alternately in Mexico and Texas, directed a trilingual, private, K through 9 school in Monterrey (where Spanish and English were the main curricular languages and French was also a part of all students' studies). She made her first visit to Dalton in January 1998. That visit and its aftermath, which were highly relevant to the subsequent fate of the bilingual curriculum component, are discussed later in this chapter.

## EARLY SUPPORT FOR BILINGUAL EDUCATION

At the December 1996 meeting between Dalton leaders and Universidad de Monterrey leaders in Mexico, the idea of creating a bilingual curriculum for Dalton was broached and accepted. The Monterrey participants in that meeting came away with an understanding that delivery of that curriculum would be a primary task of the visiting instructors. This idea probably seemed commonsensical to the Monterrey leaders—after all the teachers they were sending were trained to be bilingual educators—and perhaps prompted less reflection than it would have otherwise. The Monterrey leaders had a sense that this was an appropriate segment of the Georgia Project and might need some elaboration when the Monterrey leaders visited Dalton for the first time in January 1997.

According to notes taken by the attorney or by an assistant on the attorney's behalf at a meeting January 24, 1997, with the Universidad de Monterrey's original bilingual coordinator (and with others from Dalton and the Universidad de Monterrey involved with the Georgia Project), the original bilingual coordinator presented five possible bilingual education models that Dalton could adopt, but for each of the first four he concluded that they were not recommended.[1] After explaining the distinction between BICS and CALPs,[2] perhaps in the process using jargon as a means to signal his expertise, the bilingual coordinator discussed transitional bilingual education as his first model. By his rendition, transitional bilingual education meant that all studies would be in Spanish from preschool through fourth grade with an exception of one hour per day using an ESOL format. Students would then be mainstreamed in the fifth grade. He claimed the disadvantages were that such a model would require thirty-two bilingual teachers (presumably too many for Dalton to easily attract or for the Universidad de Monterrey to provide) and that students in such a model would lose their Spanish and CALP ability (CALP in which language was unclear) after the seventh or eighth grade.

Unless there was further commentary about this model for which no notes were taken, it appears that no one in the room hearing the presentation knew that many transitional bilingual education models gradually rather than abruptly phase out first language support and that six years of native language support—Pre-K, K, grades 1, 2, 3, and 4—is aberrantly long for a transitional bilingual education model. Nor does it appear that anyone questioned the coordinator's assumption that students would begin in this model at preschool, an assumption of population stability that was contradicted by the school matriculation records for many Hispanics in Dalton.[3]

My point is not to question the first bilingual coordinator's expertise. (Doing so on the basis of someone else's notes would be highly hazardous and, according to the evaluations of the 1997 Summer Institute participants who had him as an instructor, he was highly competent.) Rather, the various Georgia Project leaders in the room did not have a deep enough understanding of bilingual education to be able to challenge what was being presented. Had such challenges been made, the design of the adopted component—the bilingual holistic model described momentarily—might well have been clarified to a much greater degree, been better understood by Dalton educational leaders, and thus actually implemented.

The second model presented—the Maintenance/"Addition Approach"—would include all but one hour each day in Spanish from preschool through grade four and then a continuation of Spanish from fifth to eighth grade. The attorney's notes do not indicate what portion of the fifth-through eighth-graders' day would be instruction in Spanish. Though from the notes it can only be inferred, it sounds like this model and the first one would be intended only for English language learners (as opposed to a two-way model, for example, that includes English-speaking students as well). The coordinator estimated that this model would require fifty bilingual teachers.

The third model presented was called "Two Way." In this model, half of each day's lessons in all subjects would be taught in English and half in Spanish. This model would require 150 bilingual teachers.[4] According to the attorney's notes, the coordinator also explained that this was the model used in California. While there were a few such examples of two-way bilingual classrooms and schools in California (Schnaiberg 1998) and even one such public school in Cobb County, Georgia—the Argyle School—most "so-called" bilingual education in California did not follow this model (and most schooling for language minority students in California was not organized according to a bilingual model of any type [Hill 1998]). Later, a vague and inaccurate understanding of how bilingual education was enacted elsewhere contributed to the curriculum coordinator's slowly emergent general rejection of any bilingual models beyond Spanish as a foreign language. The genesis for the curriculum coordinator's misunderstanding may have begun at this meeting.

How the fourth model—Two Partial Way—differed pedagogically from the third is unclear from the attorney's notes. In it, one bilingual teacher would switch between Spanish and English while teaching the same subjects. Supposedly, this model would require seventy-five bilingual teachers. Given that two teachers using the Two Way model specified in the last paragraph could share twice as many students (two full classrooms half a day each), it is not apparent why this model would require only half as many bilingual teachers. In fact, for the regular "Two Way" model half of the instructors could be monolingual English speakers with ESOL training, meaning that model should have required fewer bilingual teachers than this one. That this mathematical discrepancy was not pursued and clarified shows again that the existing understanding of those listening to the presentation was not deep.

The attorney's notes—Figure 11.1—regarding the officially adopted bilingual holistic model were extensive, but they did not clarify how the

FIGURE 11.1    The Attorney's Understanding of the Bilingual Holistic Model

---

**Integrate Students and Teachers**

**Example:**

Pre K   Pre K   Pre K   Pre K   Pre K          K K K K K K K K K K K
Pre K   Pre K   Pre K   Pre K   Pre K          K K K K K K K K K K K

2nd 2nd 2nd 2nd 2nd 2nd 2nd          1st 1st 1st 1st 1st 1st 1st 1st

All students in the same classroom received sheltered instruction in English learning Math, Science, Social Studies and in the same class you have ESOL of both languages (so that other kids could help).

- The sheltered instruction method is to facilitate the learning process for all students. This is not a remedial approach.
- The children would be integrated so that they would learn English and they would learn Spanish.
- Don't pull the kids out to single them out.
- Every teacher should learn ESOL.
- Give normal teachers this type of training.
- Then later the English-speaking students will learn grammar, writing, reading, spelling, arithmetic, science, social studies, etc. in their own language while,
- the students who speak Spanish will be learning the same languages at the same time but in their native language so that both groups of students will achieve CALP and proficiency in their native language.
- There would be approximately one hour and a half spent on this type of learning during one school day.
- This model would take 10 bilingual teachers at [the innovative elementary school].
- Parent involvement would be a major factor to help the student learn and practice good Spanish at a good level, BICS, and culture as well.

**Recommended**

model would work. They are reproduced in the Figure 11.1 because they illustrate the confusion regarding what bilingual education could be on the part of at least one important Georgia Project leader. This confusion was symptomatic of a missed opportunity for Georgia Project proponents to develop a coherent vision of the curricular adjustments that could be part of the Georgia Project.

One element that is decipherable in Figure 11.1 was that remedial approaches were viewed warily and that pullouts were also recognized as problematic. Unlike the other presented models, the tally of required teachers for the holistic model was counted for only one school—the innovative elementary school. Whether this school was being proposed as a pilot site was unclear. Though leaders at that school would likely have been happy to pilot a program, nowhere in the agreement signed in March, nor in the newspaper stories covering the January 1997 visit, nor from accounts of my informants was this prospect separately raised. Based on his notes, it is possible this presentation was the first place/time that the attorney began to consider that all teachers could benefit from training in ESOL methodologies.

After the January 1997 visit, which was the first bilingual coordinator's only visit to Dalton (though he was an instructor during the 1997 Summer Institute in Monterrey), his designated task was to write a Spanish version of Georgia's QCC, the state's newly adopted Quality Core Curriculum. Despite the fact that the attorney disclosed in a June 1997 interview that the curriculum coordinator had assured him that the curriculum would be ready imminently, this task was never finished, so questions regarding how it would have been operationalized and how it would have meaningfully advanced Dalton's adoption of a bilingual format were not answered. As was previously noted, the visiting instructors arrived in October 1997 assuming they would implement a Monterrey-developed bilingual curriculum. The Direct Instruction curriculum they were actually asked to deliver is discussed momentarily.

The replacement bilingual coordinator who took over at the end of 1997 did not identify the QCC-conversion request as one of her tasks, though she did think she was supposed to have a curriculum development role. This was shown by her February 1998 request that Dalton administrators clarify to her what curriculum they were seeking. At that point, however, though no one stated as much at the time, the quest for curricular material had been suspended as the district-wide dissemination of Direct Instruction became Dalton's most important curricular overhaul.

## DIRECT INSTRUCTION AND THE GEORGIA PROJECT

Beyond the fact that it was a dominant language arts curriculum used by the visiting instructors (particularly at the elementary level), there are two further reasons for considering Direct Instruction as part of the Georgia

Project and as part of this chapter. First, Direct Instruction was a highly detailed, phonetically oriented, English-only model that was implemented across Dalton at the time that the Georgia Project's bilingual curriculum was supposed to be being implemented.[5] In other words, though not recognized as such by Dalton leaders, Direct Instruction functioned in lieu of the Georgia Project curriculum effort as the curriculum retooling intended to make Dalton schooling more responsive to the changed needs of Dalton students (including the needs of the Spanish-speaking student population).[6] A second reason to look at Direct Instruction is that the rapid dissemination of Direct Instruction (i.e., the training of teachers) was facilitated by the use of Title VII funds that had been secured through the grant proposal I wrote that described the Georgia Project in great detail and that mentioned Direct Instruction only once (Dalton Public Schools 1997). Money that was leveraged using the Georgia Project (though not categorized by the school district as part of the Georgia Project budget) instead supported Direct Instruction.[7]

Direct Instruction was first implemented in Dalton at an East Side elementary school (not the school referred to as "innovative" throughout this text) in 1995–1996. A primary reason for its introduction, according to an article in *The Daily Citizen-News* (Hamilton 1996a), was to help Hispanic students learn how to read English. (As noted in an earlier footnote, according to Goode's review [2002], the promoters of Direct Instruction have not marketed it or made claims about it in direct reference to helping Latinos read.) ESOL teachers were the first, or among the first, to implement it. Direct Instruction replaced a whole language model that, according to local interpretation of standardized test scores, clearly was not working for ESOL students. The pilot school's experience with the program was successful enough that when external pressure to change school practices (exemplified by the Georgia Project and by the public discourse insisting on improved test scores) combined with the availability of Title VII funds, the curriculum coordinator after some consultations determined to implement Direct Instruction at every school. At the start of the 1997–1998 school year Direct Instruction was adopted across the district.

Most Dalton teachers initially responded favorably to the introduction of Direct Instruction. It is worth thinking about why. As the attorney heard from his daughter and found when he made his initial visits to Dalton schools in the spring of 1996, at that time many Dalton teachers were frustrated by the unfamiliar challenges Spanish-speaking Hispanic students brought to their classrooms. Most did not have training specifically intended to help them understand the skills, needs, and expectations of their new student and parent populations. They were frustrated and at a loss. Indeed, it seems probable that many Dalton teachers in the mid-1990s were disconcertingly finding that they were less professionally competent mid-career than they had been earlier, if one measures professional competence from the standpoint of knowing how to engage students and to help them advance, because who their students were had changed.

In such circumstances, the strict scripting of Direct Instruction, the curriculum's requirement that students be divided into small manageable groups, and the student-engaging, constant call-and-response activity (even if rote) of the curriculum in practice all made it attractive. Furthermore, Direct Instruction's exclusive focus on English was consistent with many instructors' latent (or overt) assimilationist impulse. Direct Instruction also had a record of improving standardized test scores (a tool by which educators in turn are assessed),[8] and, in the age of exhausting "intensification" (Apple 1993:124) of teacher tasks, the minimal preparation time required for its delivery also heightened the appeal of Direct Instruction. With Direct Instruction, what and how to teach was predetermined. Uncertainty was replaced by certainty.

Whatever my own concerns about Direct Instruction (I had many after reading Adam and Engelmann's (1997) pitch for it while assembling the grant proposal in March 1997), it would be remiss to dismiss many Dalton instructors' initial satisfaction with the curriculum. However, the mode of implementation of Direct Instruction used by Dalton was contradictory to some elements of the Georgia Project. It also seemed contradictory to the school district's espoused mission to support students' development of critical thinking skills and the superintendent's espoused support of site-based management.

Having bilingual visiting instructors from Monterrey implement Direct Instruction, which they did often during my observation, begged the question why were they recruited in the first place. Direct Instruction was the embodiment of what Freire (1970) called "banking education"—predetermined content that was to be deposited into the heads of students with students proving receipt of the deposit by giving "right" answers to questions from the instructor or on the already drafted test. Because Direct Instruction predetermined all the necessary content and mandated with detailed scripts how it should be delivered, the special skills in bilingual education and the empathy for Mexican students that the visiting instructors brought with them into the classroom were marginalized. Whatever "value added" the visiting instructors had to contribute in Dalton classrooms was muted by Direct Instruction, a point that Georgia Project partners at the Universidad de Monterrey made repeatedly and with increasing shrill.

The rationale of Direct Instruction conflicted with the rationale for other components of the Georgia Project as well. The predetermination of instructors' classroom pedagogy and the curriculum content meant the advantage of sending teachers to Mexico for the Summer Institute disappeared; the acquired new skills, new materials, and additional background knowledge on students' language and sociohistorical background could not be applied. There is not a space in Direct Instruction for new skills and heightened empathy to assist the learning process. Only the Georgia Project's Parent and Workplace Involvement component escapes the reach of a closely subscribed to, fully articulated Direct Instruction program.

Despite the conclusions one would reach if only following the logic of Direct Instruction's inventors, the Georgia Project helped Dalton meet needs that Direct Instruction could not. Spanish-speaking students in Dalton (and other students as well) did sometimes get confused by Direct Instruction and/or become bored with it. In those instances, the presence of a skilled and empathetic instructor who could refocus energy, use Spanish, or make the wise decision to temporarily change tasks was of great value. According to Trueba (1994:379), "What frightens some immigrant children as they arrive to this country is not that they cannot make certain sounds, but that they cannot understand that certain things they do are considered culturally inappropriate or meaningless." The empathetic expertise of the visiting instructors and the Summer Institute participants helped immigrant students resolve their more serious questions.

There are a lot of pedagogically sound reasons for customizing the curriculum or giving instructors autonomy to build on students' existing knowledge base. Doing so helps students integrate new knowledge with existing. It avoids the perils of dismissing a student's culture, identity, and intertwined self-esteem. As a standardized curriculum not customized by district—let alone school, classroom, or individual student—Direct Instruction was not supposed to make accommodation for individual, local, regional, or non-mainstream issues of culture and identity. Again, Trueba (1994:379) clarifies the problem, "The fundamental message of success cannot be the loss of one's own linkage with the ethnic community or with one's own family." Direct Instruction did not include linkage with ethnicity and family within its framework.

On a similar theme, Ernst and Statzner (1994:202) inveighed that, "In a discussion of alternative visions of schooling, we can no longer afford an outmoded discourse that restricts definitions of success and failure to traditional measures (i.e., standardized tests, grades) or in relation to how well marginal groups assimilate to educational and cultural canons." Yet, acknowledging that acculturation can be problematic (especially if strictly assimilative), immigrant and minority students still need to be acculturated if they are to successfully negotiate the mainstream (Delpit 1988). Gibson (1988) clarified that such students need accommodation and acculturation without assimilation.

The students most directly targeted by the Georgia Project could gain from Direct Instruction's contribution to their mainstream success as marked by mainstream indicators. Though it would have meant integrating Direct Instruction with other elements rather than only buying it as a package from an externally based model developer, Dalton could have adopted Direct Instruction as another tool in the Georgia Project effort. That the curriculum coordinator was adamant that Direct Instruction was not part of the Georgia Project suggested that she championed Direct Instruction for other reasons.

The district-wide embrace of Direct Instruction was led by the curriculum coordinator. Her motives for endorsing Direct Instruction appeared to go beyond wanting to meet the interests of the children, though this was clearly one of her motives. Adopting Direct Instruction reasserted the power of her Central Office position and the rationale for her being in it. Both of these had been challenged by the Georgia Project specifically and by the district's management changes that had occurred simultaneously if not always directly because of the Georgia Project. It should be remembered that Direct Instruction was not adopted by classroom instructors but rather for them.[9]

Direct Instruction was designed to be implemented within the hierarchic, top-down management model that Puckett (1989) decried. Student tasks were scripted. Teachers made sure students followed the script while they followed one of their own. Immediate supervision of Direct Instruction required only monitoring student test scores and assuring that teachers were following their scripts. Autonomy was minimal. Oversight, censure, and correction were easy. The decisions to use the curriculum and to pay for it were singularly concentrated at the district level. Perhaps with feedback from the school sites and with the superintendent's agreement, the curriculum coordinator determined whether the curriculum should be used. That Direct Instruction fully implemented was an expensive model to operate (especially with the external consulting support provided to Dalton by J/P Associates, the Direct Instruction consultant) further concentrated the curriculum coordinator's power because an expenditure of the necessary size could not be authorized by a classroom instructor or school principal. Even if they liked the model, classroom instructors and school-based administrators were dependent on the curriculum coordinator to get it. Finally, regardless of how capable Dalton staff members might have been at curriculum design, they were not positioned to viably challenge the curriculum coordinator's authority regarding the Direct Instruction curriculum (except with individual customizations that would likely be frowned on by supervisors and external consultants). Direct Instruction curriculum decisions, apart from the decision to comply with it versus embrace it, were all made even beyond the school district by the curriculum's author and by the consultants. This made it highly unlikely that a Dalton employee could develop and display the curriculum design savvy that would threaten the curriculum coordinator's oversight of the curriculum.

In contrast, the Georgia Project initiatives presumed decentralized authority and risked exposing the curriculum coordinator's lack of expertise in various topic areas related to the learning of immigrant newcomers. The dissertation-writing principal's expertise, the celebrated educational innovations at her school, the learning of Summer Institute participants, the expertise brought by the visiting instructors from Monterrey, the Universidad de Monterrey-hired bilingual consultants (who because of the Georgia Project's complicated management structure reported to the attorney and Georgia Project oversight committee as well as to Dalton schools), and the district's unwritten site-based management philosophy, all supported school-site autonomy and school-site decision making. They combined to make a daunting challenge to the curriculum coordinator's authority and status and to the presumptions of expertise that were supposed to undergird them.

Though the combative "follow us and us only" attitude of Direct Instruction's inventors (see Adams and Engelmann 1997) and of the Direct Instruction support team at J/P Associates that served as consultants to Dalton were all disquieting, none of them had the power to insist that Dalton follow only their recommendations. The act of recommending a curriculum, the decision to choose a curriculum not endorsed by the Georgia Project, the selection of a curriculum that ignored or deemphasized the bilingual and cross-cultural skills of the visiting instructors and the Summer Institute participants, and the use of Title VII funds that would otherwise support Georgia Project initiatives, all could be read as attempts to beat back the challenges presented to the curriculum coordinator's role and status by the Georgia Project.

If this diagnosis is on target, it is still not a straightforward proposition to look upon the curriculum coordinator's actions as unexpected or irrational. The Georgia Project challenged her previous professional practices and her current professional identity in ways that no other Georgia Project architect had to negotiate. Her resistance to the dilution of her power was sensible, particularly given that the challenges to her authority were tacit and unaccompanied by any diminishment in her professional accountability. The Georgia Project was asking her to cede control, to have faith in the viability of initiatives which were ambitious and ambiguous and with which she did not have much familiarity, and to remain accountable for the resultant successes or failures as facilely marked by students' standardized test scores. Promulgating Direct Instruction was a sensible, conservative decision for her to make.

## A NEW MONTERREY COORDINATOR UNWITTINGLY PROMOTES A SCHISM

When the second bilingual component coordinator selected by the Georgia Project team at the Universidad de Monterrey visited Dalton for the first time in January 1998, she brought several operating assumptions with her. First she thought her main task was curriculum development and therefore that she needed to clarify what kind of curriculum the school district wanted. She did not anticipate this would be problematic. Second, she thought the curriculum would be implemented by the visiting instructors and perhaps others. According to the orientation she had received from the Georgia Project directors at the Universidad de Monterrey, the bilingual component and the visiting instructor component were linked. It followed that a central activity of her visit was observing how the visiting instructors were being used and listening to what Dalton administrators (school- and Central Office-based) thought of the instructor's performance to that point. Her final assumption reflected both her upbringing and her job. Because of her experience growing up in both the United States and Mexico and because of her job leading a combined trilingual *primaria* and *secundaria* in Monterrey she thought of bilingualism and bilingual education as sensible, desirable, and straightforward.

During her three-day visit, she met the attorney, the superintendent, the superintendent's assistant, and the curriculum coordinator. She saw all thirteen visiting instructors, watched many of them teach, and stopped at all eight schools in the system, even the two that since Christmas break were no longer hosting a visiting instructor.[10] She talked to principals, assistant principals, educational instructional specialists (EISs) and others who oversaw the visiting instructor's duties at the schools. In conversations with administrators, she recommended the bilingual education research of Jim Cummins and she promoted the Total Quality Management approach (TQM) developed by Deming. She saw Direct Instruction for the first time and commented to several people that she was intrigued by it.[11] She did not say and perhaps did not see that Direct Instruction was inconsistent with the decentralization of decision making that is a core tenet of TQM.

On February 19, 1998, she and the Georgia Project director at the Universidad de Monterrey faxed a report they had co-written about her visit to the superintendent. The bilingual curriculum coordinator was and was presumed to be the report's lead author, though the Georgia Project director's name was also attached, implying his review and endorsement of its contents. Reflecting both courtesy and the ongoing lack of clarity as to who in Dalton was in charge of the Georgia Project, additional copies of the report were directed to the attorney and to the curriculum coordinator. The presumption at the Monterrey end was that the report would remain a private working document. It did not, but, before the consequences of its dissemination are discussed, further contextualization is necessary.

After the bilingual coordinator's visit but before the preparation of her report, there was a public meeting of the ad hoc Georgia Project oversight committee. For this occasion, unlike some gatherings regarding the Georgia Project that the attorney had organized, there was a long list of invitees including all the visiting instructors, various business leaders, the attorney and his assistant, a representative from Dalton College, the chair of Dalton City Council's Finance Committee, the bilingual priest (noted in Chapter 8), a social worker with the superintendent and the curriculum coordinator, and four representatives of Whitfield County Schools (until this point Whitfield County Schools had not been involved with the Georgia Project since September 1997, supposedly because of anger at the unexpected cost of the Summer Institute). In all there were twenty-nine present, including me.

There was one important absence. Earlier in the day, when I told the principal of the innovative elementary school that I would see her later at the meeting, she told me that the curriculum coordinator had asked her not to come. Though it was never explained this way, the absence of the principal meant that when the coordinator presented her curriculum plan at the meeting (a plan that the coordinator had developed in consultation with the principal) those in the audience would have to direct their questions to the coordinator rather than to the Dalton employee from whom they were accustomed to soliciting advice on bilingual education.

The meeting's official agenda was surprisingly brief. There were five items listed, including the fifth entitled "Other matters for consideration." The curriculum coordinator was supposed to speak second, giving an update on the Georgia Project's "curriculum design." I knew an hour ahead of time, however, that the printed agenda was to be changed. I was asked to make a presentation about a brief "deliverables" report that I had prepared for the superintendent and dropped off just that morning. I had drafted that report as a favor for the superintendent after he had explained to me that a number of potential private Georgia Project/school district benefactors were waiting to see if the project was achieving anything (what was it "delivering") before committing any resources to it. It is worth noting that at this stage a distinction was not made between the Georgia Project and the district's actions; they were assumed, on this issue, to be one and the same.

The attorney, not the Dalton superintendent, presided over the meeting. He decided to insert me into the agenda not last in the "other items" category, nor first, but second, ahead of the curriculum coordinator's curriculum report. In the packet assembled under the attorney's supervision and distributed to all attendees, the outline which the curriculum coordinator had prepared to support her presentation was enclosed last, after the new Monterrey-based bilingual curriculum coordinator's resume, after articles from *Time,* the *Atlanta Journal-Constitution,* and *The Kiplinger Washington Letter* regarding national Hispanic education and demographic trends, after a race and ethnicity breakdown for Dalton's three East Side elementary schools and two secondary schools, after a one-page Georgia Project budget, after several letters about the Georgia Project written by the immigration attorney who had assisted with the visiting instructors' visas, and after a recent *Daily Citizen-News* story that labeled the Georgia Project as a bilingual education program. Whether the agenda-bumping and locating the outline last in the packet were intentional slights is conjectural; that the curriculum coordinator's report was de-emphasized was not.

When the curriculum coordinator finally did speak the meeting had lasted more than an hour already, She introduced the "Bilingual Transitional Plan," describing it as not having been "formally presented or adopted," but it was based on the input of "many [unspecified] people, much reading, and some experience." The Universidad de Monterrey was not mentioned in the document and it appeared unlikely that anyone from there had reviewed the document. (When I asked Monterrey staff later if they had seen it, none remembered it.) The stated goal of the plan was to have "All students achieving at grade level in English while developing skill in a second language."

The first four points all related to non-native speakers of English and varied in their specificity. The plans for instruction in English were all much clearer than for instruction in Spanish, but there was acknowledged intent to include the latter. According to the second item of the two-page plan, "All research indicates the stronger one is in his/her first language the easier the transition to a second language." Based on this research, the plan recommended beginning Spanish instruction in kindergarten, offering Spanish for Spanish speakers, and having bilingual staff and language learning related technology. This portion of the plan and all others notably excluded the idea of any academic content instruction in Spanish (apart from language arts). How language arts instruction in Spanish (a progressive step to be sure) and all other instruction being in English was intended to magically facilitate the continued broad academic achievement of newcomer students was not clarified. A vague line in the plan did promise, "Primary instruction would be in English with the students' native language (Spanish) utilized to facilitate language and academic growth."

The report drew few questions and was quickly over-shadowed by a tense exchange between the bilingual priest and the Dalton Superintendent after the priest characterized of Dalton as "incompetent" to the task of meeting the needs of its growing Hispanic population. As the meeting ended, attendees discussed this and Dalton's alleged unwillingness to hire bilingual employees.[12] A few people asked me further about my report. Eight lingered for an unannounced executive planning session. All of these were business leaders except the attorney, the Dalton superintendent, and me. The coordinator's presentation regarding the curriculum component was lost in the shuffle, only to resurface in two separate ways during the following month.

The February 19 report faxed by Monterrey's second bilingual component coordinator and its Georgia Project director clearly if unwittingly reasserted the Universidad de Monterrey collaborators' assumption that they were still leading the curriculum development initiative. It made no reference to the curriculum coordinator's outline or presentation. The report did make several pointed comments and a few subtle ones. As an example of both regarding the same issue, the report criticized the frequent casting of Monterrey instructors as assistants or paraprofessionals, saying in the recommendations section, "The Monterrey teachers are not U.S. certified, but they have been certified in Mexico. They are not at the level of para-professionals and they are not student teachers. In fact, most of them have had important experience as teachers in Mexican private, bilingual schools. Monterrey teachers could and should take a more pro-active role."[13] The regular use of terms "Monterrey teacher" and "U.S. teacher" more subtly asserted their equal footing.[14]

While acknowledging that the visiting instructors were happy and had been treated well by the superintendent and his assistants, and by the principals, administrators, and teachers in all schools, the report complained about the U.S. teachers' regular failure to pass along lesson plans and other preparatory materials to Monterrey teachers ahead of time. Monterrey teachers frequently first viewed a lesson plan at the moment they were supposed to be enacting it. The report also complained about the marginal spaces—hallways, cafeterias, and so forth—where the Monterrey instructors were frequently expected to work and about the lack of clarity regarding what the instructors' task was to be when they had first arrived.

That so much of the report was devoted to detailing the experience of the visiting instructors demonstrates how those on the Monterrey end viewed the visiting instructor component and the bilingual curriculum component as closely intertwined; there was also much in the report about the bilingual curriculum itself, but mostly questions. In a section entitled "The Dalton Model for Bilingual Education" the authors proposed an April 1998 summit (which was never held) to hasten the development of the curriculum Dalton was seeking. At the conference, four questions were to be answered:

• What do Dalton teachers, principals, superintendent want? [sic]
• What do Dalton students need?
• How will all Dalton students, Anglos and Hispanics, reach the goal of graduating at 12th-grade reading level?
• Will the "Transitional Bilingual" model be used?

Considering the first bullet, it is interesting to note how extensive the proposed group to be consulted is. Curriculum decisions are assumed not to be the prerogative of just one administrator or a small group. Unfortunately, a job category that would entail the curriculum coordinator is not included in the list, though that did not necessarily mean she was to be excluded from the process. Still if she was starting to feel slighted by the Georgia Project, this oversight would not have helped.

It is also worth highlighting that, in the fourth bullet, the bilingual holistic model vaguely defined a year earlier is not mentioned, while the reference to transitional bilingual models is a question. Monterrey Georgia Project leaders were still unsure as to what Dalton was seeking. The question about transitional models may also have reflected an unstated belief that Spanish as a foreign language and maintenance Spanish for Spanish-speaker classes did not together constitute a model that is accurately encompassed by the label bilingual education.

This segment of the report ended with a final tie-in between curriculum development and the role of the visiting instructors: "These [answers to the questions] are issues which must be carefully defined by all. Once the model is clarified, the role for the Monterrey teachers should also be easier to clarify with respect to the difference between their roles and that of the U.S. teachers, the ESOL teachers, the paraprofessionals, etc."[15]

Though blunt and perhaps indirectly critical of the absence of leadership regarding emphasis of the visiting instructors' status as credentialed educators and the planning for the visiting instructors' tasks, the Monterrey report was not dismissive or inappropriate. Assuming that it would be read only by those leading the Georgia Project, the authors' clarity was intended to be helpful not critical. These were questions that needed to be answered so that the Georgia Project could move forward and achieve the objectives that Monterrey leaders thought were desired at the Dalton end.

However, on February 27, perhaps as a maneuver reasserting his own power and attempting to mobilize external pressure for broadly inclusive planning, the attorney mailed copies of the Monterrey report to everyone on the Georgia Project Committee mailing list. As part of the same packet, a copy of the initial *Innovations in American Government* grant proposal (Dalton Public Schools 1998a) that had been generated by the superintendent's executive assistant was distributed. The attorney also updated committee members about Summer Institute 1998 preparations and about the pending March 5 visit of several partners from Monterrey. By mailing the Monterrey report, the attorney was inviting thought, feedback, and participation from many beyond the school district regarding how the identified obstacles could be addressed.

On March 5, at a luncheon meeting with the Georgia Project leaders from the Universidad de Monterrey that included the superintendent, several other district administrators, the attorney, his assistant, and me (as an observer), the curriculum coordinator again shared her Bilingual Transitional Plan. There was one change from the document she had presented previously; the words "or above" were added to the goal statement of, "All students achieving at or above grade level in English while developing skill in a second language." There were no adjustments in response to the February 19 report from the Universidad de Monterrey's bilingual coordinator and Georgia Project director.

The curriculum coordinator's March 5 presentation was not long. Nor did it draw many questions this time. The administrator did say that she had not yet had the chance to share the plan with the school board nor with the bilingual component coordinator in Monterrey (though three weeks had passed). In what likely was a reference to the February 19 report, she added that

Dalton did not want the plan the Monterrey leader had recommended, though she did not clarify what that alleged plan was. (By my read, the February 19 report did not include a recommendation.) Indicatively, she also asked the Georgia Project leaders from the Universidad de Monterrey to convey the message to the bilingual component coordinator that during the coordinator's next visit she was not to meet with Dalton principals; rather her role was to act more as a private consultant to the superintendent and the curriculum coordinator. In order to keep another appointment, the curriculum coordinator then left.

Later at that March 5 meeting, Monterrey personnel made a presentation of the proposed 1998–1999 budget for three of the four Georgia Project components. Excluding the visiting instructor's program (the accounting for which was exclusively performed by the school district), Universidad de Monterrey Georgia Project leaders outlined $183,489 of proposed costs for the coming year's program—$111,025 for the Summer Institute, $16,859 for the bilingual education curriculum design, and $55,605 for general coordination (into which the Parent and Workplace Involvement component was tucked). No one noticed the contradiction in the budget's "Anticipated Outcome of the Program" for the bilingual component and the unilateral curriculum decisions being made by the curriculum coordinator. The budget text claimed that the curriculum design needed to be accepted by the principals and still assumed that the curriculum would be put together by the Universidad de Monterrey's coordinator. When the Monterrey Georgia Project director ended the budget presentation by asking the school district's budget director if there were any problems, his answer was, "No, looks good."

Perhaps frustrated by the curriculum coordinator's exclusion of the Universidad de Monterrey's Georgia Project personnel in her preparation of the Bilingual Transitional Plan and/or perhaps convinced that curriculum input from the Universidad de Monterrey was more substantive than what the Dalton administrator was producing, on March 18 the attorney again tried to outflank the curriculum coordinator (though again not overtly). In a letter to the Georgia Project Committee and friends that announced a substantial gathering being planned for March 27, the attorney enclosed a copy of a letter written by a former Georgia Department of Education administrator that praised the insight of the Monterrey bilingual component coordinator's February 19 report. (As noted earlier, most people on the mailing list had previously been sent a copy of that report.) Of the second bilingual coordinator, the former state administrator wrote: "From an instructional point of view, I was most interested in Professor [bilingual coordinator]'s report. Her comments indicate that she has a solid foundation in how students learn within the context of multilingual, multicultural environments."[16] The attorney was not enough of an education expert to convincingly intervene directly in a curriculum methodology debate, but, as he had before, he tried to be convincing by quoting someone whose expertise was recognized.

As of May 1998, development of a bilingual curriculum component was still an espoused goal of the Georgia Project, but that curriculum did not exist, its parameters were in debate, and the development process seemed paralyzed. When Universidad de Monterrey bilingual coordinator made a return visit to Dalton that month, the curriculum coordinator asked her to send all future correspondence regarding the Georgia Project exclusively and directly to her. My informant who passed along this detail did not clarify whether the superintendent was also supposed to be excluded from the direct chain of communication.

In July 1998, Dalton Public Schools released their *Annual Report 1998*, which included an enthusiastic write-up about the Georgia Project (1998c:15). The page-long article titled "Innovation" had a subheading in large-font italics: "Georgia Project objective is to assist Spanish-speaking children in learning English." In the article's main text were the twin claims, "The first priority of the Georgia Project is to boost English-language proficiency for native Spanish-speaking children enrolled in the school system" and "Both programs have benefited all of the children in the school system." The "Both" refers to the Summer Institute component and the visiting instructors' component. Tellingly, the Parent and Workplace Involvement (relabeled "community development and research") was described as not yet fully underway and the bilingual education component was fully omitted. If an annual report tried to put an institution's best foot forward then the judgment of the school system was that bilingual education was a loser that should not be mentioned and that the community involvement piece was not generating any gains that were pertinent to the system. This last was not necessarily a negative evaluation of the Parent and Workplace Involvement component, as much of its intended efficacy—for example, the Hispanic leadership development initiative—was directed not at the school per se but at the larger community. However, it did represent a disinclination to see the Georgia Project's school and nonschool components as coequal and necessarily intertwined.

In September 1998 a Dalton contact reported that the bilingual component had been dropped. The same contact complained that the 1999 Georgia Project budget submitted by the Universidad de Monterrey still included a $16,000 allocation in that category (as it had in March). At least three months after Dalton had determined to drop the bilingual component (as evidenced by the *Annual Report 1998*) convincing words to that effect had not yet reached Monterrey. Perhaps this was indicative of a direct communication failure; perhaps instead it indicated a continuing conflict between messages emanating from the school district to the Universidad de Monterrey and those coming from the attorney's office to the Universidad de Monterrey. Maybe one was saying the component was unwanted while the other disagreed.

In August 1998, two months after the attorney had sent a letter to U.S. Representative Nathan Deal requesting his protection of Dalton's Title VII grant and thus his opposition to a pending House Bill seeking Title VII's immediate elimination,[17] and one month after Rep. Deal had responded thanking the attorney for his interest but declaring his opposition to Title VII nonetheless, the attorney invited me to give him a personal briefing on the efficacy (or lack thereof) of bilingual education. I told him then that the term was obviously a political hot potato, that it was used as a shorthand to describe vastly different programs and intentions, but that bilingual education done properly represented a useful tool for school districts to serve both English language learners and native English speakers (see Brisk 1998). He indicated that this was his impression as well.

The story does not end quite there, however, even though the bilingual curriculum component was never resurrected. It was still the case that a contingent of visiting instructors trained in bilingual education were serving in Dalton schools and were inevitably teaching at least sometimes in accordance with their training, even if the formal parameters within which they operated offered little support. The Universidad de Monterrey's second bilingual coordinator remained involved in the Georgia Project, making additional visits to Dalton, and co-authoring several reports that asked professionally appropriate but challenging questions regarding the deployment of the visiting instructors. That these reports did not lead to major policy changes at the Dalton end does not mean that they lacked penetrating insight. A better explanation is that the direct deterioration in the relationship between the attorney and the school district was also reducing the willingness of the district to regard the advice of the Mexican professionals that the attorney had so craftily brought to the table three years earlier.

Most intriguingly, in 1999, with the Georgia Project curriculum challenge over, with Dalton teachers becoming restive regarding Direct Instruction, and with none of the promised improvements in test scores, the district ended its expensive collaboration with J/P Associates for support implementing Direct Instruction, though it continued to implement Direct Instruction. The curriculum coordinator continued to personally advocate for Direct Instruction, but not necessarily with the same fervor. During my brief return visit to Dalton in March 2002, several educators in the district told me that they thought the new superintendent who had come to the district in 2001 had little regard for Direct Instruction and that, following up on her original dismantling of pieces of it, it would be gone once Dalton again received a state allocation for new textbook purchases.[18]

Goode (2002:127) sheds additional light on the Georgia Project versus Direct Instruction controversy, noting the financial hole the district got itself into with its expensive Direct Instruction consulting contract and how that meant for a logistical rather than pedagogical or ideological conflict with the Georgia Project. Part of her account follows:

Over the two years following the arrival of the first visiting instructors, Dalton began to realize how expensive the Georgia Project and the concurrent adoption of Direct Instruction was. The contract with J/P Associates dated September 2, 1998 outlines 192 days of in-classroom coaching at $1,150 per day, for a total of close to $250,000. This sum does not include the actual Direct Instruction materials, which are expensive by textbook standards. . . . In order to pay for the Direct Instruction materials, Dalton used state textbook adoption funds, as well as some of the Title VII grant money, and state generated ESOL funds, which the [attorney] found infuriating. Beginning in February of 1999, an exchange of correspondence ensued between the [attorney] and Dalton administrative staff, much of it focusing on the expenditure of the Title VII and ESOL funds. In turn, Dalton administrative staff became angered, perceiving the [attorney] as meddling in school system business.

Unfortunately, a more pointed dispute followed with the attorney requesting some very particular accountings of expenditures, generating a same-day response from the superintendent that in turn led to the attorney crafting a reply also on the same day (February 24, 1999). As quoted in Goode (2002:128), the superintendent wrote to the attorney:

I will comment on the request for Direct Instruction information. This program is a phonics-based curriculum which does meet the need for all students regardless of their background. It has proven itself over 30 years of use and has been selected for our reading series by the Board of Education, the administration, and the instructional staff. I do not believe we could select another program with the same intensive instruction, accountability component, and teacher training requirements. In other words, the decision to maintain Direct Instruction as our reading series of choice has been made. I do not anticipate any additional time spent giving this further consideration would be productive.

Again quoting from Goode (2002:128–129), the attorney disagreed with the superintendent in his reply:

I fully understand that Direct Instruction is being utilized throughout the system. Although many in the education field are not as high on Direct Instruction as you, it has been selected and nothing in my letter should be interpreted as an effort to change it in the middle of the year. However, I cannot agree that discussing Direct Instruction at this point would be counterproductive as you suggest. Dalton is using large sums for Direct Instruction from the following sources: Grant from the City of Dalton; Grant from the United States Education Department for system-wide bilingual education; and from the State Department of Education for instruction and materials for immigrant students under the Emergency Immigration Grant. . . . I am aware that, although funding for Direct Instruction was not requested in the Title VII application, that somehow and at some time, it appears to have been approved according to the documents I received from your office. . . . Consequently, since a large portion of the monies appropriated for the Georgia Project are going to pay for Direct Instruction, it is a matter that requires further discussion. . . .

Goode followed the attorney's extensive response by noting that Dalton administrators were not accustomed to having their agendas set by outsiders as the attorney was now insistently doing. As a final issue, Goode's account also explains how the school district's decision to use the visiting instructors to teach Direct Instruction was a product of (a) the high instructor to student ratio that model requires, necessitating the use of practically all available adults, including also school librarians and at least one physical education teacher, and (b) a desire to head off possible complaints by some certified teachers (including ESOL teachers), who were deeply skeptical of Direct Instruction, if the visiting instructors were exempted. In this sense, the Georgia Project was not just competing to change the status quo experienced by students in their classrooms; it was involved in tangled education politics regarding who had jurisdiction over what. The district administration's emphatic response reflected not just frustration with the Georgia Project but a kind of siege mentality as skepticism regarding Direct Instruction came louder from other quarters. The local politics of education had become unfamiliarly heated and discordant.

# 12

# The Universidad Also
# Does What It Wants

Because the Mexican scholars who led the Universidad de Monterrey's participation in the partnership were sociologists and brought a more holistic community change framework to their Georgia Project goals than just school issues, the fourth and final original component, initially known as the Parent and Workplace Involvement Initiative, encompassed a number of community development initiatives. Significantly, though much of the work conducted within this component was germane to the schooling of Latinos in Dalton—notably a Latino community needs assessment—the Dalton schools were, at best, an awkward partner for this component, attached to it largely because they were the easiest entity for the Universidad de Monterrey to partner with.

Some Universidad de Monterrey informants speculated that they thought the attorney's Georgia Project vision transcended a vision just to change local schools. Though the Parent and Workplace Involvement component had implications for the schools and its finances were coordinated by the school district's administrative services, it was the component that most overtly operated beyond the domain of the schools. Its operation came closest to substantiating the Universidad de Monterrey informants' claims regarding the attorney's larger vision, though it should be added that it largely reflected the Monterrey scholars interests and orientations with the attorney agreeing that the inquiries they wanted to engage in were useful.

Because this component was largely in the hands of the two Monterrey leaders profiled in Chapter 6, with the attorney playing a facilitating role and Dalton school personnel mostly uninvolved, comparatively little of this component's design was open to subsequent negotiation, politicking, or reinterpretation. Rather the politics emerged after the Universidad de Monterrey did what it promised—that is, conducted a needs assessment of Dalton's Latino community, examined available adult education opportunities for newcomers, identified the existing and nascent informal Latino community leadership, and initiated a leadership training seminar for those who had been identified.

The description of this component that was written by the research director in March 1997 (to clarify the component's rationale to the attorney) stands as a good summary of both its intent and deployment during my study. That text follows in Figure 12.1. As readers review it, they should note that in subsequent documents the research director and other Monterrey authors largely replaced the term "Mexican" with the term "Hispanic," which, whatever its hazards, has a U.S. reference point (Oboler 1995). One point emphasized by Monterrey scholars in most of their documents was that Dalton's Hispanic community was a permanent community. Perhaps the change in terminology was to reiterate that point.

Readers should also consider the possible discrepancy between the accuracy and candor of the promised reports that Universidad de Monterrey scholars would create and the willingness of a Dalton audience to heed and act upon the Mexican scholars' recommendations. If information was the missing ingredient impeding the mainstream community's interaction with Dalton Hispanics and limiting the provision of sufficient adult education opportunities, then these reports in remedying that information gap should also have remedied the problem. However, if communication obstacles had multiple origins (i.e., more than just absent information), if they were willfully in place (i.e., by the function of "theories in use," espoused or not, of those in the mainstream [Argyris and Schön 1975]), or if they were a result of insufficient infrastructure, then the substantive impact of the reports would be less than perhaps their authors hoped.

Furthermore, readers should consider the research director's choice of points to emphasize and the presumption they indicate about his sense (and presumably his colleagues' sense) of audience. It seems the strong emphasis on pairing Mexican inclusion with ideas such as improving the social, economic, and educational quality of life in Dalton—also referenced as "industrial, civic, and school"—was quite conscious. Having visited Dalton and spent time with some of its most powerful corporate leaders (see Chapter 8), the research director likely had already picked up on the long-standing communitarian and paternalistic impulses that were salient to Dalton's elite (see Chapter 3). It was to them, in their capacity as policymakers, that this response was directed.

Finally, readers should note that the research director's use of the term *assimilation* does not seem to match my use of that term in the rest of the

FIGURE 12.1    **Parent and Workplace Involvement Action Plan—Letter of March 7, 1997, from the Attorney to Members of the Georgia Project Planning Group**

You will recall at our meeting last week we asked Professor [Research Director] of the University of Monterrey to enlighten us in the following areas concerning the Parent and Industry/Workplace Involvement Program:

1. Design of the Parent and Industry Program;

2. What it seeks to accomplish; and

3. Why it should begin this Spring.

Professor [Research Director] has very quickly responded to our request which is enclosed.

### Georgia Project
### Parents and Industry/Workplace Involvement Program

**Goals**

The Parents and Industry/Workplace Involvement Program (PIP) is a comprehensive and multidimensional program that seeks to provide the business leadership in Dalton, the School System, and the community in general with tools to better understand and incorporate the Mexican adults and children to the social, economic, and educational life of the City of Dalton.

This program seeks to generate a) detailed knowledge and information about the social and demographic characteristics of the Mexican community, their needs and potential contribution to Dalton. This information will be used to develop b) three applied programs that will address different concerns of the business and school system leadership in Dalton in relation to the Mexican population.

As the description of the specific programs shows, one of the PIP's main goals is to enhance the contribution of the Mexican community to the industrial, civic and school activities of the larger community by means of a variety of non-formal educational programs. The four different programs comprised in the PIP have been thought as an ensemble of coordinated efforts aimed at promoting a rapid yet smooth assimilation of the Mexican population to the Dalton community.

**(continued)**

**Contents**

The PIP is composed of four different dimensions or subprograms.

(a) **Analysis of the Mexican Community**    This is a two to three week field study of the Mexican population in Dalton conducted by [the Georgia Project Director], [the Research Director], and a field assistant. The study will provide both researchers and leaders in Dalton with key information about the social, demographic and educational characteristics and needs of the Mexican community. The report of the study will include information about the literacy and skill levels and the social, economic and occupational backgrounds of Mexican families living in Dalton. The report will also generate data on the internal composition of the Mexican community and the most relevant needs and concerns of its members. It is worth noting that the study will help to establish the necessary groundwork for the ensuing subprograms and activities.

(b) **Community Leadership Program**    This program will contribute to identify potential community leaders within the Mexican population in Dalton and to provide them with needed leadership skills. These are skills that leaders can use to identify problems and needs within their communities and coordinate efforts to solve them. Leadership skills also include the ability to dialogue and work together with authorities of the larger Dalton community. During their visit to the City of Dalton last January researchers of Universidad de Monterrey were able to observe three facts in relation to the Mexican community in Dalton: (a) it is a young community that (b) appears to have settled permanently in Dalton and that (c) it contains an emerging leadership comprised of middle-class families and small entrepreneurs. Identifying leaders within the Mexican community and working with them will allow the business leadership and the heads of the school system to successfully implement almost any kind of education, civic and productivity improvement programs in Dalton.

(c) **Adult Biliteracy Program**    This program involves the design and pilot implementation of an adult literacy program in English and Spanish for Mexican workers of the Dalton industrial community. The aim of this program is to increase the literacy and numeracy skills of Mexican workers in both English and Spanish in order to enhance their current and future contribution to the economic well-being of the City of Dalton. The program suggests the use of workplaces, spaces dedicated to leisure activities and schools to recruit Mexican men and women in a creative adult biliteracy program. Researchers at Universidad de Monterrey strongly believe that this program will contribute both to the quality of the labor force in Dalton and to the success of the bilingual curriculum implemented in the public school system.

(continued)

> **(d) Parents and Schools Program** This program seeks to increase the involvement of Mexican parents with the educational experiences of their children by means of a variety of school-based activities and more frequent interaction with teachers. It was brought to the attention of the Universidad de Monterrey team by both officials and teachers of the public school system that existing language barriers (something that will be reduced with the adult biliteracy program) prevent Mexican parents from a more active participation in the educational process of children. Participation in school-based activities will help parents understand the specific learning needs of their children and will support the work done by school teachers and their bilingual assistants.
>
> The design and implementation of the various programs outlined here include the training of a Dalton-based team and continuing evaluation on the part of the Universidad de Monterrey team.

document (i.e., he is not implying that the Mexican community in Dalton should unilaterally change, erasing its distinctiveness from the mainstream to facilitate its absorption by the same). Gibson's (1988) term *accommodation* seems to better match the research director's intended meaning.

The attorney's suggestion, included at the beginning of Figure 12.1, that this component begin in the spring of 1997 proved too optimistic, but not by much. In June 1997 a team of three sociologists came to Dalton to begin their two-week survey promised as part of the "Analysis of the Mexican Community."

## A NEEDS ASSESSMENT

Almost concurrent with the departure of the first team of Dalton educators headed to the inaugural Summer Institute in Monterrey, a team of three applied sociologists from Universidad de Monterrey—the Georgia Project director, the research director, and the exchange coordinator[1]—arrived to implement a rapid community study. Halfway through their two-week stay, the research team was joined by the research director's spouse. She was a doctoral student specializing in adult education and community development at the Center for International Education at the University of Massachusetts. She would return in the fall to help conduct the community leadership seminar (described in the next segment) and to analyze adult education opportunities in Dalton/Whitfield (described in the segment after that). Like her husband, she was multilingual and had spent part of her childhood in Europe, learning Spanish and Catalan while living in Barcelona.

The research team introduced themselves with a front-page photograph and story in *El Tiempo,* a local, free, Spanish-language weekly. The article described three of the four Georgia Project components, omitting the bilingual curriculum component for unspecified reasons. Both the about-to-start Summer Institute and the then still tentative visiting instructor program were described before the community study.[2] The Georgia Project's goal was announced in the headline: "El Proyecto Georgia Empieza Para la Comunidad Hispana" (The Georgia Project Begins for the Hispanic Community). The first two sentences then clarified that the project was for the benefit of Hispanic children, parents, and families and that the researchers were looking forward to getting to know, to learning from, and to collaborating with Mexicans, Guatemalans, Salvadorans, Hondurans, Nicaraguans, Panamanians, Ecuadorians, Costa Ricans, and Americans of Hispanic origin that lived in Dalton/Whitfield. Also included in the article was the hotel phone number where the group could be contacted. Anyone seeking to share information was invited to call. The article did not say that rudimentary English was necessary to be connected through the hotel's switchboard to the scholars' room and/or to leave a message.

Taking advantage of previous experience doing research in Mexican receiving communities and also using their diverse identities to maximize their collective access (e.g., the lead female researcher contacting mothers), the team prioritized characterizing the community, discovering resources, sharing informants' articulated goals and needs, and identifying de facto community leaders. That they had much success in meeting each of the above objectives can be seen from the high response rate they received from invitees to the leadership development seminar in November 1997—if the invitations or the inviters had not seemed credible then presumably the invitations would have been ignored/rejected. Also, the report the team released in October 1997 which was based on their June visit was detailed enough, used enough primary information, and was varied enough to show that the group had successfully penetrated Dalton/Whitfield's heterogeneous Latino community.[3]

Several elements in that report are worth highlighting. Most emphatically, the Universidad de Monterrey scholars emphasized to Dalton readers of the report that Dalton's Hispanic community was a permanent community.[4] Some Anglos' nativist wishes that local Hispanics would "go back to Mexico" were characterized as racist and misguided. An emergent second generation of Hispanics, born and raised in the United States and coming to adulthood, saw the United States as their home and reference point, not Mexico. For them, Mexico was not a place that could be returned to. Hispanic parents claimed Dalton's small scale and lack of violence and gang activity made it preferable to large U.S. metropolitan areas as a location to raise a family and illustrated that much of the in-migration by Latinos to Dalton was not directly from Mexican sending communities.

The abundance of local work and the willingness of large local employers—Shaw and Mohawk/Aladdin were specifically noted—to protect worker rights and to promote Hispanics were also noted by community members as reasons for establishing local roots.

Treatment by educators and opportunities at Dalton and Whitfield County Schools were not noted as reasons to settle locally. In fact, the report noted many Hispanic secondary school students' complaints of racist treatment at local schools by fellow students, by teachers, and by school authorities (whether in Dalton or Whitfield County schools was not specified). In disputes Anglo school administrators allegedly treated Anglos preferentially to Hispanics. (As noted in Chapter 7, there were no Hispanic administrators.) Mothers noted a "modest distrust" of schools, reporting school personnels' underappreciation for the vicissitudes of local Latino employment niches. (Many jobs occupied by Hispanic parents had unpredictable schedules. Though work was readily available, obligations to work overtime, shift changes, shared child care and transportation arrangements, and other factors made scheduling and keeping weekday appointments at schools difficult.) Mothers also spoke of frustration communicating with teachers because interpreters were not always available. Children were sometimes used as interpreters. Some said that at school conferences they would be met by a social worker rather than a teacher. Incidents where Anglo school personnel alleged that Hispanics were forming gangs, using gang signs, wearing gang colors and other paraphernalia were chronicled, with the allegations dismissed as overreaction to "wannabe" gang emulation and/or the outright invention of problems and punishments without any substantive base. The researchers found no evidence of substantive gang activity involving Hispanics in Dalton. How they distinguished substantive from "wannabe" gang behavior was unclear.

How frequently any of the stated problems occurred, whether informants only included Dalton experiences or incorporated experiences from elsewhere in the United States, and whether they referred to historic or ongoing circumstances was unclear. But whether the complaints were based on just a few experiences or many, whether they were describing a local problem or a national problem brought to this local setting, the vital larger point remains that some local Hispanics did not fully trust the schools or the students, teachers, and administrators there. This suggested first that the existing Latino dropout problem could not be fully blamed on the attractiveness of work—in other words there was a "push out" dynamic also in play (Trueba 1991)—and that a challenge of the Georgia Project was to prove the school districts' sincerity and credibility to at least those Hispanic students and their parents who had doubts. In the absence of establishing such credibility, the crucial instructor/student bond of trust identified by Erickson (1987) would remain elusive, with Hispanic newcomers' school outcomes suffering as a consequence.

The Universidad de Monterrey researchers' report also catalogued a long list of local Hispanic enterprises, described household savings strategies (including informants' estimation that three to four years of hard work by multiple household members could produce enough savings to support the purchase of a $50,000 to $70,000 home), and framed the status hierarchy of employment niches available to and occupied by local Hispanics. The authors noted the paucity of public interethnic spaces and activities that brought Hispanic newcomers and established Anglo residents shoulder to shoulder. School soccer and a Hispanic-organized, elaborate, adult soccer league were both identified as exceptions. Anglo adolescent girls were also said to be frequenting Mexican "bailes" (dances) and adopting some Mexican teenager stylings. Remembering that these were exceptions, the general lack of interaction and the lack of space for interaction were both identified as factors leading either side to be suspicious of the other. The related history of exclusion of authentic Hispanic voices in community planning was also noted.[5] This was a theme that would be repeated by participants in the November 1997 Hispanic community leadership seminar and in the March 1998 survey of Dalton/Whitfield adult education opportunities. The impression of exclusion was not just one noted by outsiders, but one felt and articulated by members of the Hispanic community.

## THE LEADERSHIP SEMINAR AND THE FIFTH DALTON/MONTERREY LEADERS MEETING

In November 1997, the Monterrey research team returned to conduct more community research, to meet with school district and other Dalton-based Georgia Project leaders, to initiate a questionnaire-based survey of Hispanic parents that used the assistance of the visiting instructors to implement, and to preside over a two-day Hispanic community leadership development seminar. The questionnaire survey required a number of subsequent interventions to yield sufficient data due to both the limited Spanish-language literacy of some Dalton Hispanic parents and the skepticism/unfamiliarity that many Dalton Hispanics still felt regarding either the Universidad de Monterrey team and/or their research instrument. Despite the research team's rapid success penetrating the Hispanic community in June 1997, that visit was for only two weeks and was five months previous to the use of the questionnaire. Many Hispanics remained unaware or only vaguely aware of the Georgia Project, let alone its research component. The visiting instructors who were not trained as community researchers were still pretty new to Dalton—having arrived just a month earlier—so they were not yet well positioned to enhance the lesser known research team's credibility and thus improve the questionnaire's initial yield.

If the questionnaire process was difficult (and later on, after some tweaking, it yielded useful data), that struggle was overshadowed by the major success of the November visit: the leadership seminar. The seminar entitled "A Vision of Our Future in Dalton" had both a broad agenda— trust-building, identification of needs, initiating community action planning—and a careful attention to detail. The packets distributed to the thirteen participants (six additional invitees could not participate) each contained a Mexican *loteria* card, a symbol of good luck and, in this instance, cultural solidarity.[6] The seminar was facilitated by the research director's spouse and her Mexican colleague (also a University of Massachusetts doctoral student) with the three Universidad de Monterrey sociologists who had led the June research effort also present and involved. By arrangement of the Georgia Project's instigating attorney (who was not present), the seminar was held at the recently opened Northwest Georgia Trade and Convention Center, a site perched on a ridge of Dug Gap Mountain overlooking but away from Dalton's hustle and bustle and the homes and workplaces of seminar participants.

To avoid any public reaction and to promote a safe and trusting environment, the event maintained a low profile (no newspaper stories) and was open to invitees only. The only non-Hispanic present was the research director's spouse who could use her strong Spanish, her obvious group leading expertise, and the sanction of the Universidad de Monterrey representatives to readily establish her credibility. Dalton-based Georgia Project leaders were to varying degrees aware of the meeting's existence and purpose, but they respected the Mexican researchers' request that the event be private. They learned the details and outcomes of the meeting only several months later when they were presented with the "Hispanic Community Leadership Seminar: Final Report."

As the first sizable, coordinated gathering of Dalton's emergent Latino community leadership, the event was cathartic. Many participants met each other for the first time and were pleased to hear about previously unknown intracommunity resources and expertise as well as shared but previously unarticulated common goals for the ethnic community's future. Participants expressed a desire for more Hispanic unity in Dalton, better intragroup communication, more social action, development of creative models for problem solving, and more political and legal representation. Several education-related needs and desires were expressed: community support for youths' educational achievement (particularly college), improvement of the quality of education and the availability of educational resources, and the creation of more Adult Basic Education and ESL programs. The group also identified a need for consciousness-raising regarding family issues, specifically the provision of child care and other support for working mothers and attention to teenage pregnancy.[7]

Participants ended the seminar by initiating the development of collective action plans. They created three interest groups—Family/Youth/Education, Leadership and Political Representation, and Economic and Business

Development—to tackle the various issues and needs identified at the seminar. They also agreed on four immediate actions:

- Develop an ethnic association/Hispanic club that would provide both a social and political community forum.
- Increase the interaction and relationships with other Hispanic leaders elsewhere in Georgia and across the United States.
- Guarantee that efficient effective legal services exist for Hispanics in Dalton by attracting a Spanish-speaking lawyer to Dalton.
- Establish an educational committee consisting of Hispanic parents that would serve as a coordinating means to bring community concerns and problems to the attention of Dalton officials.[8]

The progress made toward the realization of all of these actions was not clear by the end of my research study, though neither at that point nor since have I heard of a Hispanic parent educational committee that had much communication with the school district. However, the leadership group continued to meet, under the name ACLA (Alianza Comunitaria Latinoamericana) and had by the end of my study accrued some modest broader political recognition. All of the participants in the November leadership development seminar (and those invited to attend who could not participate) were invited to the Georgia Project open house held in late March 1998 where they met with local school officials and business leaders, and school, business, and political leaders from Atlanta. Many of the Atlanta leaders were Hispanic—including business leaders and representatives from Atlanta's Hispanic Chamber of Commerce and its largest Hispanic-oriented social service agency, La Asociación Latinoamericana—which meant that the March 1998 meeting itself helped advance the networking goal on the leadership group's action agenda. Several of the local Hispanic leaders were additionally invited to a smaller meeting in May 1998 when two professors and a grant writer from the University of Georgia came to see the Georgia Project in action.

The coordination and mobilization of this group of leaders had long-term implications for the future of Dalton. It was a signal accomplishment of the Georgia Project and one that could not be taken away regardless of the fate of the other components. However, though the extension of invitations to local Hispanics to participate in Georgia Project activity represented an improvement over the previous lack of invitations, dependency on being invited did not represent full empowerment and inclusion. More satisfactory modes of inclusion had not been created as I finished my study and their development depended, to a large extent, on the resolution of the ambiguity in the Georgia Project's governance structure, another issue which was not resolved by the end of my study.

## NOT AS RECEPTIVE AS THEY FIRST APPEARED

During the November 1997 research visit, the research director's spouse and her colleague from the University of Massachusetts continued the survey begun in June regarding the availability of adult education in Dalton/Whitfield, its accessibility to local Hispanics, and its consequence. The original Hispanic community needs assessment sent to Georgia Project overseers in Dalton just before the November visit noted a limited supply of separately coordinated adult ESL and other offerings for Hispanics, a fact that was corroborated by leadership seminar participants. The separate coordination of the existing programs made linkages and referrals between programs difficult. As a follow-up to these initial communications, the Universidad de Monterrey research team released a draft report on adult education opportunities in Dalton/Whitfield in March 1998.

The authors (the two from the University of Massachusetts) identified their report as a working document that they hoped would draw comment and correction. By their account, the best chance for the document to have a meaningful local impact was through the engagement of practitioners in a dialogue about the services they provided and the considerations and possibilities raised by the report (i.e., comment and correction). The report was detailed and thorough—reviewing the programs of a range of providers from ESOL at Dalton High School, to ESL provided by Anglo volunteers at a local Baptist Church, to the multiple adult education offerings at the alternative school shared by Dalton and Whitfield County schools. However, the authors were ultimately dependent on the practitioners to enact their recommendations, including their near mantra that bilingual, bicultural individuals needed to be added to virtually every program to assist with recruitment, trouble-shooting, and teaching.

The authors' task was complicated because, with the exception of Dalton College, which had hardly been an active partner, none of the providers of adult ESL, GED, ABE, or other adult education services had been involved in the Georgia Project's planning process at the time the report was released.[9] In other words, however apt and on target the authors' diagnoses and advice, there was nothing directly compelling practitioners to change their ways. The authors could hope that their points seemed valid and viable and/or that by sharing their report with the Georgia Project committee they were mobilizing powerful local Daltonians to understand some of the challenges confronted by local adult education, to insist on their culturally responsive remedy, and to make sure resources were available to do so. They could also hope that, with information summarized and readily available, the denial of the existence of service gaps and coordination problems would be more difficult.

The immediate reaction to the working draft, however, was not friendly, nor was its working draft spirit readily honored. A number of practitioners from several of the described programs complained that it was a misrepresentation. Others simply complained that the report was sloppy and too full of spelling and typographical errors. After an angry meeting with a number of adult literacy providers, the Universidad de Monterrey researchers decided to collect all of the disseminated copies of the document. Whether this was a tactical withdrawal or a full-scale retreat was unclear. It was also unclear whether important criticisms raised in the document—for example, the insufficiency of adult ESL opportunities and the absence of Hispanic or bicultural instructors—would get the consideration they still merited. The report was pulled at a time that the Universidad de Monterrey's role in the partnership seemed to be changing from co-leader to consultant with a simultaneous reduction in its power over the project's future. The Universidad de Monterrey team never subsequently tried to re-release this report. Nor did I ever hear of a constituency in Dalton requesting it. The lesson was stark: Criticizing the workplace education opportunities and by extension criticizing Dalton's major employers was off limits.

## A SOURCE OF COMMUNITY CHANGE?

According to the research director's original description of the Parent and Workplace Involvement component (see Figure 12.1), three of the four projects within the component ultimately were to lead to the creation of programs, organizations, and/or activities. With the partial exception of the Hispanic community leadership initiative, however, the Universidad de Monterrey was not well positioned to implement more than the research phase of the proposed initiatives. In the case of the community needs assessment research was enough because that was the initiative (all of it). For the adult education initiative, the Universidad de Monterrey was dependent on not necessarily obvious partners. Unlike the three Georgia Project components being conducted in conjunction with the school district, for the Parent and Workplace Involvement initiative the district was not always a suitable partner. Adult education, including family literacy, was largely beyond the school district's mandate, jurisdiction, and expertise.

For the parent and school piece, the mechanics of operation and Dalton's possible collaboration were not clear. Though school leaders knew they needed to be responsive to parents, that was a different issue than setting up special infrastructure to ensure that Hispanic parents had representation. The possibility loomed at the end of my study both that the innovative elementary school's relative success in creating an attractive environment for Spanish-speaking parents could be created in other Dalton schools and/or that the education committee recommended by participants in the Hispanic community leadership seminar would not only be created but that it would be recognized and listened to by school and district leaders. There was little definitive proof of such happening, however.

The school district was an unwitting target for the criticism that some of these initiatives generated. The community survey initiative documented many Latino parents' mistrust and frustration at the school system. While, the promised report on Latino parents' attitudes and expectations of the school district was never written, documentation on those issues was prominent in the written summary of the community leadership seminar and informed Monterrey leaders interactions in Dalton. Perhaps the Universidad de Monterrey calculated that it was not in its interest to prepare a more definitive report that would be critical of the school district, given the fragility of its relationship with the district (exacerbated by the emerging dispute between the attorney and the district), the reception that the also critical adult education assessment had received, and the sense that the reports they were generating were not finding many readers at the school district end.

By one reckoning then the success of this component was mixed; some initiatives found traction, others did not. The adult education assessment initiative, which included a critique of several carpet industry-supported workplace literacy programs, bombed badly, generating an angry reaction from several of the employers who had helped initiate the Georgia Project. Also, the Universidad de Monterrey backed away from the original optimistic promises of the proposed parent and school initiative. However, it's worth both recognizing the original baseline and considering how some of the original goals were realized through other means. It is also useful to remember that the Universidad de Monterrey team was operating in a politically charged atmosphere where they were far from the most potent players. They needed to act tactically.

Regarding this last point, the attorney seemed to recognize that there were limits to how much a modest Mexican university would be listened to, irrespective of the accuracy of their diagnoses. In 2000, he had the Georgia Project commission a second needs assessment, this one by a well-respected domestic entity, Washington D.C.'s Center for Applied Linguistics, or CAL. Much of what CAL found reiterated what Monterrey had previously found. Like some Monterrey reports, CAL's report too suggested various strategies and possibilities with the expectation that from this menu of choices Dalton educational leaders could clarify what they wanted. Tellingly, before even a first draft had been shared, Dalton's curriculum coordinator directed the school system leadership to accept the findings as suggestions only, not mandates (see Goode 2002:53–56).

One of the striking unorthodoxies of the Georgia Project was its original premise of a community and school district contracting with a university a thousand miles away and across an international border to find out who lived down the street and what to do about them. As this component directly exemplifies, the Universidad de Monterrey seized this unlikely opportunity to raise an insistent voice on behalf of Dalton's Latino community, which ultimately, per original plan, became a self-sustaining one.

The school district could no longer delude itself with the idea that Latino parents were a broadly satisfied constituency, nor could it readily continue with the practice of engaging only Anglo proxies to illustrate its responsiveness to the newcomers. The Universidad de Monterrey had also put on the table, the idea that the existing adult education infrastructure was lacking, even though they subsequently decided they could not risk their finite political capital pursuing this point. Most importantly, a cohort—ACLA— of Latino leaders had been identified and organized.

After I finished my research study, I kept abreast of events in Dalton by making several joint presentations with the Universidad de Monterrey's research director and by routinely receiving newspaper stories, letters, and other policy documents from the Georgia Project's founding attorney. In 2001, the attorney sent me an op-ed from Dalton's daily paper penned by the chairperson of the Dalton-Whitfield County Chamber of Commerce, Sara Pierce. She described the Georgia Project as a source of favorable notoriety "beyond the community." Then added, "ACLA, a group of Latino business owners, is forging social, political, and business relationships throughout the area. These new entrepreneurs are bridging the gap in language, cultural, and business understanding" (Pierce 2001). Perhaps this reference was an attempt to preempt criticism by appearing inclusive, yet it also seems to be proof of a real change. Newcomers' contributions to the larger community were being celebrated rather than ignored or decried.

# Something Gained
# and Something Lost

After the end of my field study in mid-1998, the Georgia Project was transformed from being a promising, unorthodox grassroots partnership to being a largely stand-alone regional initiative in which both the Dalton school district and the Universidad de Monterrey played smaller parts. More conventional partners, such as the Center for Applied Linguistics and several of Georgia's leading politicians, now were counted among the initiative's supporters. In addition to being an account of the Georgia Project from March 1998 through the first few months of Dalton's first female superintendent (i.e., the first few months of 2001), this chapter notes the plurality of ways the Georgia Project has been defined, setting up consideration in Chapter 14 of how the Georgia Project has been a template upon which various entities have projected their wishes, goals, and fears. It also includes two vignettes.

## THE APEX OF THE THREE-PARTY PARTNERSHIP

On March 27, 1998, with a "coming out" party of sorts that was instigated and organized by the attorney, the Georgia Project reached an apex in Dalton. After that date, the Georgia Project and its founder would receive national accolade and would obtain substantial additional resources, but never again would the Dalton school district prove as willing and proud a partner. For the celebration, almost seventy people were involved in some or all of the two school tours and the luncheon at one of

Dalton's largest carpet company's corporate headquarters. The attorney's direction assured the attendance of a plethora of eminent and consciously diverse guests, while the school district graciously worked around the inconveniences of hosting so many visitors.

All six of the profiled Georgia Project leaders were present; the two leaders from Monterrey arrived in Atlanta at 11 P.M. the night before and in Dalton after 2 A.M. that morning. They were joined by more than sixty others, including representatives from DeKalb County Schools (in metro Atlanta), Atlanta-based Hispanic business leaders, the Mexican Consul General of Atlanta, two representatives from the Georgia Department of Education, an ESOL consultant,[1] Dalton/Whitfield business and school leaders, others from the attorney's law firm, the attorney's daughter, the bilingual priest, a local migrant education coordinator, the visiting instructors, and, most importantly, local African American leaders (that the attorney knew) and local Hispanic leaders that had been identified through the Georgia Project. This was the first time multiple members of either of these last two groups had been systematically included in a Georgia Project event. One African American invitee later explained that she was not quite sure why she had been invited but that she felt it was an honor. She subsequently spoke in glowing terms regarding the Georgia Project.

That morning, after most attendees had convened at the attorney's office, the group formed a loose caravan to the innovative elementary school where they were met out front by the superintendent, the curriculum coordinator, and a school-based administrator. Guests were ushered downstairs to the cafeteria/auditorium. After a greeting from the principal that was mostly intended to call the audience to attention, an African American student stood up on the stage and said "Bienvenido." A Latino student followed with the translation "Welcome." An Anglo student then exclaimed "Soy un estudiante bilingüe." A second Hispanic student followed with "I am a bilingual student." This bilingual, expectation-fighting juxtaposition of language and students' apparent phenotype continued for a few more speakers until, at the lead of one of the visiting instructors from Monterrey, the assembled student group (of fifteen or so) began singing in Spanish and also signing the lyrics (presumably in American Sign Language). When the students, all grade 2 or younger, sang the chorus in English—"No more hunger/No more war/We want peace on this earth"— they continued signing. The attorney watched from the front row.

After the students finished their presentation with another song—their all-English school song—the superintendent stood up and welcomed the visitors. He offered that the Georgia Project was a model not just for North Georgia, but for the whole state, and perhaps the country. He then hailed the attorney as a visionary leader and said, "If you could have only seen [the awe and pride on the attorney's] face when those children were singing."

Speaking next, the attorney deferred the personal accolade and noted the involvement of several others in the project. He then asked the bilingual priest to come forward and introduce the local Hispanic leaders. The priest did so starting with the line, "I'm pleased that this will be the final time I am called on to do this." He clarified that from that moment forward the local Hispanic leaders would not need an introduction by a mediator. They would be known directly and be approachable as such.[2] The attorney then introduced and thanked two visitors from the Georgia Department of Education for coming.[3] After introducing me as someone "who had been with the project from the beginning," he introduced the two Georgia Project leaders from the Universidad de Monterrey. He then acknowledged the former Georgia Department of Education employee who, among other things, had offered the favorable appraisal of the February 1998 report by the second bilingual education coordinator from Monterrey (see Chapter 11). The attorney characterized the ex-state employee as a friend and "a source of information that I'll draw from for as long as I live." Last he introduced a Hispanic business leader who had come up from Atlanta and who spoke briefly.

Thanking the attorney and the superintendent, this leader explained that he had grown up as a migrant worker in the United States and was pleased to see an effort reaching out to students who started in similarly difficult circumstances. Then he introduced the ten Latino leaders who had accompanied him from Atlanta. Though the events of the day were only thirty-minutes old at this point, already we had witnessed a choreographed demonstration by primary school students of one vision of multiculturalism and inclusion, an endorsement of the attorney by the superintendent that played to the broadly appealing theme of the attorney being moved to help the children, the attorney's very subtle editorializing about the Georgia Department of Education's current and previous staffing, and the brief comments of a Latino leader from Atlanta that presumably offered a Latino validation of the Georgia Project's white leaders' intentions to lend a hand to the newcomers.

Before the audience was divided into tour groups, the principal gave an overview of the educational philosophy in her building and the various programs operating there. Careful to say that acquisition of English was a priority, she then described using Spanish as "a means to English" for many students. She also proudly recounted her school's successful efforts to be accessible to parents. Her loudest point was that in her building, "We do not lower standards. . . . We *know* all children can learn." While such a message was clearly welcomed by the audience, it also served, however ephemerally, as the principal's bid to claim a rationale that united the vastly divergent programs and policies that were in play in her building. Her final comments characterized the Georgia Project as "giv[ing] voice to the Hispanic community." The subsequent tours of her school lasted about forty minutes with visits to Spanish classrooms, demonstrations of Direct Instruction, and a stop at a Pre-K class out in one of the school's three portable trailers.

The group then headed over to the high school. The reception there contrasted significantly with the almost stealth-like, accord-signing ceremony of the previous March. This time Dalton Ambassadors—students in formal, school-color, red dresses—greeted each visitor, welcomed them, and guided them into the auditorium. There the formal welcome was led by the Dalton ESOL coordinator. (As had been the case for the accord-signing a year earlier, the principal was again away from the building.) Also offering a vision of inclusive multiculturalism, she started by showing a video of an Anglo student performing with a Mexican student folkloric group. She then spent twenty minutes describing the history of ESOL in Dalton, the dimensions and staffing of the program, and its goal of "as much intensive English as quickly as possible." She discussed the Spanish-for-Spanish-speakers classes, Direct Instruction, and the four tiers into which ESOL students were divided. She then explained how Georgia's required graduation tests were a major obstacle for ESOL students and that free summer remedial classes for those who wanted to retake the tests often conflicted with ESOL students' family or work priorities. What she did not say was anything specifically about the Georgia Project. The gap between the Georgia Project and the ESOL program and perhaps a sense that the Georgia Project was taking attention and accolade away from the ESOL program were subtexts of the presentation. Goode (2002) later identified this ESOL/Georgia Project fracture line as one that ultimately contributed to the derailing of the Georgia Project within Dalton several years later.

When the two visiting instructors from Monterrey gave brief descriptions of their activities at the high school, their remarks seemed off topic even though they were supposed to be the topic. Both visiting instructors described the counseling function they had taken on with Hispanic newcomer students. Referring to her own and her students' culture shock and sense of dislocation, one visiting instructor summarized the empathy she had for such students: "I'm living the same thing."

The Dalton Ambassadors then reappeared, split the audience into tour groups, and took the visitors to see ESOL classes, Direct Instruction, and the media center. On several walls a flier was posted: "Voten por [student name] nuestra voz hispana." As tour groups drifted back from their tours, the high school's front lobby became noisy with visitors introducing themselves to each other and commenting favorably about what they had seen so far. (I heard no negative comments.)

The final meeting place for the day was in the corporate dining room of a major local carpet company. After the bilingual priest offered grace (in English) and the buffet lunches were eaten, there were more presentations. The CEO who was hosting the event, the same CEO who had initially contacted his business partner in Monterrey leading to the partnership with the Universidad de Monterrey, noted how pleased he was by the Georgia Project and its response to "a need, not a problem, a need." Then the research director from Monterrey (who was more comfortable speaking publicly in English than the project director) described the Georgia Project's Hispanic leadership development initiative that, given the guest list, was on display in the room.

The attorney then offered lengthier remarks, returning the superintendent's morning compliments and noting of the Georgia project director from Monterrey, "I think he's fallen in love with the project as much as I have." Of the leadership initiative, he declared that it was "organization of Hispanic leadership on its own terms." Of the visiting instructor program, he claimed, "Nothing that Monterrey has done has exceeded the quality of the visiting instructors." (The visiting instructors were scattered throughout the room; at the beginning of the lunch the superintendent's executive secretary had reminded them not to all sit together.) The attorney then claimed that the litany of public and private support the Georgia Project had garnered was "not a product of begging and pleading." He acknowledged that one particularly active member of the oversight committee was developing a video, partially about the Georgia Project, entitled, "Dalton: A City Unafraid to Change."[4]

His most intriguing comment followed up on the well-developed and widely known rendition of how the Georgia Project was started because of his daughter's complaint. After pointing out his daughter in the audience, the attorney said that the morning tour of the innovative elementary school had been her first return visit to the building in two years. He said she was amazed, impressed, and pleased at the major changes that had allegedly taken place there because of the Georgia Project. According to the story line: There had been a problem; then the Georgia Project was created; now the problem was remedied. The accuracy of the rendition did not matter; its public accessibility did (as did its repetition of the implied criticism that the old order, the one that had prevailed two years before, was inadequate).

Afterwards, the assembled visitors were slow to leave. As at the high school, conversation groups formed and split and formed. Some of the conversations were in Spanish; more were in English. Many business cards exchanged hands. Promises of future contact were made. It seemed like a new era was dawning, the era of the Georgia Project as a model. Indeed a new era was dawning—that of the Georgia Project being relevant beyond Dalton—but the existing era of the Georgia Project as an unorthodox assemblage of local educators, transnationally connected executives, Mexican scholars, and wily politicians was starting to fracture, with the consensus to "do something" no longer a sufficient source of unity. Differences regarding what to do and why and, as importantly, under whose governance and by what authority had all emerged. Still, the claim that Dalton had become more responsive to its newcomers seemed plausible.

## Vignette 4: No Going Back

In June 1998, there was a bilingual dedication of two new Astro-Turf soccer fields. Though ostensibly not part of the Georgia Project, it drew the three nonschool district leaders described in Chapters 5 and 6 (i.e., the attorney and the two directors from the Universidad de Monterrey) as well as several of the members of the Georgia Project oversight committee. Consistent with the long-standing pattern of local businesses supporting local recreation (Brown 1976),[5] a pattern that matched the business community's involvement in the Georgia Project, all of the land and much of the materials and labor for the new fields had been donated by private interests.

The public speeches and private comments that were made at the dedication were telling and sometimes poignant. An Anglo carpet executive who was centrally involved in both the fields' construction and in the Georgia Project responded to his impatient son's query about when they could leave by saying, "Not yet, it's important that I be here." Though perhaps romanticizing the moment, I felt that I was seeing what was possible in an inclusive multicultural Dalton: a father showing communitarian spirit trying to accommodate the interests of newcomers (helping build a soccer field) and in the process teaching his son that actions like this mattered.

## FOR WHAT PURPOSE(S)?

In 1997 and 1998, as the Georgia Project was converted from an idea into a well-funded, multifaceted initiative, its future seemed bright, but the comprehensiveness of its proposed action plan hid the fact that project initiators, project implementers, and various portions of the general public all had different specific ideas regarding the particularities of the challenges Dalton faced because of its demographic change. They similarly differed in their visions for how those challenges should be resolved. Was professional development the main challenge for the Georgia Project or other Dalton school initiatives? Was the biggest need an emergency temporary teacher exchange that could bring bilingual, bicultural teachers from the Universidad de Monterrey to Dalton? Was the biggest need a research need—a need for clearer understanding of the dynamics of the newcomer community and of the newcomers' backgrounds, aspirations, circumstances, and self-identified problems? If a clear depiction of such dynamics were generated, what would the educators and other members of Dalton subsequently be expected to do? All of these questions were on the table in the spring of 1998 as my field research ended; that they would lead to a schism even as the project won broader accolade only became clear later.

Cohen (2000:84) wrote "Programs that advocate changes in the modes of socialization and education must be congruent with the cultural realities for which individuals are being prepared." With Dalton as a site of fractious ontological variation—that is, fundamental differences in viewpoint related to different identifications and affiliations—the cultural realities that the Georgia Project needed to prepare its various target populations for were contested. Thus how to seek congruency was also unclear.

Despite the skeletal outline provided by the original accord signed by the Georgia Project partners in March 1997, what the Georgia Project was supposed to be was never fully clear. To some extent this was a product of competing interpretations and agendas, but not fully; there was also a kind of "big tent" inclusive political logic to this vagueness. Perhaps on the part of the Monterrey scholars and the attorney there was an incipient sensibility that in a community dominated by the pro-immigration script and, to a lesser extent, its echo the anti-immigration script (Suárez-Orozco 1998), the pluralist or cultural-relativist aspects of portions of the Georgia Project did not need emphasis. Highlighting them would jeopardize them.

As Hatch (1998) would predict, what was highlighted or prioritized varied from one Georgia Project collaborator to another, and each component of its four-component architecture was not given equal emphasis when the partnership was shown to inquirers. From its very beginning it was a challenge to define the Georgia Project's goals at a level more detailed than the variously interpretable generality of: helping Dalton and its school district negotiate their sudden, substantial, continuing influx of Hispanic newcomers. Help how?

The ambiguity of the Georgia Project helped it avoid concerted criticism. Criticism at the microlevel (e.g., anger at a visiting Monterrey instructor's printed claim that she and her colleagues were more approachable to Hispanic students because of a cultural affinity) did not quickly convert into a systematic challenge of the Georgia Project. But the ambiguity of the Georgia Project's goals and plans of action left a number of its contradictions unacknowledged and unaddressed. Just as there were no targets to take more than crude aim at, there were no obvious, articulated benchmarks by which to mark project success. (Per the initial request-for-proposal, the Title VII grant proposal I assembled did promise that the grant oversight committee would develop an evaluation plan during the grant's first two years, at least for the Title VII-supported portions of the project. But that oversight committee was never convened.)

Figures 13.1 and 13.2 illustrate the multiple, partially overlapping ways the Georgia Project was characterized by different parties at different times. Figure 13.1 includes quotes from the Georgia Project leaders identified in the field study, plus one from the two Monterrey-affiliated University of Massachusetts doctoral students who wrote the assessment of local adult education opportunities for newcomers that was so poorly received (see Chapter 12). Figure 13.2 includes only quotations from the print media, mostly from the local paper, *The Daily Citizen-News*. Those show the multiple ways the Georgia Project was characterized to and by the broader Dalton/Whitfield English-reading public.

As a project intended to counter the multiple challenges raised by the new coexistence of Hispanic newcomers and established Daltonians, the Georgia Project was helpfully multifaceted and able to derive a synergy

FIGURE 13.1  Varying Definitions of the Georgia Project from Its Principal
Architects

- The purpose of the Georgia Project is to cause the non-English speaking
  students to become English speaking much sooner and to insure [sic] that
  the quality of instruction of English speaking classmates remains high.
  —from a December 1996 letter by the Georgia Project's founding attorney
  to an INS officer as part of an (unsuccessful) request to obtain
  visas for a pilot group of visiting instructors

- This is the heart of the Georgia Project: Our purpose and goal is to
  expand the educational horizon of all children in the local school system.
  —from a letter by the Georgia Project's founding attorney written in
  early 1997 to a different INS officer in hopes of expediting the ultimately
  unsuccessful visa approval process for a Spring 1997 pilot group of visiting
  instructors from Monterrey

- Much research, study, and observation has resulted in the determination
  that bilingual education is the model of choice for increased academic
  achievement for both bilingual and monolingual students. It is the route
  to develop globally competitive students. It is the "Georgia Project"—
  fueled by the support of community leaders [sic] it is the vision of an
  existing school system in the northwest corner of Georgia determined to
  be successful on behalf of all students!
  —from the *Title VII—Systemwide Bilingual Education* proposal abstract
  written by the curriculum coordinator in April 1997

- The Georgia Project is a research and community development project started
  by researchers of [the] Universidad de Monterrey that seeks 1. to understand
  the incorporation and experiences of inter-ethnic interaction of Mexican
  immigrants in Northwest Georgia; 2. to contribute with applied knowledge
  and programs to the development of Mexican communities in their newest
  areas of resettlement and immigration; and 3. to device [sic] community
  development methodologies to promote positive inter-ethnic interaction.
  —from an October 1997 letter of inquiry to the Ford Foundation by a Georgia
  Project leader at the Universidad de Monterrey

- One of the central goals of the Georgia Project has been to initiate
  dialogue and discussion around the educational strengths, needs and
  concerns of the Hispanic community with Dalton industries, the Dalton
  school system and the community in general.
  —from the introduction to *Adult, Community, and Workplace Education:*
  *A Working Document*, a report prepared by researchers affiliated
  with the University of Massachusetts and the Universidad de Monterrey
  [Released March 1998]

- In the public today, we sometimes get a lot of beating up of public schools, that
  schools aren't doing a good job. But I don't think you could be in the audience
  you're in this morning and not get the feeling that public schools are the future
  of our nation. . . . The Georgia Project is, and will continue to be I think, one
  of the most significant initiatives not only in North Georgia, but in the state
  and perhaps the nation through the visionary leadership of [the attorney].
  —from the superintendent's welcoming of 60+ people from several parts of
  Georgia to a March 1998 tour/"coming out" for the Georgia Project

**FIGURE 13.2** Varying Public Definitions of the Georgia Project
(in Chronological Order)

- Not only will [the Georgia Project] boost the school system's curriculum, the program will help break into the typically reserved Mexican community here.
  —from a December 1996 article in *The [Dalton] Daily Citizen-News* describing the Georgia Project just after the first visit by DPS officials and the attorney to Monterrey (Hamilton 1996c)

- The Georgia Project is more a business community initiative than a school-based effort, though leaders are working hand in hand with educators.
  —from a January 1997 article announcing the arrival of researchers from the Universidad de Monterrey for a first visit to Dalton (Hamilton 1997a)

- The Georgia Project is designed to help the growing number of Hispanic students in Whitfield County learn to speak English.
  —from a July 1997 article in *The [Dalton] Daily Citizen-News* announcing the return of the 24 Dalton and Whitfield County educators who attended the inaugural Summer Institute at the Universidad de Monterrey (C. Quinn 1997)

- . . . the Georgia Project, a combined effort of local businesses, industries, and schools seeking ways to merge the Mexican and American cultures.
  —from an article in the *Chattanooga Times* describing the Georgia Project and focusing on its impact at the East Side elementary school that had most welcomed it (Denton 1997)

- The Georgia Project is in an interesting phase, one we hope pays the kind of dividends organizers of the bilingual teaching program envisioned.
  —from an editorial about the Georgia Project in *The [Dalton] Daily Citizen-News*, December 1997 (*Daily Citizen-News* 1997d)

- **Issue:** The bilingual education program the Georgia Project is now in full swing in Dalton schools. **Our Opinion:** Its success in keeping Spanish-speaking students up to speed is critical for the future of the community.
  —from a *Daily Citizen-News* side-bar next to a December 1997 editorial about the Georgia Project (*Daily Citizen-News* 1997d, bold print in original)

- Less than two years after its creation, the Georgia Project may become a model bilingual education program for the state and possibly the nation.
  —from a front-page story in *The [Dalton] Daily Citizen-News*, March 1998 (Surpuriya 1998a)

- Mohawk also is a supporter of the Georgia Project, a cultural exchange program that sends teachers from Dalton to Mexico and from Mexico to Dalton to learn the language and culture.
  —from a lengthy May 1998 profile of Dalton that was part of a 3-part "1998 Southern Economic Survey" in the *Atlanta Journal–Constitution*. The series focused on the impact of Latino immigration into the South (Poole 1998)

- A unique bilingual education program might earn Dalton Public Schools an Ivy League award and a $100,000 check.
  —from *The [Dalton] Daily Citizen-News* front-page story announcing that the Georgia Project had been selected as a semifinalist in the Innovations in American Government award competition, May 12, 1998 (Surpuriya 1998d)

from the varying orientations of its promoters. However, there is a fine line between functioning in a complementary fashion and operating for disparate or uncoordinated purposes (Hatch 1998). However sincere and diagnostically accurate, the University of Massachusetts doctoral students' call for "dialogue and discussion" echoed the terminology of liberal university training and had "Freirian" and "Sengian" antecedents (see Freire [1970] and Senge [1990]). It was alien to the modus operandi of the attorney with his informally organized, "old boys' network" oversight committee (Hunter 1963) and, even more so, to the curriculum coordinator who had "read the research, looked at the facts, and made the decision." The University of Massachusetts doctoral students' assumptions regarding appropriate process were not matched in the assumptions of the attorney or the curriculum coordinator, nor were the attorney's and the curriculum coordinator's assumptions matched with each other.

The Georgia Project's initial multiple partner structure was thus simultaneously one of the initiative's key strengths and greatest weaknesses. As Hatch (1998) would predict, the different espoused theories of action employed by the different partners meant that they sometimes talked past each other and, at the level of theories in use, acted in contradictory fashions. Yet this same arrangement meant the Georgia Project incorporated two of the facets Sarason identified as essential to viable school reform. He wrote, "On the level of action you should always be dealing with more than one group" (1990:33) and "If I am right in saying that no major educational problem is only a 'within system' problem, then attacking the problem must never be conceived of as only a school problem" (1990:36). Redress of the different espoused theories of action problem required explicitly tending to those differences, tending that happened, at best, only intermittently and semi-intentionally during my study period.

That said, the overlap, complementarity, and discrepancies in the espoused theories included in Figure 13.1 did not reveal the full difference between and within the leaders' theories in use (Argyris and Schön 1975). Conflicts regarding who should do what and in consultation with whom emerged in parallel with the different partners' growing realizations that they differed in how they calculated the *for whats* and *for whoms* of the Georgia Project. The attorney and curriculum coordinator were both confident (or at least decisive) in their courses of action, but not in agreement as to how to proceed, as the routine overlooking of the curriculum coordinator's input and then her fading affection for bilingual education both illustrated. Though, like her colleagues, the coordinator was interested in the ideas generated by the team from Monterrey, she and other district personnel felt less obligation to heed their advice than did the attorney.

School district personnel's theories of action differed from the attorney's who felt it was his prerogative to comment on and intervene in the activities of the schools. Initial tolerance of his activity by district personnel did not indi-cate agreement with this presumption, but rather, at least sometimes, indicated deference to his social status and the presumed hazards of crossing him and his allies. Indeed, the district only ultimately crossed the attorney, well after 1998, after (1) a number of his allies had sold their carpet businesses and left the area, (2) the attorney had challenged the appropriateness of actions by the school board, (3) the district had hired a superintendent whose management style did not match the "old boys' network" style of either her predecessor or the attorney, and (4) the attorney had obtained independent federal funding for the Georgia Project (and thus was not beholden to a relationship with the district for the project's continued existence).

If the Georgia Project could be characterized differently by its own lead-ers, it is not hard to see how it could be understood differently and even contradictorily by the broader public. The brief comparative listing of print media representations of the Georgia Project in Figure 13.2 illustrates some of that public confusion and likely also contributed to it.

Without the Georgia Project leaders' articulated intentions fully recon-ciled and coherent (Figure 13.1), it is not surprising that the public descrip-tions of the Georgia Project varied (Figure 13.2) and that troubling public sphere characterizations like "typically reserved Mexican community" were not publicly challenged. Intriguingly, characterizations of the Georgia Project as a bilingual education were common even though that element of the original action plan was never enacted.

As a consequence of the simplifications and contradictions regarding the Georgia Project's intentions and plans, the broader public understandings of the project's purposes, including the understandings of some enactors (e.g., teachers), were vague. This limited and simplified local public sup-port of the Georgia Project. Potential supporters were not sure what to support and when they did endorse the Georgia Project they did so often in a facile way that promised little more than support for teaching English to Spanish-speaking students (using Mexican instructors if necessary). Their support did not include problematizing the "pro-immigration" and "anti-immigration scripts" (Suárez-Orozco 1998) nor diagnosing those scripts' interdependency and it did not include "penetration" (Willis 1977) into the play of hegemonic social reproduction forces that maintained Dalton's stratification. While all that would have been a tall order, to be sure, one point here is that characterizations of the Georgia Project in the Dalton public sphere were limited in their transformative prospect. Sarason (1990) emphasized that alteration of power relations was an essential component of viable school reform. In the face of facile public understanding of the project, most Dalton educators and the larger com-munity could offer little deep and stable support for the project's address-ing of community power differentials.[6]

## MULTIPLE DEFINITIONS ENABLE NEW LINKAGES
## BUT FRUSTRATE OLD PARTNERSHIP

As noted in earlier chapters, by the summer of 1998 several of the initial Georgia Project initiatives were on shaky footing and personal relationships between erstwhile partners were fraying. The district had resolved against adopting the bilingual curriculum component, participation in the Summer Institute was low enough that that component seemed in jeopardy, and the parent and workplace involvement piece had poked a hornets' nest. As a modest example of faltering communication, in September 1998 I received an invitation to a United Way forum scheduled to be held in Dalton in early October 1998 that included the Georgia Project as one of the programs that would be discussed. When I asked the superintendent's executive secretary (who was most involved with the district's Georgia Project business) what the event was about, she said she did not know. The only thing she had heard about it was a question from the superintendent asking whether the district was supposed to be part of the event. Given that she had heard nothing, she speculated that it must be a Georgia Project event that had been negotiated by or in contact with the attorney's office.

During the course of the 1998–1999 school year, relations between the attorney and district administration worsened as the attorney became indignant that Title VII funds appropriated for the Georgia Project were being used by the district for programs external to the project. In turn, district personnel were increasingly resenting both the ongoing external scrutiny of their affairs and the negative publicity that much of it seemed to generate. This came to a head when a dispute about the funding of Direct Instruction led the attorney to request an outside audit of how the district had supported Direct Instruction and how it had accounted for all the funding it had received ostensibly for the Georgia Project. The audit request was covered by local media, generating negative publicity for the district even when no illegal expenditures were uncovered. The district had legally expended monies in ways that the attorney (and I as writer of the Title VII grant proposal) disagreed with, but bringing that truism to light did little to relieve any acrimony.

According to Goode (2002), the district's anger at the attorney was linked to their effort to reduce the number of visiting instructors to six, a proposition the superintendent advanced at a June 1999 school board meeting, thinking he had the support of the board. However, when the proposal was made, the board rejected it, agreeing on a sum of eleven visiting instructors, and simultaneously undercutting the superintendent. For the board to publicly disagree with the superintendent was an exceedingly rare event in Dalton and began the chain of events that less than a year later led to his encouraged retirement. The expense and other complications related to Direct Instruction and the steady decline in test scores were also reasons that led to pressure for his departure. Goode also notes that prior to the

Georgia Project the district had never been subject to sustained public scrutiny or criticism; no doubt this was also a source of pique.

In 1998–1999 as acrimony grew in Dalton, the Georgia Project began sending visiting instructors to serve in Whitfield County schools, expanding to two the ways the county system was involved in the project (the Summer Institute being the other). The attorney also made initial contacts with the Center for Applied Linguistics (CAL) that year. That began a relationship that led to a fully Georgia Project-funded needs assessment that the school district tolerated and to subsequent CAL-organized professional development activities, also offered under Georgia Project auspices. Dalton educators participated in both these endeavors but partnered in neither. Nor did the Universidad de Monterrey partner in these new activities. In essence, the Georgia Project began to function as its own entity with important relationships with various partners, but no indispensable ones. It had also found a conventional expert source of support, CAL, in addition to its unorthodox one, the Universidad de Monterrey. This mattered as the Georgia Project sought financial support from further afield.

As a spectacular example of such funding, in December 2000 the Georgia Project announced that through the bipartisan efforts of Georgia's two U.S. senators—Senators Cleland and Coverdell—it was to receive a special $650,000 appropriation. Unlike the 1997 Title VII grant, and unlike the City Council's 1997 appropriation, this time the funding was directed exclusively to the Georgia Project without the school district playing any role as either a recipient or financial intermediary. However, the relatively new Georgia Project Teacher Advisory Committee, which had been organized after 1998 and included several Dalton teachers, did play a central role in determining how to allocate this support. As Goode explains, "Virtually every suggestion made by the Teacher Advisory Committee was approved by the Georgia Project's Executive Committee" (2002:133). At least some teachers who were working with Dalton's newcomers had a substantially powerful role they had not had in the original three-party governance of the Georgia Project. That said, with the district bitter and skeptical of the Georgia Project, those Dalton teachers who participated on the Teachers Advisory Committee were in a politically awkward position.

The accepted Teacher Advisory Committee recommendations for expenditures included CAL-provided professional development, scholarships to support teachers' attendance at national conferences on second language learning, the special Cleland/Coverdell scholarships described next, and a special Georgia Project conference that would convene educational, governmental, business, and faith-based organizations who were all negotiating the region's new demography. Subsequently, Spanish classes for Dalton and Whitfield County teachers were also organized by the Georgia Project.

The new Cleland-Coverdell Scholarships were awarded to bilingual graduates of local high schools who sought to become educators. Scholarship recipients were expected, once their studies were completed, to return to teach in the area. In short, the new scholarships were proposed as a longer-term solution to the original problem diagnosis upon which the Georgia Project had been founded, namely that the newcomers merited instruction from bilingual, empathetic educators who could gain their trust and engagement.

The first scholarships were awarded in August 2001 with both Dalton's daily newspaper and several of the Spanish-language weeklies giving the award's ceremony prominent play. Six students who were bilingual (three from Dalton High, one from Southeast High in Whitfield, and two from Murray County High), accepted the scholarships, agreeing to return as teachers to the systems from which they graduated (Mahony 2001). One of the winners was quoted in the local paper to the effect, "When they told me I had been chosen for a scholarship I was really thrilled. I know it's hard to learn another language because I had to start from the very bottom. . . . We [recipients] know what it feels like to be there and to feel what it's like to be alone" (Starks-Winn 2001).

As had increasingly become a signature of the Georgia Project, in addition to the local renderings of the event (e.g., reports of the award ceremony) there were articulated tie-ins to a broader public sphere. As the back of the scholarship award ceremony program reproduced in Figure 13.3 indicates, the Georgia Project had become a template for politicians to illustrate their responsiveness to Dalton and its Latino newcomers. With politicians committed to trying to serve the public good and attuned to their own needs for reelection, the Georgia Project was becoming a vehicle through which to demonstrate responsiveness to and support of a new fast-growing portion of the electorate.

The politicians' assumptions, assumptions that my very writing of this book indicate I share, was that the Georgia Project mattered locally *and* elsewhere. Its larger significance is discussed in the next chapter; however, this chapter closes with a moving vignette, a speech by a Dalton student, that offers an ultimately optimistic assertion that a transformed Dalton might be all right.

In November 2001, in an event that formally had nothing to do with the Georgia Project—the opening of Dalton's new middle school—an eighth grade student offered an evocative welcome that seems worth repeating here both as a hopeful indicator of how Dalton is responding to its demographic change and as an embodiment of the spirit that the Georgia Project has tried to foster. Her comments, included in Goode (2002:139) follow as Vignette 5.

**FIGURE 13.3  The Senators' Public Support: Back Cover of Program for Inaugural Awarding of First Six Cleland/Coverdell Scholarships, Aug. 20, 2001**

Multicultural education is one of the most pressing matters facing our state today. With a 300% increase in Hispanic population over the past decade, Georgia needs leaders, both public and private, who will step up to the critical challenge of educating all young Georgians. With this in mind, we express our appreciation to Senator Max Cleland and the late Senator Paul Coverdell, who made a joint effort to promote the goals of The Georgia Project and who took major steps in addressing the realities of Latino immigration in Georgia. The fruits of their labor culminated in much of what you will see here tonight.

"You all are on the right track and have devised a marvelous response here. You have a lot of positives here. You've got our support. We're available to you for grant writing."
—Sen. Cleland, *The Daily Citizen-News*, September 3, 1999

"The Georgia Project is creating laboratories of innovation in Dalton's classrooms, and I am proud to help in any way I can."
—Sen. Coverdell, *The Daily Citizen-News*, February 5, 2000

"The program as it has existed in Dalton has promoted positive community relations and an appreciation for ethnic and cultural differences."
—Sen. Cleland, *The Daily Citizen-News*, April 30, 2000

"Our nation's communities are being transformed by the diverse culture of their citizens. By working together in a bipartisan manner to pass this important legislation, which will provide communities with the resources they need to reach out to the population, Sen. Cleland and I hope to better serve our children—the best guarantee we have of ensuring America's strength well into the 21st century and beyond."
—Sen. Coverdell, *The Daily Citizen-News*, April 30, 2000

## Vignette 5: This Is Our Home

When you look at me or any of my 1,172 fellow students, you look at the face of Dalton Middle School. We are black and white and every shade of brown in between. There are 32 different countries represented by students of our school. We are Baptist and Catholic and Presbyterian, Episcopalian and Jewish, Methodist and Muslim. We are wealthy and we are welfare and everything in between. We come to school from every kind of home you can imagine: two parent homes, single parent homes, no parent homes, foster homes. We are Challenge students and challenging students and everything in between. We are gifted academically and athletically, artistically and musically. We are every kind of kid you can imagine and by going to school together everyday, we are learning to get along with each other which will prepare us well for the real world where we know that not everyone looks the same as we do. We are the face of public school, we are the face of Dalton Georgia. We are the face of the future, but right now we are Cougars and this is our home. Welcome.

In March 2002, a team of Georgia Project representatives, including the attorney, the executive director, two Latino members of the now more formalized advisory committee, an administrator from the Whitfield County school system, and even an administrator from the no-longer-very-involved Dalton system all went to Chapel Hill, North Carolina, to lead a seminar on school and community responsiveness to Latino newcomers. Three hundred teachers and interested others assembled for the event. The title was "From Nothing to Something."

# Part Four

# Ephemeral Opportunity
# or Inclusive New Order

# The Politics of Latino Education Policy: Implications of the Georgia Project

In this last chapter, as I attempt to reconcile many of the themes broached previously, it is important first and foremost to remember how rapidly Dalton changed in the fifteen years prior to this writing (i.e., since 1987). The school district's Hispanic enrollment alone in 2001–2002 of 2,987 was more than three-quarters as large as the entire district population in 1989–1990 when the enrollment totaled 3,876, including just 151 Hispanics. Though the composition of Dalton's teaching force also changed during this time, it did so achingly slowly. Until the Georgia Project, mostly the decade of the 1990s was a time when talented, successful, veteran instructors slowly became less successful as the demographics of their enrollments and the pertinence of their previously developed skills both changed.

The same demographic changes impacting the schools were consequential in the larger public sphere, making Dalton the "border city," or transnational city, that the attorney alluded to in his January 1997 toast. Sometimes this change spawned the rage of the anti-immigration script (Suárez-Orozco 1998), as illustrated by protests, hostile letters to the newspaper, and the threatening words of a landlord noted back in Vignette 2 (see Chapter 1). More commonly, Dalton's demographic transformation yielded articulations of disquiet and the pro-immigration script (Suárez-Orozco 1998). In all cases, previous assumptions about community, including who was part of it, what mores it embraced, and even what languages were to be used in it, seemed no longer to fit well.

Yet against this backdrop some long-standing local habits proved relevant to the question of how to respond. Sensibilities that the schools should remain preeminent, that business had a role in ameliorating community challenges, and that unorthodoxy and entrepreneurism were signs of pluck and promise each were exploitable as leaders and others considered how to respond to the newcomers.

As a field of inquiry, ethnography of educational policy emphasizes that by highlighting the place and role of values, beliefs, and identities in the policy process, one obtains the analytic tools to broadly understand sociocultural activity (Levinson and Sutton 2001). In this case the goal is to understand the response of a few to demographic change that in turn led to the mobilization of a binational partnership and that partnership's later transition into a multiply tied but autonomous community organization.

Before we get to a final analysis of these responsive few, we must remember that the responsive few were, in one sense, not just a responsive few. Rather, the six Georgia Project leaders focused on in previous pages were embedded in "webs of significance" (Geertz 1973:5) that were socially created. Those leaders had access to various tropes, or cultural frameworks of interpretation, that had been created and perpetuated sometimes by dozens, sometimes by millions.[1] The local ethos of corporate paternalism was an example of the former scale and the pro-immigration script an example of the latter. In other words, when any of the six leaders acted, they brought to bear opinions, understandings, and recommendations acquired from others.

Though a complicated act that required the complicity of others for dissemination, the six leaders could create new tropes that had new morals even as they referenced existing ones. The attorney's oft-repeated tale of visiting his daughter's school and witnessing miscommunication and missed opportunity was an example of this. It referenced an existing sensibility—that teachers should not be endlessly frustrated and that they needed to be able to communicate with their students—and added a new understanding: that remedying a communication mismatch was necessary. The six leaders could also transfer tropes from elsewhere into Dalton, not being originators of particular ideas per se, but clearly being the originators of certain ideas' circulation in Dalton. Ideas from the innovative elementary school and its dissertation-writing principal fit into this category, as did many of the suggestions from the scholars in Monterrey. Unlike these two examples, however, acquisition and embrace of tropes was not always conscious and witting; indeed it usually was not (Borofsky 1994).

Tropes are both local and nonlocal. They are the cultural tools—the metaphors, taxonomies, and frameworks for seeing and acting—that are socially created and then re-created every time they are employed.[2] As tools, they are used by individuals as those individuals negotiate their world, do their jobs, and identify and try to solve problems. Thus tropes link the actions of individuals, like the six profiled in Chapters 5 and 6, with the larger sway of events. This link matters because it suggests why the actions and evolving understandings of these six matter not just for the current and future generations of Daltonians directly impacted by the Georgia Project, but also for those studying and/or entwined in the dynamics of community change and newcomer education. As cultural beings (like all the rest of us), those in Dalton and Monterrey who helped found and steer the Georgia Project did so according to sometimes explicit, sometimes deeply internalized understandings of *what should be*. Among the tropes in play were ones regarding how and by whom educational decisions should be made, ones regarding what linguistic and cultural skills were needed to become educated, and ones regarding what the community encompassed and what it should propose to be.

## WINDOWS OF POLICYMAKING OPPORTUNITY

Writing a new epilogue in 1996 to her 1983 study *Ways With Words* (Heath 1996), Shirley Brice Heath recognized that there had been a window of policymaking opportunity that had given teachers she worked with atypical and ephemeral control over how they organized their school practices. The actions these teachers took were all inexorably tied to the time period that Heath documented, the late 1970s. Heath noted that the recent desegregation of the Carolina district she worked with had put many issues in flux. District administrators who had climbed career ladders under the previous operating assumptions of segregation had little idea about what pedagogy and classroom management needed to look like in the face of sudden demographic transformation of their district's classrooms. At that historic moment, those who had compelling ideas regarding how to proceed were encouraged to pursue them. There was a window of policymaking opportunity. Later on, those in administrative positions stopped being so permissive, reasserting in the early 1980s their prerogative to control educational decision making. The window closed.

Dalton in the mid-1990s was not desegregating, but in many ways its changes paralleled those that Heath had described. When the attorney visited the not-yet-so-innovative elementary school in 1995–1996 and heard the teachers' poignant laments about communication challenges, the retiring superintendent conceded that he and his colleagues had no good idea regarding how to respond and welcomed efforts to develop any. If anything, the change in superintendents in the summer of 1996 added to the school district's willingness to hear and enact exogenously created ideas for response to the newcomers. With an instinct honed in Bulloch County to please the electorate and those local leaders who helped shape the electorate's sensibilities, the new superintendent's first impulse was to respond favorably to the nascent ideas of the attorney and local corporate leaders. Thus when an unlikely chain of personal connections brought a parapro's complaint to the attention of Mexican sociologists, the Dalton schools were willing to partner in the response. There was a window of policymaking opportunity.

Having little background in immigrant education, ESOL, bilingual education, and so forth, the superintendent and other district administrators had little understanding of what an orthodox response to newcomers might look like, so they also had little appreciation of how unorthodox partnering with a Mexican university was (Lorey, personal communication). They did, however, trust their eyes and ears and were sufficiently impressed by their encounters with the Mexican university leaders in December 1996 and January 1997 to forge forward with that relationship when closer sources of support seemed unresponsive. They also trusted the principal at the innovative elementary school whose research and practice both seemed to indicate that the proposals being generated by the Monterrey scholars and the attorney were not so far-fetched.

The Georgia Project became binational because Georgia institutions including state government and universities failed to respond quickly to Dalton leaders' impatient requests for assistance, thus compelling Dalton to look for help from farther afield. That Dalton could look further away hints at a changing relationship between U.S. school districts and universities. Though initially only vaguely aware of the region and unaware of Dalton itself, as the name they created—the Georgia Project—indicates, the Monterrey scholars recognized very early on that the nebulous prospect of a partnership was something they should respond to favorably and quickly. A plethora of very different rationales supported this course of action, ranging from indicating respect for one of the Universidad's founding families, to being excited at finding a case so compelling to their scholarly interest in transnational migration, to perhaps even a sense of poetic justice that a U.S. entity recognized that it needed to go to Mexico to find help. Though scholars not development officers, the scholars were also aware that Dalton could become an exemplar of the ways that Mexican universities might bring to other U.S. school districts, a point expounded upon by Zúñiga et al. (2001).

In her Carolinas research site, Heath (1996) and the teachers she worked with initially met with great success as they collected knowledge from historically underserved communities (in that case working-class white and African American communities) and developed novel inclusive pedagogical strategies. Though she does not dwell on this point, it seems possible that at her research site these initiatives were welcomed for the political cover they provided in the face of ephemeral pressure to prove that the schools were responsive to all sectors of the newly desegregated enrollment. (That such pressures at least temporarily existed are illustrated by the fact that desegregation actually was enacted, despite more than twenty previous years of not honoring *Brown vs. Board of Education* requirements.)

Similarly, in Dalton there was an ephemeral coalition that included all six profiled founders (and several other key people) who commonly agreed something needed to be done. Teachers were voicing frustration and enrollment data was showing sharp demographic change. At this early stage, the attorney and others frequently retold the story of the attorney's original school visit and thus the actual experience that precipitated his action was converted into a trope that others could access to rationalize their actions. As Levinson and Sutton (2001) wrote, policies are both problem statements and strategies of action intended to respond to the purported problem. As the Georgia Project was being launched in 1997, the attorney's story was sufficiently broadly embraced that it served as the espoused problem statement justifying the four-component mobilization. That it did not provide an equal rationale for each of the components, that it was not equally adhered to by different project leaders, and that those same leaders also believed in other and differing problem diagnoses all had not yet become obvious or consequential, but at least three hints of it were visible in the winter and spring of 1997.

First, the Universidad de Monterrey scholars were asked by the Dalton community leaders group to reiterate the purpose and procedure for the Parent and Workplace Involvement component. From what they had learned from the attorney's description and the January visit by four leaders from Mexico, the match between the attorney's problem diagnosis and that component's proposed action plan was not obvious. The Monterrey scholars were envisioning the initiation of a local Latino political organization, responding to a gap or problem they had identified in Dalton, but not one that was straightforwardly reconcilable with the attorney's teacher/student miscommunication story.

Second, the emptiness of the Dalton High School auditorium at the Georgia Project's original signing ceremony suggested that if that building's administration even knew of the attorney's story, they did not find it sufficiently compelling to direct their attention or that of their students and faculty to the ceremony. Celebrating the creation of an unprecedented, unorthodox, binational entity that was supposed to help Dalton schools address the challenges of their changing enrollment was less important than the ordinary practice of school.

Third, intertwined with the Georgia Project's first large success to raise funds, in April 1997 when the City Council designated $750,000 to the Georgia Project, the local newspaper report of the funding offered an alternative problem diagnosis ostensibly rationalizing the Georgia Project. It asserted that the Latino newcomers needed to learn English and that the Georgia Project proposed to accomplish this task (*The Daily Citizen-News* 1997c). This problem diagnosis was much simpler (and overtly assimilationist) than the attorney's miscommunication story. It also differed from the newspaper's own January 1997 story (Hamilton 1997b), published concurrent with the

Monterrey scholars' first visit to Dalton, that described a Latina student who lit up and became engaged in response to the Spanish-language inquiries of one of the Mexican visitors. Allegedly, that girl's teacher had previously speculated that the student might have a learning disability. If one were to align the attorney's story, the January story, and the April editorial on a continuum, the April editorial would be at the colonialist or assimilationist end (assuming that the newcomers came with needs rather than assets) and the January story on the other pluralist or additive end (assuming the newcomers had untapped but relevant skills). Perhaps one reason the attorney's story resonated so much is that it sat beguilingly in the middle of the continuum.

From the summer of 1997 through the March 1998 celebration described in Chapter 13, the unlikely consensus among the six profiled leaders seemed to be holding and the Georgia Project was broadly visible and celebrated. The first Summer Institute participants had found their experience exhilarating and had come home to enthused attention from the local media. The visiting instructors had finally obtained visas and come to Dalton to begin serving in its eight schools. The Universidad de Monterrey had identified a cohort of incipient Latino leaders and succeeded in having most accept an invitation to a first-ever Latino-only leadership retreat.[3] Even the bilingual curriculum was seen as delayed rather than dead. In turn, the superintendent had made a successful effort to have the attorney be one of fifty Georgians honored at the "Build a Better Georgia" ceremony in February 1998 and his executive assistant drafted an application to have the Georgia Project honored in Harvard's "Innovations in American Government" award ceremony. It was one of 100 semifinalists, out of 1,600+ applications.

However, beneath the surface, some of the pressures that would damage the Georgia Project as a three-party partnership were beginning to build. The attorney presided over a meeting where a local priest called the district's response to Latinos "incompetent." Even though the superintendent deftly parried that challenge practically at the moment it was made, the charge still represented unfamiliar and unprecedented public criticism of the district's performance. At the same time, the curriculum coordinator (perhaps tired of finding her views disregarded within Georgia Project circles) began circulating an alternative bilingual transition plan without consulting the second Monterrey-designated bilingual coordinator who, based on her briefing in Monterrey, still thought the curriculum development was a task the Universidad was supposed to be completing. Shortly thereafter, to pressure the district, the attorney made public a critical Monterrey-authored report suggesting the utilization of the visiting instructors was not making sufficient use of their training and skills. A story line of criticism of the district's performance was emerging (replacing a less accusatory account that the district had been caught off guard and deserved assistance from corporate and other leaders), as were different operating assumptions regarding how and by whom the project was to be managed. It was also becoming apparent that various leaders had different sensibilities regarding what Latino newcomer students needed.

According to Heath's (1996) experience in the Carolinas, windows of opportunity do not remain open. There, supported by the conservative restoration embodied by Reagan's rise to the presidency, back-to-basics-oriented school administrators reasserted their control over the experimenting teachers who had been adjusting their practices based on what they had learned through action research. In Dalton, too, several central office administrators moved to reassert their power, backing a back-to-basics curriculum, as their lack of control over the Georgia Project felt increasingly problematic.

In 1998–1999, the increasingly obvious conflict between partners began to focus on the controversial and expensive implementation of Direct Instruction. The attorney ordered an audit of district expenditures, particularly those pertaining to how the Title VII funds had been spent, as he was concerned that the promise of the Georgia Project described in the grant proposal was now being used for other very different ends. While he was right that some Title VII funds were going to pay for Direct Instruction and thus district practice was deviating bluntly from the grant proposal, it is also true that this change in expenditures had been accepted by the U.S. Department of Education, the source of the Title VII funds.

Meanwhile, the Universidad de Monterrey communicated that it did not think using the visiting instructors to lead lessons in English phonetics was wise. Fair as that point was, Goode (2002) notes that because district administrators were facing resistance to Direct Instruction from some regular teachers and, because of the high staffing demands of the Direct Instruction design, these leaders felt that for political reasons they had to have the visiting instructors help with Direct Instruction. Otherwise, they would face challenge from other Direct Instruction skeptics asking why the Monterrey instructors did not have to do Direct Instruction when they did.

At the end of the 1998–1999 school year, several months after the superintendent's executive assistant had angrily handed over the Georgia Project checkbook to the attorney, saying neither she nor the district had any further interest in co-signing cheques for project expenses, the fracture came to a head. The superintendent approached the school board saying he intended to reduce the number of visiting instructors to six. That intent was made public before the meeting and compelled one teacher from the innovative elementary school to write a letter insisting on how valuable the visiting instructors had been to her and her colleagues. The attorney subsequently circulated that letter. The attorney also mobilized several of his powerful allies. So, though going into the meeting the superintendent thought he had a majority of board members willing to agree with the reduction in visiting instructors, his proposal was rejected by the board. This marked the first time in anyone's memory that the Dalton board had publicly differed with a superintendent regarding policy.

The writing was on the wall for the superintendent and within a year he resigned/retired. One Dalton informant characterized the departed superintendent as "the last of the good old boys." He was replaced by another external candidate, Dalton's first woman superintendent, who had previously led a fast-growing suburban Atlanta school district and had a no-nonsense kind of reputation.

The window of opportunity that had given the Georgia Project entrée into Dalton schools was fast closing. Simultaneously, a second window of opportunity that had also enabled the Georgia Project was also closing. This one had nothing to do with the schools but it seemed yet further evidence to longtime Daltonians of the loss of home and community (just as the newcomer influx was sometimes regarded). From 1997 onward, the local carpet industry went through a wave of consolidations that, among other things, also meant for the consolidation of Dalton's autonomous corporate executive class (several former company heads after selling their companies left Dalton). In 1996 and 1997, the attorney was able to mobilize this executive class, obtaining in-kind partnership supports (like the use of corporate jets and frequent flier vouchers) and illustrating clearly to the new superintendent that crossing the project meant crossing Dalton's most powerful contingent. While there are several factors related to why the attorney could not or did not mobilize this same group again in 2001 when Dalton refused to continue its extra compensation (beyond parapro levels) for the visiting instructors, one was that the group to be mobilized had grown smaller.

Yet if the local window of opportunity closed doubly, that meant neither the end of the Georgia Project, nor even the end of its local consequentialness. The attorney's local mobilization of project support had sufficed to get the project started with his initial entrees into the school district securing visiting instructors' access to Dalton classrooms and local teachers' access to needed in-service training at Summer Institutes in Mexico. Once this was accomplished, the project existed, and the attorney and other project champions could engage outsiders in considering and often supporting something tangible. Thus, an initiative that had originally attracted limited attention and no support from Georgia's institutions of higher education had, by 2002, engaged in serious planning with Kennesaw State University, Berry College, and Dalton State College. It had also gained, if less tangibly, from collaboration with scholars at the University of Georgia and Georgia Southern University.

Once the Georgia Project was a tangible, active effort, the attorney could also assure that scholars at CAL and advocates at the National Association for Bilingual Education and the National Council of La Raza (all of whom were engaged in the national Latino education policymaking discourse) were aware of the Georgia Project and could reference it. In the spirit of courting serendipity, this indirectly enabled the Georgia Project to gain support of national lawmakers from both sides of the aisle, notably Georgia's U.S. Senators Cleland and Coverdell and Congressman Johnny Isaacson (who replaced Newt Gingrich). Taking advantage of one window of opportunity led to the opening of others.

With major further local financial support of the Georgia Project unlikely, obtaining external resources for local and regional use meant the transformed project was still viable. It also meant the Georgia Project was no longer quite so unorthodox. Instead of being an unlikely partnership of a school district, a community initiative, and a Mexican university, by 2002 it was better characterized as a stable 501(c)3, not-for-profit community organization. The Georgia Project still worked with the Universidad de Monterrey, several school districts, and some other entities, but it was no longer an interdependent partnership, a three-legged stool that would topple if one of the partners were to leave.

## HOW THE GEORGIA PROJECT WAS LOCALLY CONSEQUENTIAL

The attorney used a power politics strategy to guide his Georgia Project efforts. By broadly publicizing the Georgia Project's intentions, emphasizing its central ethical concerns, contributing his own tireless volunteer energy to it, and daring anyone to come forward with doubts, he raised the scrutiny of the school district's practices and mobilized a powerful community contingent. Even though there was a history of business and community involvement with education in Dalton, until the Georgia Project, there had not been a coordinated external voice that insisted on a role in program design, program enactment, and oversight.[4]

Through his involvement, the attorney found a Mexican institutional partner for the Georgia Project, oversaw the elaboration of a four-component program design, and assured that both Dalton and the Whitfield County school systems signed the Georgia Project accord in March 1997. Moreover, the attorney kept arranging for outsiders to see the success of the Georgia Project and hear repeated renditions of the miscommunication problem diagnosis. Thus he compelled the superintendent, the curriculum coordinator, and others in the district to accept accolades for facets of the project they were not always privately enthusiastic about. From this perspective, Dalton's unwillingness to remain deeply engaged in the Georgia Project does not constitute an ultimate failure of the attorney's strategies; rather that the district remained engaged as long as it did is a measure of his political acumen.

Eventually, however, the school district-based resistance to the Georgia Project rose sufficiently that both the district and the attorney faced a kind of crossroads. The attorney was faced with fully ceding control to the school district, a prospect that he did not seriously consider because of both his faith in his initial problem diagnosis and his subsequent experience with the district's reallocation of what he thought of as Georgia Project resources. Instead he figured out ways to formalize the Georgia Project and secure the needed external resources for it to operate autonomously.

The school district, however, faced a crossroads as well. Goode (2002:132) suggests that the negative exposure of district practices that the attorney's Georgia Project maneuverings kept exposing/alleging made for a "no-win" situation. Faced with competing priorities and the skepticism of at least some leaders and other stakeholders regarding the Georgia Project, the district was never going to implement the project to the attorney's satisfaction, even if it made what by its own reckoning seemed like substantial efforts. Moreover, the conflicts between the attorney and the school district that had emerged initially unwittingly had been exacerbated rather than resolved, thus supporting a nonvirtuous circle of mistrust followed by a clash followed by greater mistrust.

Dalton's no-win situation was not only a clash of personalities, however. In some senses, the district was caught between the Georgia Project and the Universidad de Monterrey on one side and the imperatives of the Georgia Department of Education and its allies on the other. From the perspective of the former, bilingual education was a good idea because it led to bilingualism and the opportunities that were afforded by such. Similarly, knowledge of Mexico and a Mexican cultural sensibility were assets that visiting instructors brought to Dalton classrooms and that were worth cultivating among Summer Institute participants. Acquiring such background knowledge enabled educators to support students' construction of knowledge, acquiring new skills and content knowledge by building on what they already understood. Collecting the perspectives of Latino newcomers regarding both the schools and the larger Dalton community in a needs assessment was also logical because it was presumed that what these individuals thought mattered.

In contrast, the Georgia Department of Education to which the district was formally accountable was bent on demonizing bilingual education and discounting the value of linguistic skills and other funds of knowledge that Mexican newcomers brought to the table. Beck and Allexsaht-Snider (2001:50) describe how the 1999 revision of the Georgia ESOL guide (Georgia Department of Education 1999) insisted that "we do not have bilingual education in Georgia," though Dalton had funding for just that and a dual-language immersion public school was operating in suburban Atlanta. In a gesture that would seem absurd if it were not so symbolically hostile, that same guide excluded the term bilingual education from the glossary that listed a number of instructional methods for English language learners. The guide's chapter on "Accommodations for ESOL Students in Regular Education Classrooms" stated "Label items in the classroom **in English-only**. The student's [sic] already know their own language and would ignore the English if you displayed their first language in addition to English. Leave foreign language education of your American students to the foreign language class" (1999:60, bold in original).

While a review of the right-wing ideology of the senior administration at the Georgia Department of Education can be harrowing, it is worth noting three salient factors that are less about the particular views of powerful administrators there and more about Georgia generally. First, Linda Schrenko, the state superintendent of instruction who led the Georgia Department of Education from 1994 through 2002 was an elected official. There was a substantial constituency in Georgia, including Dalton, that either overtly favored these policies or at least was sufficiently untroubled by them that they were willing to support Ms. Schrenko for other reasons. The school district would have been aware of this constituency and some district employees were no doubt part of it. Acting contrary to this framework risked generating the ire of this constituency.

Second, as Goode (2002) points out, Georgia's English-only laws, which predated the Schrenko administration, were also salient reasons for Dalton educational administrators to favor English-immersion type curricula. Not versed well on English language learner issues, they made commonsense (though not necessarily accurate) calculations that if all assessment was going to be in English, then English acquisition deserved to be the primary perhaps even exclusive focus of instruction. Unfortunately, as demographic change continued to correlate with test score declines, the appeal of an "English-at-all-costs-for-test-score-improvement" logic only grew.

Third, as an operator with a long history of active involvement with the Democratic Party in Georgia, the attorney was disposed to being skeptical of the Schrenko administration for partisan reasons as well as pedagogical ones; this was not necessarily true of other Dalton-based Georgia Project leaders. Though hardly his major motive, championing the Georgia Project meant defying the state's Republican educational leader, clearly an opportunity the attorney would favor. The school district, however, could not as readily be as partisan (even if it were disposed to). The divergence between Monterrey/Georgia Project viewpoints and Georgia Department of Education viewpoints was not obvious as the project started, but as it became so, district leaders had choices to make.

Continuing this idea that the district was at a crossroads, we can reconsider elements of the biographies and contextual circumstances of the Georgia Project's three leaders who were district based—the principal, the superintendent, and the curriculum coordinator. Of these three, the curriculum coordinator was the one who appeared to be the most disposed toward the Georgia Department of Education vantage point.

Though the principal's dissertation research, favorable experiences with the Summer Institute, and support for innovations in her school would all appear to dispose her to advocating for the Georgia Project side of the split, several factors dampened such an effort. For one, the principal and the curriculum coordinator were close friends and, as such, the principal seemed unwilling to publicly cross the curriculum coordinator, whatever feelings she might have had regarding the district's growing skepticism of the Georgia Project. Relatedly, the curriculum coordinator seemed to go along with the idea that some native language support and responsiveness at the principal's school was appropriate per the bridging logic of transitional bilingual education (different from the logic of the value of long-term bilingualism that informed the participants from Monterrey). Co-opting in a way the attorney's story about the need to remedy miscommunication, the curriculum coordinator could support practices the principal endorsed not under a logic that cultivating biliteracy and biculturalism were long-term goods, but rather that, in the short term, with children just starting their school careers, catering to their existing communicative competencies was expedient. Moreover, the first norm-referenced tests that were externally reported and thus for which the curriculum coordinator and superintendent would be politically accountable did not occur until the Stanford 9 test was administered to third graders, a grade level the principal's pre-Kindergarten to Grade 2 school did not include. There was less need for the curriculum coordinator to pressure the principal and less need for the principal to feel compelled to try to do the same back. In short, if the district was considering dropping its relationship with the Georgia Project, the principal was not as likely to resist this notion as one might think.

In turn, the superintendent and the curriculum coordinator were faced with starker choices. While the recommendations of the Universidad de Monterrey might have seemed plausible to both of these leaders, they were recommendations in content areas that neither knew well and they remained recommendations from a source that Georgia educators were unaccustomed to soliciting expertise from (i.e., a Mexican university championed by an attorney and local business leaders). The district leaders did not so much reject the Monterrey recommended policies as find them less compelling than the policies that seemed more overtly consistent with Georgia's educational accountability infrastructure and other related state guidelines. Both had spent much more of their careers trying to adhere to these guidelines than those proposed by Monterrey.

Moreover, as an ironic outcome of the negative publicity the attorney had generated to mobilize support for the Georgia Project, the superintendent and curriculum coordinator had to negotiate a very difficult political climate. As the Dalton resistance to a Dalton-Whitfield merger described in Chapter 3 illustrated, there was still a broadly extant belief that Dalton was and could continue to be a superior school system. Yet rapidly declining test scores, apart from SAT averages, belied this public expectation. District leaders needed to be seen as moving to stanch the decline. From that perspective, Direct Instruction made more sense than the unorthodox, untested Georgia Project.

Direct Instruction corresponded with the worldview of the curriculum coordinator (Goode 2002). Moreover, perhaps because it substituted a clear plan of action for the befuddlement that had greeted the demographic change in many classrooms, it was initially popular among many teachers. Direct Instruction allegedly had a research base suggesting it worked well for poor kids and it came recommended by consultants who seemed knowledgeable and thus credible.[5] This contrasts with the Georgia Project whose advocates included business leaders, an attorney, and foreign nationals, several of whom were sociologists rather than educators. At the same February 1998 meeting where the priest labeled Dalton's response to Hispanics "incompetent," business leaders and the priest both joined in haranguing the district for not hiring a Spanish-speaking Colombian associate of the priest "even as a janitor." I mention this because, though the district response was polite, it highlights how little these business leaders actually knew about the *how to's* of education. What exactly was the expected pedagogical impact of hiring a janitor of whatever linguistic background?[6] That district leaders were not automatically receptive to each idea of the Georgia Project committee should hardly be surprising or troubling. Discounting the curricular and pedagogical recommendations of the Universidad de Monterrey according to an ignore-the-message-because-of-the-messenger standpoint (i.e., ignoring the Georgia Project oversight committee) was not all that different from ignoring the janitor hire recommendation.

Ignoring recommendations was a politically different act than challenging or rejecting them. Unlike the shrug off of the janitor hire recommendation, in 1999 when the superintendent opted to favor the educationists and stand beside his curriculum coordinator by defending Direct Instruction and the related need to strip resources from other programs (including by some interpretations the Georgia Project) to cover its expenses, he began challenging the presumptions of the Georgia Project's community leaders. This challenge set up the school board's subsequent rejection of his desire to reduce the number of visiting instructors that, in turn, led to his encouraged retirement. The failure of test scores to go up in the two-plus years of intensive implementation of Direct Instruction sealed his fate. He was defending an expensive program for which he could not demonstrate effectiveness.

What then was the local legacy of the Georgia Project efforts during the period described in this book? One not implausible answer is that it led to a superintendent's encouraged departure. More favorably, it led to the acquisition of substantial external resources (e.g., the Title VII money and the Cleland-Coverdell appropriation). Four other ways of appraising the local effectiveness of the Georgia Project all suggest it was effective. First, though it was not the purpose of her inquiry, in a dissertation that referenced the Georgia Project, Haynes' (2000) comparison of teaching methods used by Dalton ESOL teachers, visiting instructors from Monterrey, and two other groups, suggested that the visiting instructors were as likely to teach in a student-responsive fashion as the district's trained ESOL teachers, despite the constraints of their paraprofessional status. Thus the goal of growing the supply of newcomer-responsive educators was met at least for the duration of the visiting instructor program.

Second, Goode (2002) notes that when Dalton scaled back and ultimately ended its participation in the visiting instructor program, it replaced the departing Monterrey educators with bilingual paraprofessionals. This gesture failed to recognize the training and expertise of the Monterrey visitors, but did account for the idea that the schools needed staff who could communicate with newcomer students and their families. This was a step forward from the hiring practices that had brought monolingual paraprofessionals like the attorney's daughter into educational setting with high numbers of not-yet English proficient Latino newcomers. This marked a change in the district's ethos. Indeed, in November 2002 I had a chance to visit several Dalton schools, including a new "newcomer school" that acted as a transitional academy for new arrivals. I was told repeatedly by district personnel that they had not rejected the Georgia Project so much as "moved beyond it." What was abundantly clear was that district and school-based personnel both felt compelled to illustrate that turning away from the Georgia Project did not mean turning away from hiring Spanish-speaking personnel, from attending to students' backgrounds, and other goals that the Georgia Project embedded.

Third, at the time the Georgia Project was inaugurated, the only substantive response to newcomers had been the creation of an ESOL program that was not sufficiently large to keep all English language learners from encountering teachers who were untrained in how to communicate with them, let alone teach them. Five years later, in what is perhaps the most substantive legacy of the Georgia Project, there were two community organizations—ACLA and the Georgia Project itself—that both took the task of meeting newcomer needs seriously. ACLA did this through political organizing. The post-partnership Georgia Project did this by organizing a broad range of services for numerous constituencies, ranging from Spanish and other professional development for teachers, to English classes for newcomer adults. These services were available to a broader region than just Dalton and Whitfield County. (Murray County Schools and Calhoun City Schools were two other Georgia districts that had become involved with the stand-alone Georgia Project.)

Finally, looking specifically at the Georgia Project's local impact on Latino newcomers in Dalton, high school enrollment data from September 2001 showed the ratio of Hispanic twelfth graders to tenth graders had improved to 35.6/51.7 or 68.9 percent from the September 1996 ratio shared in Chapter 7 of 11.8/30.0, or 39.3 percent.[7] That is to say, concurrent with the  implementation of the Georgia Project, Dalton schools got better at preventing the dropout of Latino students. As the 68.9 percent figure indicates, however, the problem had been reduced not solved. Attributing this improvement exclusively to the Georgia Project seems inappropriate, but similarly excluding it also seems unfair. The Georgia Project put Latino-responsive educators in each Dalton school, helped some veteran Dalton teachers learn more about Mexican newcomers by way of the Summer Institute, and, more generally, increased the local focus on the fate of Latino students while helping change public sphere sentiments about responding to the newcomers. Previously, offering no more response than a hastily assembled ESOL program had been deemed sufficient.

## HOW LATINO IDENTITY MATTERED IN THE NEW SOUTH

Looking at the Georgia Project in regards to its broader implications for Latino education is both complicated and important. As a rather straightforward point, the Georgia Project proved that Mexican universities are sites of competence and expertise that can help U.S. school districts meet the needs of their growing Latino enrollments (Zúñiga et al. 2001). As I was finishing this manuscript, the Universidad de Monterrey was involved in some very preliminary discussions with the Sindicato Nacional de Trabajadores Educativos and some other Mexican partners about trying to make Mexico-trained teachers more broadly available to U.S. districts. The Georgia Project also suggested the potential value of various particular practices and the limits of those practices if they were not subsequently supported (like the valuable learning at the Summer Institutes).

However, the Georgia Project also reveals a rather uncomfortable paradox about Latino education. To mobilize the requisite support for the Georgia Project, the attorney and other community leaders needed to paint the district as falling short, as being inadequate, hence the need for external resources and a new plan of action. Such criticism was unfamiliar to Dalton, which since the district's very founding had been accustomed to its favorable reputation as the region's preeminent district. In partial consequence, and I think contrary to the intentions of all six leaders profiled here, as the Georgia Project continued and as the district enrollment became increasingly students of color, the public image of the district faded (and white flight accelerated). A typical student in Dalton in 2002 (likely a Latino student) who was academically successful, would find that success undercut by the public perception that the "schools are not what they used to be," implying that this student's success must be less than the success of previous (likely white) students. Absent the Georgia Project's challenge to the district, there may have been no mobilization and no significant response to the newcomers, but with the challenge, something was lost. As evidenced by the new prevalence of public criticism and by white flight, the value of a Dalton education was presumed to be reduced.

As of 2002, Dalton had become a community where many Latino students were prospering, but still not at the rate of their white classmates. The district had become a place where a few of their teachers now came from backgrounds that more closely matched their own; four former Georgia Project visiting instructors had been employed by Dalton as of 2001–2002. Yet it was still a place that had not systematically agreed to value the linguistic and cultural funds of knowledge Latino students bring with them to school. It was not yet a place that consistently favored "additive biculturalism" (Gibson 1997a) over "subtractive schooling" (Valenzuela 1999). Most importantly, it was a place that has seen its previous myth expire of shared sensibilities between corporate leaders, educators, and the families attending schools. A new vision of what school is for has not been agreed upon and the constituencies that would need to agree seemed less disposed to do so than when I started.

The ongoing challenge for Dalton, but also for American society writ large, is to figure out how to respond to growing Latino populations such that educational change can be constructed as necessary but not dire. Marleen Pugach (1998) argues for a new trope—"border as opportunity"—that suggests a needed challenge to the pro-immigration script, a valuing of skills pertinent in Mexico and the United States, or in Latino cultural contexts as well as Anglo ones. By and large this trope was not available in Dalton. When the attorney tried to introduce it in his January 1997 toast it resonated with the Monterrey scholars, but not, as far as I can tell, with the remainder of the audience. Perhaps, however, the task of making "the border as opportunity" a viable trope in Dalton requires the work beyond Dalton that the attorney has helped the Georgia Project more recently engage in. Here I mean not just the involvement with other districts, but also the tie-ins with the Georgia Association of Educators, CAL, the National Council of La Raza, the National Education Association, the National Association for Bilingual Education, the U.S. Senate and Congress, and even my employer, Brown University (which highlighted Dalton and the Georgia Project at an April 2000 teacher training institute). The official policies of the Georgia Department of Education during the past decade have argued against the "border as opportunity" trope, while changing the political ecology within which Dalton educators operate, making embrace of the trope hazardous. Perhaps the Georgia Project's new links set up a way of outflanking the Georgia Department of Education or supporting its transformation. (As of this writing the department's leadership was up in the air, as State Superintendent Schrenko was finishing her tenure, having not sought a third term, instead devoting her energies to a failed bid for the governorship.)

The Georgia Project's relevance in this new millennium may be as much nonlocal as local. Its capacity to engage the imagination and advocacy of mainstream politicians and national advocates for Latinos and second language learners may be more salient. The lessons for them are that a Mexican university can help a United States school district, that interethnic and international coordination is possible even in the face of disconcertingly rapid demographic change and state-level resistance, that teachers need professional development if they are to respond well to the interests, needs, and orientations of newcomer students, and that rapid multifaceted mobilization is possible. That's an impressive (and incomplete) list of accomplishments for the complaints of one monolingual parapro, even if much work remains to be done.

# Epilogue

For the entirety of my research period in Dalton and much of the time since then (i.e., from July 1998 through 2002), Dalton's economy, like the rest of America's was booming. As a related issue, for most of that same time immigration into Dalton was largely tolerated because it was not economically threatening to most of the population, indeed it was benefiting the top. Also, pre-September 11, 2001, exotic, little understood foreign nationals were not seen as menacingly as perhaps they are now. However, in ways this manuscript has little space to explore, I am quite cognizant that the context of host community/newcomer relations in which the Georgia Project operates must now be different.

During a brief visit to Dalton in the fall of 2001, the Universidad de Monterrey's former research director for the Georgia Project started hearing tales from Latino newcomers in Dalton that some were mulling returns to Mexico and that others had already left because it had become a little harder to find work and a lot harder to pick up extra earnings from extra shifts. Dalton was not about to see a net out-migration of Latinos, but the flow in was no longer going to quite so thoroughly outpace the flow out. In February 2002, the *Boston Globe* carried a front-page story (Robertson 2002) with the title "An Economic Retreat: Worried About Jobs Some Immigrants Return to Mexico" that mentioned Dalton and some other key sites in the economy of the New South (e.g., Durham, NC, Charlotte, and Chattanooga). A Knight-Ridder newspaper story a week before the *Globe* article (Recio 2002) carried the headline: "Recession Hits Hispanics Hard,

Study Finds" and cited data from the Pew Hispanic Center illustrating that
the 2001 recession was disproportionately impacting Latinos, because of
Latinos overrepresentation in the vulnerable service sector of the economy.

In Chapter 2, I promised to largely constrain the telling of my autobiography to a few pages of that chapter. As I finish this manuscript, however,
I have two additional thoughts about my role that seem salient, even though
I do not have enough perspective on either of them to be sure how. First, as
long as I was closely involved with the Georgia Project, the six leaders profiled here, as well as other relevant project enactors (e.g., the superintendent's
executive secretary, the second bilingual coordinator from Monterrey), succeeded at getting along. While this may well have been coincidence, I cannot
shake the idea that my rapport with all of them somehow made me an intermediary and that, absent my mediation, snafus became conflicts.

Conversely, during 1998–1999, I remember receiving a phone call from
the attorney asking me what I thought about the expenditure of Title VII
monies on Direct Instruction. With a sense of both pride in the original
grant proposal and betrayal—ideas I believed in and had written into the
proposal were ignored—I concurred with his diagnosis that the expenditures seemed inappropriate. Thus, I cannot reject the idea that my input
then hastened the deterioration of relations between the attorney and the
school district. As I hinted in Chapter 14, I now have more of an appreciation for the dichotomy between the Georgia Project, Title VII proposal, and
Monterrey ideas on the one side and the ideas of the Georgia Department
of Education on the other. In the face of declining test scores and growing
community pressure, the district officials were in a bind that, even in retrospect, I cannot think of an easy way out of. Their not adhering closely to
the Title VII proposal should be seen in this larger context.

In November 2002, I returned briefly to Dalton to attend "Diversity in the
21st Century," the first conference that the Georgia Project had ever organized. The event drew over 100 participants from across the state of Georgia,
including founders of Latino community organizations, scholars from many
of Georgia's major universities, school and district officials, business representatives, and others. Also participating were Delia Pompa (Executive
Director of the National Association for Bilingual Education), Donna
Christian (Director of the Center for Applied Linguistics [i.e., CAL]), and a
large contingent from the Universidad de Monterrey. In ways similar to,
though far grander than the original, this event was similar to the March
1998 Georgia Project celebration described in Chapter 13. Though I cannot
well measure the dividends from the information exchanged and the interpersonal contacts initiated or reestablished, I have little doubt that this more
recent event will be remembered as another milestone in the expansion of a
Latino-community-responsive infrastructure in the New South.

# Notes

## CHAPTER 1

1. Dalton and Whitfield County are both the actual place names for the site of my study. See Hamann (2001b:93) for a short discussion of the ethical considerations used in various write-ups of this research, sometimes "naming names" and other times using pseudonyms. Readers should know that I never promised blanket anonymity to any Daltonians or others involved in the Georgia Project and I was always explicit that, whatever additional roles I was enacting, I was present as a researcher and taking notes. In instances, like the surveys of visiting instructors from Mexico or the interviews of Georgia teachers who participated in the summer training programs in Mexico, I have, however, fully protected the anonymity of respondents. Such informants have comparatively less power than those who initiated the Georgia Project and there is an ethical obligation to assure that use of their insights does not jeopardize them.

Readers should also know that I take seriously Erickson's (1984) characterization of the findings of educational ethnography as "provisional knowledge." In other words, though the findings offered here are empirically grounded, it is always possible that I never collected some pertinent data that would have led me to different findings. I have named Dalton in part as an invitation to readers to go where I went, to see the community I saw, and determine if they would draw the same conclusions. If readers did not know where I had studied such attempts to verify or falsify my research claims would be impossible. Finally, readers will see that, though I am more sympathetic to the actions of some than others, no identifiable person here is accused of acting maliciously.

2. In considering what terminology to use in this book, I have had to confront the contemporary contentiousness regarding whether "Latino," "Latino/Latina," or

"Hispanic" is the more appropriate or politically correct term. In my research site, "Hispanic" and "Mexican" were more common terms than "Latino," but I have chosen to use "Latino" most often here to honor two arguments of David Hayes-Bautista and Jorge Chapa (1987). First, they assert that Latino is a chosen term (rather than assigned one). By using Hispanic only when quoting or paraphrasing an official document or a government categorization from the Census, for example, I can bring emphasis to the act of assigning a label. See also Oboler (1995). Second, Hayes-Bautista and Chapa assert that "Latino" does not apply to Iberian Europeans (i.e., to the historic colonizers as opposed to colonized), but it does apply to all of the peoples who trace descent to areas south of the United States that were targeted by the Monroe Doctrine. In using Latino, I am acknowledging the neo-colonialist economic and governmental interventions into Latin America made by the United States that, ironically, have initiated many of the links as well as the dislocations that have brought many from Mexico and elsewhere to the United States. Though in Spanish, Latino is a masculine form, albeit one used to refer both to males and to mixed gender groups, I have decided to use Latino rather than the awkward Latino/Latina. If referencing an all female group, like the group of visiting instructors from Mexico who worked in Dalton, I use Latina/s in place of Latino.

3. Given that the Georgia Project is ongoing as I write these words, readers may find the insistent use of the past tense peculiar, even awkward. Nonetheless, echoing Delgado-Gaitan (1990:3), I have consciously rendered the field study using the past tense because it would be misleading to have the audience of this document believe that what I observed was static and unchanging.

4. "Anglo" is a term used by the principal in this building. Though elsewhere in Dalton "white" is a more common term, Anglo is used and understood broadly. "Redneck" and "poor white trash" are derogatory terms frequently applied to and used by low-income whites in Dalton/Whitfield.

5. The often negative characterization that I offer later of the Georgia Department of Education's problematic response to Mexican newcomers emphatically does not apply to the state employee referenced here.

6. Dalton is squarely in Appalachia, with Whitfield County being included in William's (1996) definition of "core Appalachia," which meant it was included in all six of the definitions determining Appalachia's border that he reviewed. But at the time of my study, Dalton and Whitfield were also somewhat anomalous from much of Appalachia as the preponderance of locally owned business was exceptional to the region and because its per capita income nearly matched the national average in 1989, making Whitfield one of the ten wealthiest counties in Appalachia (Cuoto 1995).

7. Only Mississippi, Louisiana, and Texas did not substantially follow this trend. In the case of Texas this was because a large existing Latino population base meant that the proportional growth between 1990 and 1998 was smaller, though actual growth was substantial. In contrast, Mississippi's and Louisiana's economies were less robust and generated less growth and fewer new jobs.

8. According to a recent report by the General Accounting Office (1999:7), a 1993 study found that 80 percent of U.S. school districts reported difficulty in recruiting bilingual teachers and 53 percent had difficulty finding trained ESL teachers.

9. See Hamilton (1996b) and Dalton Public Schools (1997) for written versions of this account.

10. Some Dalton educators used the title "Accelerated Cognitive Growth" as the name for this program. Because "Direct Instruction" is a much more familiar term in the district and the research literature, that is the term I use throughout this document.

11. As noted in Endnote 1, I have chosen to name roles rather than names of the key personnel who figure in this study. As exceptions to this identifying but not naming, I have included the names of three Dalton educators—Lisa Goode, Amy Haynes, and Frankie Beard—when I refer to their Georgia Project-relevant, in-the-public-domain scholarship, that is, their dissertations.

12. One of my dissertation readers—Kathy Hall—suggested I include myself in the mini-biography section because my role with the Georgia Project was not just as a "detached" observer. I have opted, however, for the biographical information included in Chapter 2 to suffice as a characterization of my role.

## CHAPTER 2

1. One could assert that, in my roles as applied researcher in Dalton and now author of this manuscript, I wrote what I wrote because of my own understandings of what was salient and what was needed. Though this study is empirically grounded, no doubt this assertion is true. I broach this topic more toward the end of this chapter.

## CHAPTER 3

1. It is intriguing to ponder both how deep and how widespread this sympathy for black redress was and to what extent it might have been related to the new presence of a substantial Hispanic community. My data, however, offer no ready answer. According to data from the 2000 U.S. Census, Dalton's African American population totaled 2,153 (or 7.7 percent), while Whitfield County overall was home to 3,214 (or 3.8 percent) African Americans.

2. Dalton's experience matches the long-term African American emigration from all over the Appalachian core region noted by Williams (1996).

3. See Banker (1996), Plaut (1983), and Puckett (1989) for more on how low-income Appalachian whites have been marginalized by the local middle-class and elites, as well as by middle-class and elite outsiders.

4. Tufted products are made by sewing loops of yarn into a fabric base and usually clipping the loops to create a surface of bushy or puffy fiber ends.

5. Several of my Dalton informants, none of whom worked as mill laborers, emphasized that mill wages were generous, well above the minimum wage.

6. At the time of my study, ConAgra was the largest meatpacking company in the world and in that capacity the company's strategies for staffing its plants had a profound and widespread effect. As part of a process that Griffith (1995:129) calls the "Latinization of low-wage labor" and that Hackenberg (1995:261) refers to as the "Latin-Americanization of the secondary labor sector," ConAgra was centrally involved in the recruitment of Latino labor, particularly Latino newcomer labor, in many parts of the country. The company's motives for recruiting immigrant labor were multiple. Several of the factors that initially attracted the poultry industry to the rural Southeast were gradually disappearing. According to Griffith (1995:130), the rural Southeast used to provide a poorly educated, low-income,

racist, anti-union surplus labor force that was docile, unlikely to organize, and agriculturally oriented enough to be accustomed to the seasonality of labor demand.

7. If one includes the word-of-mouth informal recruitment of new Mexican laborers by present carpet industry workers, then the industry was directly recruiting in Mexico. But allegations of sending buses and/or recruiting agents to Mexico were probably inaccurate. Given the efficacy of informal recruitment methods, why would a company decide to pay for something it could get at no cost?

8. The category "carpet and rug industry" excludes support industries like yarn mills.

9. At the time I investigated this question, in the winter of 1998, no data newer than the 1994 figures were available. During the 1989 to 1994 time frame, the overall number of people employed in the carpet and rug industry in Georgia fell minimally from 33,999 to 33,388 which strongly suggests that there was not a significant expansion in carpet industry jobs near Whitfield County that could explain Dalton's influx of Hispanics (U.S. Department of Commerce 1991:4, 1996:4).

10. The Crown Point School operated until 1946 when it was closed and its students incorporated into the Dalton Public Schools (Thomas 1996).

11. Mohawk/Aladdin was the second largest floor covering maker in the world and World Carpet was the twelfth (Jackson 1997).

12. This practice ended when that company was bought out by a larger local carpet producer. Dalton Public Schools then formally hired the former teacher to continue in his same role.

13. The racial/ethnic categories and terminology match those used in the *Report Card*.

14. The per-student expenditures noted in the 1996–1997 *Georgia Education Report Card* claim that Dalton spent $6,581 per student and that Whitfield spent $4,968 (Georgia Department of Education 1998), but those figures, unlike mine, excluded the Title Programs and the Lottery K–12 and all Other K–12 budget categories that, like the General Fund, directly supported instructional services.

15. According to the Georgia Department of Education's (1998) *Georgia Public Education Report Card, 1996–97,* when the Georgia Project began the average Dalton teacher had 13.18 years of teaching experience.

16. Putting a different twist on the "white flight" scenario, a few carpet executives who were well known in Dalton (because their companies are prominent and Dalton is not a large city) told me they decided to send their children or grandchildren to Chattanooga private schools because the environment there was more anonymous—the students did not feel known for or judged by their family's prominence or wealth. One Dalton executive told me that, during a fund-raiser at Dalton High, his child's teacher had suggested to his child that she get her father to buy all the magazine subscriptions that the students were attempting to sell, because, the teacher explained, the executive had the means to do it. The incident made the student quite uncomfortable and the father quite angry.

17. I acknowledge that there are many problems with using SAT scores to compare and rank the school districts; here I am merely echoing local practice. See Cumming (1998).

18. See Trueba's (1991) distinction between "push" and "pull" factors that lead to dropping out.

19. Of the eighty-one mothers of Hispanic students, fifty were born in Mexico, twelve in the United States, and the birthplace of nineteen was unknown. Claiming that 80 percent were born in Mexico requires discarding the unknowns.

20. Counting generations differently, Padilla (1996) found that Hispanic school attainment improved between first and second generations while progress stagnated between second and third generations.

21. I realize these brief sentences risk insinuating that Hispanic students are responsible for whatever limitations they encounter at school. Though I do not want to deny their agency, I echo Valenzuela (1999) in her claim that the culturally sub-tractive nature of schooling engenders the alienation felt acutely by many second-generation Latino students.

## CHAPTER 4

1. I weighed whether to delete or change the names of the individuals named in this segment, but decided that, because they are elected public figures and these were on-the-record comments, there was no need to invent anonymity on their behalf.

2. Regarding this language and identity dynamic, Galindo has written, "English is equated with 'America' as if other languages did not have a historical presence in the United States before English and as if any language other than English was 'unAmerican'. . . . For many, the English language is a symbolic marker of 'Americanism' rather than the social and political ideas behind democracy" (cited in Beck and Allexsaht-Snider [2001:44]).

3. During my research period, among dozens of stories in the *Atlanta Journal-Constitution* about Georgia's increased links to Latin America were reports that Mexico was the third leading country for Georgia exports, valued at $252 million for the first quarter of 1997, a 93 percent increase from the first quarter of 1996 (M. Quinn 1997), and that Delta Airlines was making Atlanta a hub for its expanded operations throughout Latin America (Thurston 1997a, 1997b).

4. To clarify, this idea states that secondary-sector householders do not have experience with schooling contributing to their earnings or job security. It does not say that householders do not believe in such a link.

5. Since announcement of this budget resulted in a public outcry (albeit from only limited quarters), the State Superintendent of Education in March 1998 promised that in January 1999 she would seek supplementary funds to make up the difference, but she determined it was too late to try to repair the "complex" problem when it "came to her attention" during the final week of the then-operating state legislative session (Kurylo 1998a, 1998b). Beck and Allexsaht-Snider assert, however, that at best Schrenko's claim was misleading. They write, "It is important to note that the 'complex formula' for ESOL funding referred to in the [Kurylo] article is little more than a standard FTE (full time equivalent) count of student segments, a common formula used in funding nearly every level of education from kindergarten to the university" (2001:60).

6. I base this claim on the account of several reliable informants who asked that I hide their identities. It is echoed, however, in Beck and Allexsaht-Snider (2001). Several of these informants have qualified their characterization by saying that anti-immigrant sentiment at the Georgia Department of Education is just one facet of a more general anti-multiculturalism, anti-diversity, ostensibly assimilationist perspective. On the

State Superintendent's 1998 reelection website, one of the two issues she highlighted was her support for the Republican platform proposal to make English the official language. (The Democratic candidate's platform argued for "English-plus.")

7. This legislation ultimately did pass in the House, but subsequently died, as similar legislation did not pass in the Senate. In the federal Elementary and Secondary Education Act (ESEA) passed in January 2002, Title VII was formally eliminated.

8. As of the spring of 1998, a few professors in the College of Education and the School of Social Work at the University of Georgia were in the initial stages of arranging an agreement entitled "The Pan-American Project" with a Mexican university in Xalapa, Veracruz. In 1999, through this program the University of Georgia supported several current Georgia teachers' summer study in Mexico.

9. Villenas (personal communication) who studied a similar small Southern city in the North Carolina Piedmont (see Villenas [2001]) says a similar dynamic had not occurred in her research site.

10. Villenas did find characterizations of Hispanics as familial, hardworking, and loyal in her North Carolina research site.

11. This was a lesson learned by white elites in Atlanta in the 1950s and 60s when partnerships with a few prominent African Americans offered political cover from claims that they were racist or segregationist (Hunter 1963).

## CHAPTER 5

1. Several informants speculated that this may have been the primary motive of the attorney.

2. The "old-boy network" operating style is amply reflected in Hunter's (1963) classic analysis of Regional City [Atlanta]. While Dalton is much smaller than Regional City, the tacit but real roles and rules that Hunter documented forty years ago aptly describe Georgia Project oversight committee functions with the attorney at its helm.

3. A Mexican immigrant newspaper editor and an African American woman at Dalton College were inconsistently invited to various oversight committee activities.

4. Several of the Universidad de Monterrey informants remarked on how surprisingly happy and at ease he appeared in audiences that were entirely Mexican and Mexican immigrant except for him. They were with him in such situations both socially and formally as part of the development of Dalton's Hispanic leadership council within the Parent/Workplace Involvement framework.

5. For one year, 1998–1999, I was a "temporary assistant professor" in the University of Georgia's Educational Psychology Department. I was filling in because an attempt to attract a senior researcher to resurrect the College of Education's qualitative research methods initiative had foundered. During that year, I not only initiated the contacts that led to the *Georgia Magazine* story (Wexler 1999), I also invited several Georgia Project leaders to travel down to Athens to be interviewed by my graduate students. The subsequent April (in 2000) when I had begun working at Brown University, another team from Dalton was invited up to Rhode Island (under my coordination) to be a focal case study of our *2nd Institute on Cultural and Linguistic Diversity*. For both the magazine article and the presentations, my motives included promoting an initiative that I thought, on balance, was both compelling and instructive. I also supported the forging of links between Dalton-based educators and those with expertise and experience elsewhere.

6. Gradually the attorney transferred more and more of his legal work to the partners in his firm to free up more time for Georgia Project activities. At the time of this writing (in 2002) the attorney is fully retired from his legal practice and all his work is voluntary work on behalf of the Georgia Project.

7. Because of the cultural bias of standardized tests and other factors, Hispanics tend in aggregate to do less well on these instruments than whites. See Damico and Hamayan (1991) and Cloud (1991) for an introduction to cultural and linguistic test bias and other assessment issues. See also Fischer et al.'s (1996) *Inequality by Design*.

8. Because he left, it was never clear whether he would ultimately have been appointed.

9. When the superintendent came to Dalton, there was an assistant superintendent who had failed in his bid for the top spot who might have been able to help in this arena, but that assistant and the superintendent never developed much of a relationship.

10. Though most or all of the participants were there either because they were invited or were representing someone who had been invited, the meeting appeared to be open to the public.

11. This second administrator left the Dalton school system in August 1998.

12. Arguably, some ESOL personnel in the district were also relative experts on the topic of successful education strategies to use with language-minority children (including immigrant Mexicans, but not necessarily focusing on them), but no ESOL personnel were deeply involved with the Georgia Project's design and implementation.

## CHAPTER 6

1. Rifkin's typology also fits me reasonably well.

2. *Cultural ecology* refers here to people's use of and interaction with their physical environment. Too many people trying to use too few resources in a given place constitutes a cultural ecological explanation for displacement. The concept of *political ecology* pays heed to the idea that availability of resources in a particular place may be a product not only or not mainly of that place's natural history but instead of that place's location in regards to arbitrary (created) political boundaries. The availability of higher or more stable wages on the other side of a political border may constitute a rationale for displacement from this perspective.

3. Mendez Lugo (1997) cites Mexico's national teacher union data that claim that 20,000 SNTE members are presently working—presumably as immigrant laborers—in the United States (where their credentials are unrecognized). This is one example showing a consequence of Mexico having more credentialed professionals than attractive job niches for them.

According to Lorey (1995), in 1990 in Mexico almost 40 percent of egresados with four or more years of university education held nonprofessional jobs. Thirty-six percent of those with four or more years of university experience earned less than three times the national minimum wage.

4. According to Lorey (1995), "The Mexican university developed increasingly distinct public and private components in order to allocate ever larger numbers of aspirants between available professional and technical positions. Public universities increasingly performed the function of providing social status to rapidly growing

entering classes, keeping alive the revolutionary goal of widespread mobility into the middle class or at least keeping up appearances."

5. While it is plausible that U.S. teaching experience could augment a Universidad de Monterrey graduate's bid to find a public education job in Mexico—not necessarily the goal of most—indexing of public education salaries by the government means they could command a salary no better than any other Mexican public school teacher.

6. The specific text in Spanish of the Universidad de Monterrey's founding principios can be found on the Internet at: http://www.udem.edu.mx/institucion/filosofia/index.htm (Accessed 6/18/02)

## CHAPTER 7

1. The term *limited English proficient*, or LEP in shorthand, has come into common usage since the 1974 U.S. Supreme Court *Lau v. Nichols* decision which, under a logic of equal protection, required schools to formally identify all students who were not fully proficient in English and assure that those students had additional assistance that allowed them equal access to the curriculum. Since that decision, the term has been criticized for its deficit implications, identifying students by what they do not know. Here I use limited English proficient when quoting or paraphrasing and when referring to formal identification of such students by schools, but when I do not need to highlight someone else's classificatory schema, I use the substitute term *English language learner*.

2. Summer school and some additional logistic and academic supports were available to some students and their families through their qualification for the federally funded, state-administered Migrant Education Program. However, many Latino families in Dalton were not involved in agricultural or food-processing labor and thus were not eligible for migrant services.

3. This teacher (and most or all of her colleagues) may indeed have felt quite overwhelmed. Ironically, as is noted later in this chapter, they worked for the most innovative school in the district (at least most innovative in relation to responsiveness to Latino newcomers). Prior to the Georgia Project, their school piloted a number of initiatives that were similar (if on smaller scale) to Georgia Project initiatives. These pilot efforts likely were integral to Dalton school administrators' initial acceptance of the Georgia Project.

4. The SAT averages presented here were all based on student's most recent score, not necessarily their best (Georgia Department of Education 1998).

5. Traditionally the celebration of the Virgin of Guadalupe marks the beginning of Mexico's extensive Christmas celebration, so it is worth noting that the Mexican Georgia Project collaborators deferred the beginning of their holiday in deference to their eager Dalton partners.

6. Three years after this meeting, the attorney's recollection of the rationale for the Georgia Project supported the interpretation that importation of bilingual and bicultural teachers was the Dalton initiator's primary goal: "We decided we needed instructors who were of the same ethnic origin as the bulk of the students, who were wise in the culture and bilingual. That's a very simple proposition. Now, how do we find them?" (Wexler 1999:34).

7. Whether this had been the original plan, whether this was an optimistic misrepresentation on the part of the attorney, or a misinterpretation on the Universidad

de Monterrey side is a delicate question that none of my contacts would/could satisfactorily answer. According to the carpet executive, he was happy to pledge his support to the Georgia Project, but he had never promised to be its main financier. Perhaps lending to the executive-as-benefactor interpretation, the executive did support the use of his corporate jet for bringing Monterrey-based partners to Dalton for a reciprocal January 1997 visit further described in Chapter 8.

8. Admitting to his impatience, the attorney was quoted in the Dalton newspaper as saying: "Logic says you need preparation time, but we don't have preparation time. We've got to do this" (Hamilton 1996c).

9. Students were enrolled in these two-language classrooms only at their parents' request. When I last inquired about the topic, there was more demand for these classes than available space.

10. In 2000, when the sponsoring carpet company was bought out, the school district did decide to add this educator to regular payroll (still as a parapro).

## CHAPTER 8

1. That the original *Daily Citizen-News* article mentioned only one program, while the second mentioned four, gives added credibility to the claim by Universidad de Monterrey personnel that school district officials had initially only seriously envisioned the recruitment of bilingual teachers from Monterrey to Dalton.

2. The participation of this one local Hispanic in the early stages of the Georgia Project was intermittent and appeared to be by invitation on an event-by-event basis.

3. Non-white, nonbusiness owners were for the first time systematically included in active ways in several Georgia Project activities as I was finishing my research in mid-1998, but these individuals were not at that point added to the oversight committee, nor did the newly included represent all the previously excluded segments of the population affected by the Georgia Project. One African American woman representing Dalton College did attend the February 28, 1997, Georgia Project Planning Committee meeting, as did one locally based Hispanic newspaper editor. No Dalton teachers were involved.

4. The meeting group's title was unofficial. Different terms—including *Committee, Planning Committee,* and *Ad Hoc Oversight Committee*—were used by the group.

5. Because the state Title VII director position was vacant (and had been for more than a year), Title VII was also within this coordinator's purview.

6. I had some previous experience writing Title VII proposals and evaluating Title VII programs in Kansas and mentioned this experience to the Georgia Department of Education administrator during a visit in October 1996.

7. Centro Latino closed in 2001. By then both ACLA and the Georgia Project could make viable claims that they were Latino community-based organizations. Even at its apex, Centro Latino seemed to be more *for* local Latinos than *of* their community.

8. Punctuation and verb-tense errors in the following text match the original which, it should be remembered, was just a preliminary draft text.

9. At the invitation of since-departed Georgia Department of Education officials, in March 1996 Virginia Collier led a one-day workshop for representatives from Georgia's ten districts with the highest ESOL student enrollments. Dalton was

invited to this presentation. Thomas and Collier's work was disseminated through additional activity by Georgia Department of Education officials at that time. That this administrator was aware of this research was not surprising. Her understanding of and loyalty to its implications may not have been very deep, however.

10. I use the term *limited English proficient* here to reflect the terminology of both the request for proposal and the grant proposal I drafted (instead of the more contemporary term *English language learner*).

11. See Cummins (1993), Garcia (1992, 1994), and Saville-Troike (1976).

12. See Grant (1988) and Muncey and McQuillan (1996).

13. See Ramirez (1991) and Cazden (1992).

14. Though he did not say so, NAFTA had facilitated the link between the Dalton carpet manufacturer and the Mexican conglomerate that was the original linkage around which the Georgia Project was constructed.

## CHAPTER 9

1. See also Polinard, Wrinkle, and Meier (1995).

2. Tied to Meier and Stewart's observations regarding Hispanic political power, Hackenberg (1995) notes that the relative lack of Hispanic political power in proportion to their group size in newcomer situations is, in effect, democracy without representation; that is, the larger community may be democratic yet newcomers, as noncitizens and nonvoters, are excluded from participation.

3. This finding needs an important caveat; as Erickson (1987) points out, there are multiple examples of minority students learning in an exemplary fashion from nonminority instructors. Neither Erickson nor I would disagree with Meier and Stewart's general premise as long as their claim is not misapplied on a case-by-case basis. It does not necessarily follow that in specific Dalton classrooms and schools the relative lack of Hispanic educators led to pedagogies and outcomes that disadvantaged specific Hispanic students, but systemwide that prospect seemed likely. Arguably, the creation of the Georgia Project was an admission of this problem.

4. The database does not clarify what the national origin or descent of this one teacher was, nor does it clarify what his/her linguistic skills were.

5. Dentler and Hafner (1997) found in a comparative study of eleven districts with rapidly growing immigrant enrollments that only in the three where administrators were well versed in newcomer education issues (e.g., second language acquisition) did the academic performance of students improve. While it is simplistic to infer that an absence of Hispanic administrators in Dalton meant for an absence of empathy toward Hispanics, the idea should not be entirely disregarded.

6. That there was a regional shortage of Hispanic candidates is clear (Schaerer et al. 1996); whether this shortage provides a full explanation for the low number of Hispanic educators in Dalton, however, was less certain.

7. In the sheltered English science class, advanced ESOL students were taught from the same textbook as mainstream students by a teacher who also had mainstream classes. Sheltered English referred to the teachers careful use of English and the expectation in the class that terms would more often be unfamiliar and require clarification. Valdés (1998) worries that classrooms like this can be language minority student ghettoes, with students' access to mainstream English speakers (apart from the teacher) limited. While I generally agree with her premise, in the classroom of this type that I observed, the lesson seemed to be working well.

8. Crawford (1991:121) notes that completely dichotomizing bilingual education and ESOL is awkward and misleading as bilingual education programs that include the instruction of English include the instruction of ESOL.

9. My use of the word *flawed* here echoes both the Dalton curriculum coordinator's characterization of the effort in her early Title VII drafts and Thomas and Collier's (1997) research findings.

10. All thirteen instructors who answered my questionnaire said their main task was to work with Hispanic students. If their main task was to support a two-way bilingual model (as originally described in the Title VII grant), I suspect they would have answered this question differently.

11. *Assimilation* and *acculturation* are being carefully contrasted here, with assimilation referring to the process of becoming part of a new culture and acculturation referring to the process of learning the ways and habits of a new culture. Acculturation is silent in regards to whether one becomes part of a new culture, becomes bicultural, or maintains one's original culture. For further terminological clarification, see Redfield et al. (1967), Gordon (1964), Park and Burgess (1970), Teske and Nelson (1974), Grey (1991), and Hamann (1999a:xxiii–xxix).

12. The Monterrey instructors were not opposed to teaching English. To the contrary, many identified the improvement of their own English skills as a primary reason they had been interested in coming to Dalton. However, in the questionnaires, a few instructors volunteered that one of their goals for their students was to teach them pride in their Mexican heritage and identity. Had I asked this question directly, I suspect others would have said this was a goal of theirs too. If we remember that many of the Hispanic newcomer students in Dalton were "sojourner students" (Hamann 2001a) and likely to have to negotiate both U.S. and Mexican environments, the visiting instructors' orientation was not only nationalistic or patriotic, but also functional.

13. See Corson (1995) for a nice distinction between formal and functional authority. By his reckoning and mine, the former refers to power wielded because of official position or status, while the latter refers to power that comes from credibility.

14. As with any Dalton schools employee, the visiting instructors were also supposed to be eligible for the Grant-in-Aid program which would permit them to study in local colleges and universities. Despite the fact that several instructors were interested in course work that would qualify them for Georgia teaching certification, during my research period Monterrey instructors never did get access to higher education opportunities as delays in getting their Mexican transcripts translated and reviewed forced the deferral of their wishes.

15. This attitude may have partially reflected the fact that the original discussion about the visiting instructors had focused on the idea of bringing student teachers from Monterrey. This idea received a lot of press before being rejected because student teachers could not be compensated. For some teachers, however, the attitude was more likely a retreat to formal authority—if their professional competence was not obviously ahead of the visiting instructors they could still pull rank.

16. According to Hernández León (1997) Monterrey does have well-developed, high-volume migration links with Houston, Texas.

17. To clarify, Dalton officials claimed that for some time they had been seeking certified instructors who spoke Spanish and English. Dalton had not necessarily

been seeking instructors with a bilingual certificate or bilingual endorsement, categories recognized by educational officials in some states, but not in Georgia.

18. Keyes' tentative dissertation title was: Fullerton's Linguistic Challenge: Educators Creating Language Policies and Plans. As of April 1998, he was hoping to defend his dissertation in December of the same year.

19. A needs assessment carried out in Dalton by the Center for Applied Linguistics in February 2000 found that "Teachers and staff in the Dalton Public Schools believe strongly in teaching all ESOL students through English and oppose bilingual education" (2000:27).

20. It is worth noting again that a small majority of Hispanic students in Dalton had been born in Mexico and that nearly all of Dalton's Hispanic students' parents were born in Mexico.

21. Drawing such a conclusion, however, ignores two key limitations of Haynes' study, one of which she readily acknowledges. As she notes, her study does not look at student achievement to test whether instructors from different groups doing similar things did so with different consequences. More fundamentally, her study through its very design focuses only the question of what teachers do, as if that independently has bearing on student learning. Clearly what teachers do matters, but from a constructivist understanding of learning (Erickson 1987) the context of the teacher/learner interaction and the point of view of the learner regarding both teacher and context are inseparably pertinent.

22. School reform promoter Philip Schlechty reiterates this point, "It is commonplace to assume that teaching is the cause of learning and to argue that when learning has not occurred, teaching has not occurred. That is nonsense. What has not occurred is that students have not been brought to expend the effort needed to learn. Teaching occurred, but too few students cared or became engaged" (2001:215).

## CHAPTER 10

1. As it worked out, only seventeen Dalton educators (including one English monolingual paraprofessional) applied for the district's eighteen available slots. Anyone willing to go could go. There was no further selection process beyond this.

2. Of the eleven Dalton participants in 1999, there was one administrator, the principal at the school into which the innovative one fed.

3. See Argyris and Schon (1975), Hatch (1998), and Hamann (2001b) for a clarification of the distinction between espoused theories and theories in use.

4. This final suggestion responds to but does not fully resolve Muncey and McQuillan's (1996) dilemma that change efforts that benefit only a portion of the staff risk bifurcating the staff rather than benefiting all through a neutral dissemination process. The successful adoption of Summer Institute lessons at the innovative elementary school that had two administrators attend the Summer Institute suggests that there were ways, short of training for all, that allowed for school-site transformation.

5. As sociologists who were not particular experts in school management and as project advisors who were infrequently in Dalton, the two Universidad de Monterrey Georgia Project leaders highlighted in this chapter were also not well positioned to contribute to Summer Institute follow-up activities.

## CHAPTER 11

1. For brevity, for the remainder of this section these are referred to as the attorney's notes, but, as acknowledged here, they may well have been produced by his bilingual assistant who was closely involved in the project. The notes were passed along to me by the attorney's office assistant, but their authorship was not credited.

2. BICS stands for Basic Interpersonal Communication Skills. CALP refers to Cognitive Academic Language Proficiency. Language educators and researchers distinguish between these two categories to clarify that apparent oral proficiency in language (i.e., the apparent ability to converse) is not the same as sophisticated comprehension of a language. The latter level and range of skills is necessary for academic success. Without caution and/or an assessment instrument distinguishing between the two levels of capability, a language minority student's display of BICS skills can be misinterpreted to mean that the student is ready to work unassisted in mainstream classrooms.

3. This hints at a point raised earlier: To what extent were Georgia Project leaders planning designs that would accommodate the mobile portion of the student population?

4. Though it would not have been politically viable in Dalton to have instructors who only knew Spanish, that such teachers could be used to implement the Spanish-immersion part of this model seems not to have been considered. The Universidad de Monterrey could have provided an abundant supply of such teachers.

5. The Direct Instruction model adopted by Dalton fully scripted teachers' tasks, detailing exactly what instructors should say and when. These scripts were all in English. Promoters of Direct Instruction (Adams and Engelmann 1997) warned that they were not responsible for failures of the Direct Instruction model if it was not followed exactly. However, in Dalton classrooms, I saw implementation of Direct Instruction that was not exclusively in English. This was just one way that I witnessed implementers of Direct Instruction in Dalton deviating from their scripts.

6. It is worth noting here, however, that the creators of Direct Instruction made little reference to Hispanics or English language learners in both their claims for their model and their selective review of research that "showed" how viable it was (Goode 2002).

7. During a July 28, 1997, phone call informing me that Dalton had received the Title VII funding, the administrator who called me said that the funding would pay for ten visiting instructors, Direct Instruction training for 200 teachers, and other indirect costs. According to the semifinalist *Innovations in American Government* grant proposal (Dalton Public Schools 1998b), slightly less than $74,000 of the $150,000 first-year Title VII funds were budgeted for the Georgia Project.

8. Education researchers who are as philosophically opposed to Direct Instruction's mind-numbing roteness as Erickson, have conceded (1987:342) that it often succeeds within the narrow parameters of improving standardized test scores in early grades. However, students who experience it as their only reading curriculum often experience a fourth grade slump that persists thereafter (Chall, Jacobs, and Baldwin 1990). In fourth grade the reading tasks at school change from decoding to comprehension (Nation and Coady 1988) and Direct Instruction seems poorly suited to support this transition.

9. At the innovative elementary school certified instructors were technically given the choice of adopting Direct Instruction or not, but, administrators have told

me that the two or three Direct Instruction holdouts felt isolated and frustrated. (I did not interview them directly.)

10. One of the original fourteen visiting instructors did not return to Dalton after going home to Monterrey for Christmas 1997. The redeployment of the remaining thirteen instructors left two schools without an on-site visitor, except on an as-needed basis. This reconfiguration did not indicate, as far as I could tell, any negative judgment of the visiting instructors' performance at those two schools during the fall of 1997.

11. She apparently was unaware at that time that Cummins (1996:201–203) opposed the use of Direct Instruction with LEP students because empirical data showed that the method helped such students only minimally with sustained academic gains and that it was significantly less effective than a properly implemented bilingual program.

12. This charge was based primarily on the story of an associate of the priest who, though he had a master's degree from a university in Colombia, had been told there were no openings in Dalton at the time he applied for work there. While the administrator in charge of hiring was vilified in absentia, nonschool affiliated attendees, notably but not exclusively the priest, asked why the candidate could not at least have been hired on as a janitor with his instructional role created improvisationally as opportunity permitted. This particular debate is illustrative of a number of issues, but one worth highlighting is what it says about the noneducators' sensibility about how schools do and should organize instruction.

13. According to the questionnaires I gave them, a few also had experience as student teachers and in other roles at Mexican public schools.

14. Though the report acknowledged elsewhere that instructor certification in the United States is done at the state level, note the slip here with the reference to "U.S. certified." In Mexico teachers are nationally certified.

15. The report had acknowledged the existence of some mistrust of the visiting instructors by both some ESOL teachers and some paraprofessionals.

16. This was the same individual who the attorney had saluted at the March 1997 Georgia Project Accord signing ceremony. As an administrator at the Georgia Department of Education, she was the only one from there to substantively contribute to the Georgia Project during my research period. Since resigning her position with the state, she has remained in contact with the attorney (and with me) and thus stayed abreast of the Georgia Project.

17. The attorney first learned that the Title VII monies were in jeopardy after I sent to the superintendent an e-mail I had received to that effect from a former employee of the Georgia Department of Education. The superintendent had relayed my e-mail to the attorney.

18. If I understand Georgia procedure on this issue correctly, on a rotating basis school districts receive extra money for textbook replacement.

## CHAPTER 12

1. The job title Georgia Project Exchange Coordinator referred to the administrative supervision this Monterrey employee performed related to all Georgia Project components (especially her tasks related to the logistics of the visiting instructor program). The title does not capture well her role, as a researcher, neither

as part of this needs assessment nor previously in her career when she had written a masters thesis on women in the Mexican *colonias* in south Texas for the University of Texas-PanAmerican's sociology program.

2. The visiting instructor program was still tentative because, despite efforts by the school district and at the Universidad de Monterrey, the legal requirements of the program (i.e., visas) were still up in the air.

3. *Heterogeneous* here refers to a diversity in length of time in Dalton and the United States, a range of experience in other U.S. locales, differing degrees of residential stability (ranging from recent arrival at the Little Mexico trailer park to the purchase of a home), and differing work experiences (ranging from the introductory or lowest tier work at ConAgra's poultry plant up the continuum to the opportunities provided by small and, even better, large carpet producers, plus the entrepreneurial endeavors of several dozen). It does not refer to the national origin or descent of Dalton's Hispanic population, approximately 90 percent of whom were Mexican by birth or descent.

4. Emphasizing that some Dalton Hispanics desired to settle permanently in Dalton/Whitfield reflected both what the researchers were told and the researcher's recognition that a stumbling block limiting previous mainstream recognition, outreach, and inclusion of Dalton's Hispanic community was the belief that the Hispanic community was impermanent. That some Hispanics in Dalton would not settle there permanently, perhaps never intended to, and yet still merited services from the schools and elsewhere was not directly broached (Hamann 2001a).

5. *Authentic* voices were the voices of local Hispanics in contrast to the voices of non-Hispanic mediators who were often sought as supposed representatives of the Hispanic community. (Such as when the school district pointed me to the bilingual priest when I was crafting the Title VII grant proposal in March 1997.)

6. Except for the research director's wife, the seminar leaders and participants were all either Mexican born or of Mexican descent. The two Daltonians of Guatemalan descent who were invited did not participate.

7. Though the community needs assessment identified Hispanic fathers' frequent child care role as spouses alternated work shifts and being at home, the report summarizing the leadership development seminar identified only a need to support working mothers. Whether this discrepancy reflected cultural beliefs ideationally assuming child care as a female responsibility (even if in practice it was often a shared duty) or whether it only represented an inadvertent word choice by the report's authors was unclear.

8. Dentler and Hafner (1997) identified the presence of such committees as a common factor among the three school districts successfully negotiating newcomer influxes in their study of eleven similarly situated districts. One challenge limiting local Hispanics ability to use conventional methods (i.e., voting) to gain representation was that the community's collective voting power was tiny in relation to its size. A high proportion of Dalton Hispanics were not voting age U.S. citizens. As Hackenberg (1995) recognizes, newcomer Hispanics in many communities are residents without representation.

9. Leaders of some of the companies that did provide work site education programming were involved with the Georgia Project, but in those instances those actually coordinating the education programs were not part of the Georgia Project.

## CHAPTER 13

1. This ESOL consultant was the former Georgia Department of Education employee who had previously advised the Georgia Project and who had written the March 1998 letter, distributed widely by the attorney, that praised the Universidad de Monterrey bilingual coordinator's February 1998 report.

2. Despite this claim, two months later, at a ceremony to inaugurate the opening of two artificial turf soccer fields that was not a Georgia Project event but that was nonetheless attended by the attorney and two project leaders from Monterrey, the priest again was an intermediary, introducing several Hispanic leaders.

3. This introduction was a polite and tactical formality. These two Georgia Department of Education employees were outspoken skeptics of bilingual education who had never offered any support or assistance to the project. Their role in relation to the education of Hispanic newcomers across Georgia was negatively characterized by Beck and Allexsaht-Snider (2001). I suspect at this event, they were in attendance to learn more about what the Georgia Project was; not to be won over by it.

4. This video was produced but, according to contacts who have seen it, it was not of sufficient quality to be of much use.

5. The words used by Brown, the former chairman of Dalton's Recreation Commission, to introduce his article echo the discourse that described community and business involvement in the Georgia Project twenty years later. Brown starts his article (1976:38): "The growth of the Dalton, Georgia, park and recreation system is attributable to a continuing spirit of harmony among elected officials, lay contributors, community groups, and professional recreation and park personnel."

6. It is worth remembering here that Sarason (1990) called the alteration of power relations a necessary but insufficient condition of sustainable useful reform. Other factors also needed tending to.

## CHAPTER 14

1. There is an extensive anthropological literature on trope theory (e.g., James Fernandez' 1991 book *Beyond Metaphor: The Theory of Tropes in Anthropology*), but in using this term I am not trying to insert myself into any debates regarding tropes, versus schemas, versus cultural models. I see these as substantially overlapping ideas and want my definition of trope provided in the text to suffice as a clarification of how I am intending the term, that is, to reference a cultural framework that combines understandings and ideas in a way that shapes observation and thus the lessons drawn from interacting in the social world. Tropes are metaphors that point to particular understandings and thus suggest particular courses of action.

2. This idea is consistent with situated learning and activity theories. Rogoff wrote, "Rather than examining context as an influence on human behavior, I regard context as inseparable from human actions" (1990:27). In other words, the actor does not determine the context and the context, including all of the frames of seeing, doing, and assigning meaning, does not determine the action; rather actor, action, and context are all intertwined.

3. At the request of the Monterrey project leaders, Dalton-based Georgia Project leaders had successfully kept the convening of this conference at a low profile until it was finished. While the idea of creating a Latino political organization may not have been a goal of many of the corporate leaders who comprised the Georgia

Project's initial ad hoc oversight committee, this group readily accepted the idea of a strategic retreat where conversations could be speculative and candid away from probing eyes and ears. Such a convening matched practices that the executives themselves engaged in leading their companies.

4. For this statement to be true, the Dalton school board needs to be seen as part of the district.

5. See Cummins (1996), Heshusius (1991), and Allington and Woodside-Jiron (1999) for at least three challenges to the research claims favoring Direct Instruction.

6. One could posit that diversifying the school's workforce would contribute to a generally more inclusive culture, regardless of the position being offered. This could have favorable classroom effects, however indirect. However, one could counter such an argument by claiming the hiring of a Latino janitor would merely extend the reproduction of an ethnically marked status hierarchy, contributing to an unfortunate association between Latino identity and low-status work.

7. This number is generated by dividing the proportion of the twelfth grade class that is Hispanic by the proportion of tenth graders that are Hispanic. With the potential number of tenth and twelfth grade Hispanics equal, the discrepancy between these numbers becomes an indicator of dropout rates.

# Bibliography

Aberle, David. 1962. Millennial Dreams in Action. In *Comparative Studies in Society and History, Supplement II.* Sylvia L. Thrupp, ed., pp. 209–214. The Hague: Mouton & Co.

Adams, Donald K., Mark B. Ginsburg, Thomas Clayton, Martha E. Mantilla, Judy Sylvester, and Yidan Wang. 2001. Linking Research to Educational Policy and Practice: What Kind of Relationships in How (De)Centralized a Context? In *Policy as Practice: Toward a Comparative Sociocultural Analysis of Educational Policy.* Margaret Sutton and Bradley Levinson, eds., pp. 59–76. Westport, CT: Ablex.

Adams, Gary L., and Siegfried Engelmann. 1997. *Research on Direct Instruction: 25 Years Beyond DISTAR.* Eugene, OR: Association for Direct Instruction.

Allington, Richard L., and Haley Woodside-Jiron. 1999. The Politics of Literacy Teaching: How "Research" Shaped Policy. *Educational Researcher* 28(8): 4–13.

Altwerger, Bess, and B. L. Ivener. 1994. Self-esteem: Access to Literacy in Multicultural and Multilingual Classrooms. In *Kids Come in All Languages: Reading Instruction for ESL Students.* K. Spangenberg-Urbschat and R. Pritchard, eds., pp. 65–81. Newark, DE: International Reading Association.

Ambert, Alba N., ed. 1991. *Bilingual Education and English as a Second Language: A Research Handbook 1988–1990.* New York: Garland Publishing, Inc.

American Association for Employment in Education. 1997. *Teacher Supply and Demand in the United States: 1996 Report.* Evanston, IL: American Association for Employment in Education.

Amidon, E. J., N. A. Flanders, and I. G. Casper. 1985. *The Role of the Teacher in the Classroom: A Manual for Understanding and Improving Classroom Behavior,* 3rd ed. St. Paul, MN: Paul S. Amidon and Associates.

Anderson, Benedict. 1991. *Imagined Communities: Reflections on the Origin and Spread of Nationalism*, rev. ed. London: Verso.

Apple, Michael W. 1993. *Official Knowledge: Democratic Education in a Conservative Age*. New York: Routledge.

Argyris, Chris. 1998. How Organizations Change: Implications for School Reform. Invited Presentation. SIG/Organizational Theory Division A Membership Meeting, American Educational Research Association Annual Meeting. San Diego, CA.

Argyris, Chris, and Donald A. Schön. 1975. *Theory in Practice: Increasing Professional Effectiveness*. San Francisco: Jossey-Bass Publishers.

Ball, Stephen J. 1990. *Politics and Policy Making in Education*. London: Routledge.

Banker, Mark. 1996. Unraveling the Multicultural Riddle: Clues from Southern Appalachia and Hispanic New Mexico. *Journal of Appalachian Studies*, 2(2):277–298.

Barnett, H. G., Leonard Broom, Bernard J. Siegal, Evon S. Vogt, and James B. Watson. 1954. Acculturation: An Exploratory Formulation. *American Anthropologist*, 56:973–1002.

Barry, Tom. 1997. Carpet Rebound Creates Need for More Workers in Northwest. *Georgia Trend*, 12(8):27–29.

Barth, Fredrik. 1969. Introduction. In *Ethnic Groups and Boundaries: The Social Organization of Cultural Difference*. Fredrik Barth, ed., pp. 9–38. Boston: Little, Brown and Company.

———. 1997. Commentary: How Others See Us: An Interview with Fredrik Barth. *Anthropology Newsletter*, 38(2):60, 59.

Beard, Frankie. 1996. Georgia Elementary Principals' Perceptions of Administrative Preparation and Its Impact on Their Attitudes for Dealing With Language Minority Students: Implications for Staff Development. Ed.D. Dissertation, University of Alabama.

Beck, Scott A. L., and Martha Allexsaht-Snider. 2001. Recent Language Minority Education Policy in Georgia: Appropriation, Assimilation, and Americanization. In *Education in the New Latino Diaspora*. Stanton Wortham, Enrique G. Murillo, Jr., and Edmund T. Hamann, eds., pp. 37–66. Westport, CT: Ablex Press.

Borman, Kathryn M., Peter W. Cookson, Alan Sadovnik, and Jean Spade, eds. 1996. *Implementing Educational Reform: Sociological Perspectives on Educational Policy*. Norwood, NJ: Ablex.

Borofsky, Robert. 1994. On the Knowledge and Knowing of Cultural Activities. In *Assessing Cultural Anthropology*. Robert Borofsky, ed., pp. 331–346. New York: McGraw-Hill.

Brisk, Maria E. 1998. *Bilingual Education: From Compensatory to Quality Schooling*. Mahwah, NJ: Lawrence Erlbaum.

Broadway, Michael. 1994. Beef Stew: Cattle, Immigrants, and Established Residents in a Kansas Beefpacking Town. In *Newcomers in the Workplace*. Louise Lamphere, ed., pp. 25–43. Philadelphia: Temple University Press.

Brown, George H., Nan L. Rosen, Susan T. Hill, and Michael Olivas. 1980. *The Conditions of Education for Hispanic Americans*. Washington D.C.: National Center for Education Statistics.

Brown, James. 1976. A Million Dollars' Worth of Growth. *Parks & Recreation*, 11(6):38, 49–50.

Carter, Thomas P., and Michael L. Chatfield. 1986. Effective Bilingual Schools: Implications for Policy and Practice. *American Journal of Education*, 95(1):200–232.

Cazden, Courtney B. 1992. Language Minority Education in the United States: Implications of the Ramirez Report. National Center for Research on Cultural Diversity and Second Language Learning. (http://www.ncbe.gwu.edu/miscpubs/ncrcdsll/epr3/index.html)

Center for Applied Linguistics. 2000. Serving the Needs of Limited English Proficient Students in Dalton and Whitfield County. Washington, D.C.: author.

Chall, Jeanne S., Vicki A. Jacobs, and Luke E. Baldwin. 1990. *The Reading Crisis: Why Poor Children Fall Behind*. Cambridge, MA: Harvard University Press.

Chavez, Leo R. 1994. The Power of the Imagined Community: The Settlement of Undocumented Mexicans and Central Americans in the United States. *American Anthropologist*, 96(1):52–73.

Chavez, Linda. 1995. One Nation, One Common Language. *Readers Digest*, August: 87–91.

Cloud, Nancy. 1991. Educational Assessment. In *Limiting Bias in the Assessment of Bilingual Students*. Else V. Hamayan and Jack S. Damico, eds., pp. 219–245. Austin, TX: Pro-ed.

Cloud, Nancy, Fred Genesee, and Else Hamayan. 2000. *Dual Language Instruction: A Handbook for Enriched Education*. Portsmouth, NH: Heinle & Heinle.

Cohen, Yehudi A. 2000 [1971]. The Shaping of Men's Minds: Adaptations to Imperatives of Culture. In *Schooling the Symbolic Animal: Social and Cultural Dimensions of Education*. Bradley A. U. Levinson, ed., pp. 83–107. Lanham, MD: Rowman & Littlefield.

Coles, Gerald. 2001. Reading Research and Skills-Emphasis Instruction: Forging "Facts" to Fit an Explanation. In *Literacy as Snake Oil*. Joanne Carson, ed., pp. 27–44. New York: Peter Lang.

Collier, Virginia. 1987. Age and rate of acquisition of second language for academic purposes. *TESOL Quarterly*, 21, 617–641.

———. 1995. Acquiring a second language for school. *Directions in Language and Education*. Washington, D.C.: National Clearinghouse for Bilingual Education.

Corson, David, ed. 1995. *Discourse and Power in Educational Organizations*. Cresskill, NJ: Hampton Press.

Crawford, James. 1991. *Bilingual Education: History, Politics, Theory, and Practice*. Los Angeles: Bilingual Education Services, Inc.

Cumming, Doug. 1998. Dismal SATs: Spin Aside, Georgia Ranks 49 of 51. *Atlanta Constitution*, September 2: A1.

Cummins, Jim. 1981. The role of primary language development in promoting educational success for language minority students. In *Schooling and language minority students: A theoretical framework*, pp. 3–49. California State Department of Education.

———. 1993. Empowering Minority Students: A Framework for Intervention. In *Beyond Silenced Voices: Class, Race, and Gender in United States Schools*. Lois Weis and Michelle Fine, eds., pp. 101–117, 367–372. Albany: State University of New York Press.

———. 1996. *Negotiating Identities: Education for Empowerment in a Diverse Society*. Ontario, CA: California Association for Bilingual Education.

Cuoto, Richard A. 1995. The Spatial Distribution of Wealth and Poverty in Appalachia. *Journal of Appalachian Studies,* 1(1):99–120.

D'Agostino, Jerome V. 2000. Achievement Testing in American Schools. In *American Education: Yesterday, Today, and Tomorrow, Ninety-ninth Yearbook of the National Society for the Study of Education, Part II.* Thomas L. Good, ed., pp. 313–337. Chicago: University of Chicago Press.

Daily Citizen-News, The. 1995. Lifestyle: Times Change. *The [Dalton] Daily Citizen-News,* January 15: 5A.

———. 1996. [The attorney] Leads Effort to Help Educate Hispanic Students. *The [Dalton] Daily Citizen-News,* December 20: 4A.

———. 1997a. Business Involvement Aids Georgia Project. *The [Dalton] Daily Citizen-News,* January 23: 4A.

———. 1997b. Georgia Project Off to Promising Start. *The [Dalton] Daily Citizen-News,* March 20: 4A.

———. 1997c. Georgia Project's Aim Is to Teach English. *The [Dalton] Daily Citizen-News,* April 24: 4A.

———. 1997d. Georgia Project's Success Important. *The [Dalton] Daily Citizen-News,* December 19: 4A.

Dalton Public Schools. 1997. Systemwide Bilingual Education Program: Dalton Public Schools Commitment to a Changing Population. Title VII Bilingual Education: Systemwide Improvement Grants (Catalog of Federal Domestic Assistance number: 84–291R). Grant application. Dalton, GA: Dalton Public Schools.

———. 1998a. [Initial] Innovations in American Government Grant. Grant Application. Dalton, GA: Dalton Public Schools.

———. 1998b. Semifinalist Application #988 1998 Innovations Award. Grant Application. Dalton, GA: Dalton Public Schools.

———. 1998c. Dalton Public Schools: Excellence, Diversity, Caring. Annual Report 1998. Dalton, GA: Dalton Public Schools.

Dameron, Rebecca J., and Arthur D. Murphy. 1996. Becoming an International City: Atlanta, 1970–1996. *Research Applications,* Center for Applied Research in Anthropology, Georgia State University 5(1):1–3.

Damico, Jack S., and Else V. Hamayan, eds. 1991. *Limiting Bias in the Assessment of Bilingual Students.* Austin, TX: Pro-Ed.

Datnow, Amanda, Lea Hubbard, and Gilberto Q. Conchas. 2001. How Context Mediates Policy: The Implementation of Single Gender Public Schooling in California. *Teachers College Record,* 103(2):184–206.

Deaton, Thomas M. 1993. *Bedspreads to Broadloom: The Story of the Tufted Carpet Industry.* Chattanooga, TN: Color Wheel.

Deck, Ben. 1997. State School Chief Praises Local Programs. *The [Dalton] Daily Citizen-News,* September 3: 1A.

De La Rosa, Denise, and Carlyle E. Maw. 1990. *Hispanic Education: A Statistical Portrait 1990.* Washington, D.C.: Policy Analysis Center, Office of Research, Advocacy, and Legislation, National Council of La Raza.

Delgado-Gaitan, Concha. 1990. *Literacy for Empowerment: The Role of Parents in Children's Education.* New York: The Falmer Press.

Delpit, Lisa D. 1988. The Silenced Dialogue: Power and Pedagogy in Educating Other People's Children. *Harvard Educational Review,* 58(3):280–298.

Dentler, Robert A., and Anne L. Hafner. 1997. *Hosting Newcomers: Structuring Educational Opportunities for Immigrant Children*. New York: Teachers College Press.

Diwan, R. 1999. Gandhian Economics. In *Encyclopedia of Political Economy*. Phillip Anthony O'Hara, ed.,. pp. 387–388. New York: Routledge.

Durrenberger, E. Paul, and Kendall Thu. 1998. Coming in from the Margins. *Anthropology Newsletter,* October: 60, 58.

*Education Week*. 2000a. Uneven growth. *Education Week* (Nov. 8):44.

———. 2000b. Dropping Out. *Education Week* (Nov. 8):44.

Erickson, Frederick. 1984 [1973]. What Makes School Ethnography 'Ethnographic'? *Anthropology & Education Quarterly*, 15:51–66.

———. 1987. Transformation and School Success: The Politics and Culture of Educational Achievement. *Anthropology & Education Quarterly*, 18(4):335–356.

Ernst, Gisela, and Elsa L. Statzner. 1994. Alternative Visions of Schooling: An Introduction. *Anthropology & Education Quarterly*, 25(3):200–207.

Fernandez, James W., ed. 1991. *Beyond Metaphor: The Theory of Tropes in Anthropology*. Stanford, CA: Stanford University Press.

Fine, Michelle. 1989. The Politics of Research and Activism. *Gender and Society*, 3(4):549–558.

Fischer, Claude S., Michael Hout, Martin Sanchez Jankowski, Ann Swidler, and Samuel R. Lucas. 1996. *Inequality by Design: Cracking the Bell Curve Myth*. Princeton, NJ: Princeton University Press.

Flamming, Douglas. 1992. *Creating the Modern South: Millhands and Managers in Dalton, Georgia, 1884–1984*. Chapel Hill: University of North Carolina Press.

Foley, Douglas E. 1990. *Learning Capitalist Culture: Deep in the Heart of Tejas*. Philadelphia, PA: University of Pennsylvania Press.

———. 1991. Reconsidering Anthropological Explantions of Ethnic School Failure. *Anthropology & Education Quarterly*, 22(1):60–86.

Foucault, Michel. 1977. *Discipline and Punish: The Birth of a Prison*. Alan Sheridan, trans. New York: Vintage Books.

Francis, Norbert, and Phyllis M. Ryan. 1998. English as an International Language of Prestige. *Anthropology & Education Quarterly*, 29(1):25–43.

Freire, Paulo. 1970. *Pedagogy of the Oppressed*. New York: Seabury.

Garcia, Eugene E. 1994. Bilingual Education: A Look to the Year 2000. Washington, D.C.: National Clearinghouse for Bilingual Education.

———. 2001. *Hispanic Education in the United States: Raìcesy Alas*. Lanham, MD: Rowman and Littlefield.

Gaventa, John. 1990. From the Mountains to the *Maquiladoras*. In *Communities in Economic Crisis: Appalachia and the South*. John Gaventa, Barbara Ellen Smith, and Alex Willingham, eds., pp. 85–95. Philadelphia: Temple University Press.

Geertz, Clifford. 1973. *The Interpretation of Cultures*. New York: Basic Books.

General Accounting Office. 1999. Public Education: Title I Services Provided to Students With Limited English Proficiency. Washington, D.C.: Author.

Georgia Department of Education. 1996a. Georgia Public Education Report Cards: State, Systems and Schools, 1994–95. (CD ROM) Atlanta: Georgia Department of Education, Research, Development and Accountability Unit.

———. 1996b. Georgia Public Education Report Cards: State, Systems and Schools, 1995–96. (CD ROM) Atlanta: Georgia Department of Education, Research, Development and Accountability Unit.

———. 1998. Georgia Public Education Report Cards: State, Systems and Schools, 1996–97. (CD ROM) Atlanta: Georgia Department of Education, Research, Development and Accountability Unit.

———. 1999. English to Speakers of Other Languages Resource Guide, 4th ed. Atlanta: Author.

———. 2002. 2000–2001 Georgia Public Education Report Card. Atlanta: Author. (Electronic document accessed on July 18, 2003, at: http://accountability. doe.k12.ga.us/Report01)

Gibson, Jane W. 1996. The Social Construction of Whiteness in Shellcracker Haven, Florida. *Human Organization,* 55(4):379–389.

Gibson, Margaret A. 1988. *Accommodation without Assimilation: Sikh Immigrants in an American High School.* Ithaca, NY: Cornell University Press.

———. 1997a. Introduction: Exploring and Explaining the Variability: Cross National Perspectives on the School Performance of Language Minority Students. *Anthropology & Education Quarterly,* 28(3):318–329.

———. 1997b. Complicating the Immigrant/Involuntary Minority Typology. *Anthropology & Education Quarterly,* 28(3):431–454.

Gitlin, Andrew, K. Bringurst, M. Burns, V. Cooley, B. Meyers, K. Price, Robyn Russell, and P. Tiess. 1992. *Teachers Voices for School Change: An Introduction to Education Research.* New York: Teachers College Press.

Gonzalez, Norma, Luis C. Moll, Martha Floyd Tenery, Anna Rivera, Patricia Rendon, Raquel Gonzales, and Cathy Amanti. 1995. Funds of Knowledge for Teaching in Latino Households. *Urban Education,* 29(4):443–470.

Goode, Judith G., Jo Anne Schneider, and Suzanne Blanc. 1992. Transcending Boundaries and Closing Ranks: How Schools Shape Interrelations. In *Structuring Diversity: Ethnographic Perspectives on the New Immigration.* Louise Lamphere, ed., pp. 173–213. Chicago: University of Chicago Press.

Goode, Lisa. 2002. Policy to Practice: An Analysis of the Influence of a Community-based Project for English Language Learners and Its Effect on Local School Policy. Ed.D. dissertation, Graduate School of the University of Alabama.

Gordon, Milton M. 1964. *Assimilation in American Life: The Role of Race, Religion, and National Origins.* New York: Oxford University Press.

Grant, Gerald. 1988. *The World We Created at Hamilton High.* Cambridge, MA: Harvard University Press.

Green, Larry. 1996. Influx of Hispanics could change DHS athletics. *The [Dalton] Daily Citizen-News,* May 15: 1B.

Grey, Mark A. 1991. The Context for Marginal Secondary ESL Programs: Contributing Factors and the Need for Further Research. *The Journal of Educational Issues of Language Minority Students,* 9:75–89.

———. 1995. Pork, Poultry, and Newcomers in Storm Lake, Iowa. In *Any Way You Cut It: Meat-Processing and Small-town America.* Donald D. Stull, Michael J. Broadway, and David Griffith, eds., pp. 109–127. Lawrence, KS: University Press of Kansas.

Griffith, David. 1993. *Jones's Minimal: Low-Wage Labor in the United States.* Albany: State University of New York Press.

———. 1995. *Hay Trabajo:* Poultry Processing, Rural Industrialization, and the Latinization of Low-Wage Labor. In *Any Way You Cut It: Meat-Processing and Small-town America*. Donald D. Stull, Michael J. Broadway, and David Griffith, eds., pp. 129–151. Lawrence, KS: University Press of Kansas.

Griffith, David, and Ed Kissam. 1995. *Working Poor: Farmworkers in the United States*. Philadelphia, PA: Temple University Press.

Griffith, David, Donald D. Stull, and Michael J. Broadway. 1995. Introduction: Making Meat. In *Any Way You Cut It: Meat-Processing and Small-town America*. Donald D. Stull, Michael J. Broadway, and David Griffith, eds., pp. 1–15. Lawrence, KS: University Press of Kansas.

Grundy, Thomas. 1992. ESL/Bilingual Education: Policies, Programs, and Pedagogy. *Oregon School Studies Council Bulletin*. 36(4). (ERIC No.: ED 355786).

Hackenberg, Robert A. 1993. Reflection on the Death of Tonto and the New Ethnographic Enterprise. *High Plains Applied Anthropologist*, 11:12–27.

———. 1995. Joe Hill Died for Your Sins. In *Any Way You Cut It: Meat-Processing and Small-town America*. Donald D. Stull, Michael J. Broadway, and David Griffith, eds., pp. 232–264. Lawrence, KS: University Press of Kansas.

———. 1997. The U.S.–Mexico Borderlands in Century XXI: Hispanics and Indians Move from Local Ecology into the Global Economy. *Culture & Agriculture*, 19(3):94–100.

Hakuta, Kenji, Y. G. Butler, and D. Witt. 2000. How Long Does It Take English Learners to Attain Proficiency? Santa Barbara, CA: University of California Linguistic Minority Research Institute.

Hall County Schools. 1998. Bilingual Education: Project B.A.B.E. Title VII Grant Proposal. Hall County, GA: Hall County Schools.

Hamann, Edmund T. 1995. Creating Bicultural Identities: The Role of School-Based Bilingual Paraprofessionals in Contemporary Immigrant Accommodation (Two Kansas Case Studies). Masters Thesis. University of Kansas.

———. 1997a. The Future Is Now: Latino Education in Georgia. Paper presented at the American Anthropological Association annual meeting. Washington, D.C.

———. 1997b. Georgia on the Fault Line? Looking at the Education of Latinos Statewide. *Research Applications,* Center for Applied Research in Anthropology, Georgia State University, 6(1):1–2, 6–8.

———. 1999. The Georgia Project: A Binational Attempt to Reinvent a School District in Response to Latino Newcomers. Ph.D. dissertation, Graduate School of Education, University of Pennsylvania.

———. 2001a. ¿Theorizing the Sojourner Student: (With a Sketch of Appropriate School Responsiveness). In *Negotiating Transnationalism: Selected Papers on Refugees and Immigrants,* Vol. IX. MaryCarol Hopkins and Nancy Wellmeier, eds., pp. 32–71. Washington, D.C.: American Anthropology Association.

———. 2001b. ¿Un Paso Adelante? The Politics of Bilingual Education, Latino Student Accommodation, and School District Management in Southern Appalachia. In *Education in the New Latino Diaspora*. Stanton Wortham, Enrique G. Murillo, Jr., and Edmund T. Hamann, eds., pp. 67–97 Westport, CT: Ablex Press.

Hamilton, David W. 1994a. Opponents Say Bond Failure Sends Message. *The [Dalton] Daily Citizen-News,* March 17: 1A.

———. 1994b. Dalton Teachers Ranked No. 1 in state. *The [Dalton] Daily Citizen-News,* April 24: 1A, 9A.

———. 1995a. One Year Later: Tax Fear Doomed Bond. *The [Dalton] Daily Citizen-News,* March 15.

———. 1995b. Jobs Analysis Complete. *The [Dalton] Daily Citizen-News,* April 6: 1A.

———. 1995c. Merger May Be Dalton's Last Chance at Education. *The [Dalton] Daily Citizen-News,* September 8: 1A.

———. 1996a. Instruction Turns Teachers into DIs: Hispanics May Read English But Not Always Understand It. *The [Dalton] Daily Citizen-News,* January 10: 6A.

———. 1996b. Educators Seek Ways to Reach Hispanics. *The [Dalton] Daily Citizen-News,* December 12: 1A, 6A.

———. 1996c. Trip to Mexico May Lead to Historic Deal. *The [Dalton] Daily Citizen-News,* December 17: 1A, 5A.

———. 1997a Communication Revolution Arrives in Dalton Today. *The [Dalton] Daily Citizen-News,* January 22: 1A.

———. 1997b. Visiting Professors Shocked by Size of Communication Problem. *The [Dalton] Daily Citizen-News,* January 25: 1A, 3A.

———. 1997c. Dalton in Historic Pact with Mexican University. *The [Dalton] Daily Citizen-News,* March 20: 1A

Hatch, Thomas. 1998. The Differences in Theory That Matter in the Practice of School Improvement. *American Educational Research Journal,* 35(1):3–31.

———. 2000. What Does It Take to "Go to Scale"? Reflections on the Promise and Perils of Comprehensive School Reform. *Journal of Education for Students Placed at Risk,* 5(4):339–354.

Hayes-Bautista, David E., and Jorge Chapa. 1987. Latino Terminology: Conceptual Basis for Standardized Terminology. *American Journal of Public Health,* 77:61–68.

Haynes, Amy E. L. 2000. An Analysis of Classroom Discourse in Relation to Teachers' Cultural Training: Teaching Implications of the Georgia Project. Ed.D Dissertation, University of Tennessee-Knoxville.

Heath, Dwight B. 1988. Introduction: Social Groupings and Authority. In *Contemporary Cultures and Societies of Latin America.* 2nd ed. Dwight B. Heath, ed., pp. 230–240. Prospect Heights, IL: Waveland Press, Inc.

Heath, Shirley Brice. 1996 [1983]. *Ways With Words: Language, Life, and Work in Communities and Classrooms.* Cambridge: Cambridge University Press.

Hernández León, Rubén. 1997. El Circuito Migratorio Monterrey-Houston. *Ciudades,* 35:26–33.

Hernández-León, Rubén, and Victor Zúñiga. 2000. "Making Carpet by the Mile": The Emergence of a Mexican Immigrant Community in an Industrial Region of the U.S. Historic South. *Social Science Quarterly,* 81(1):49–66.

Heshusius, Lous. 1991. Curriculum-Based Assessment and Direct Instruction: Critical Reflections on Fundamental Assumptions. *Exceptional Children,* 57(4):315–328.

Hill, David. 1998. English Spoken Here. *Education Week,* January 14:42–46.

Hoffman, Carl. 1993. Education: Practicing What They Teach. *Appalachia,* 26(2):31–35.

Hoffman, Valerie A. 1993. In Search of Home: Schools Key to Assimilating Hispanics. *The [Dalton] Daily Citizen-News,* November 1: 1A, 5A.

Howe, Kenneth R., and Jason Berv. 2000. Constructing Constructivism, Epistemological and Pedagogical. In *Constructivism in Education: Opinions and Second Opinions on Controversial Issues, Ninety-ninth Yearbook of the National Society for the Study of Education, Part 1.* D.C. Phillips, ed., pp. 19–40. Chicago: University of Chicago Press.

Huberman, A. Michael, and Matthew B. Miles. 1984. *Innovation Up Close: How School Improvement Works.* New York: Plenum Press.

Hunter, Floyd. 1963. *Community Power Structure: A Study of Decision Makers.* Garden City, NY: Anchor Books.

Jackson, Robert. 1997a. Shaw No. 1 Ranked Top Floor Covering Maker. *The [Dalton] Daily Citizen-News,* September 13: 1A.

———. 1997b. WBLJ to retain English format. *The [Dalton] Daily Citizen-News,* September 17: 1A.

———. 1997c. Local Radio Station Goes All-Hispanic. *The [Dalton] Daily Citizen-News,* October 17: 1A.

Jones-Correa, Michael. n.d. Under Two Flags: Dual Nationality in Latin America and Its Consequences for the United States. David Rockefeller Center for Latin American Studies Working Paper No. 99/00–3. (Accessed electronically 10–4–01 at: http://www.fas.Harvard.edu/~drclas/programs/immigration.html)

Kelley, Kathryn A. (Kitty). 1996. On Their Own: American Working Class Women Married to Mexican Immigrant Men in the Rural South. Masters Thesis. Georgia State University.

Kurylo, Elizabeth. 1998a. Error Leads to School Funding Cut: English programs for immigrant students take $1.7 million hit, but superintendant vows to eventually put it right. *Atlanta Journal-Constitution,* March 19: C4.

———. 1998b. Schrenko Will Seek to Repair Slip-up. *Atlanta Journal-Constitution,* March 28: D2.

———. 1998c. Overcoming Barriers: Hispanics Look Within to Curtail Dropout Rate. *Atlanta Journal-Constitution,* September 22: C1–C2.

Lamphere, Louise. 1992. Introduction: The Shaping of Diversity. In *Structuring Diversity: Ethnographic Perspectives on the New Immigration.* Louise Lamphere, ed., pp. 1–34. Chicago: University of Chicago Press.

Lamphere, Louise, Alex Stepick, and Guillermo Grenier, eds. 1994. *Newcomers in the Workplace: Immigrants and the Restructuring of the U.S. Economy.* Philadelphia: Temple University Press.

Levinson, Bradley A., and Dorothy Holland. 1996. The Cultural Production of the Educated Person: An Introduction. In *The Cultural Production of the Educated Person: Critical Ethnographies of Schooling and Local Practice.* Bradley A. Levinson, Douglas E. Foley, and Dorothy C. Holland, eds., pp. 1–54. Albany: State University of New York Press.

Levinson, Bradley A. U., and Margaret Sutton. 2001. Policy as/in Practice: Developing a Sociocultural Approach to the Study of Educational Policy. In *Policy as Practice: Toward a Comparative Sociocultural Analysis of Educational Policy.* Margaret Sutton and Bradley A. U. Levinson, eds., pp. 1–22. Westport, CT: Ablex Press.

Levy, Daniel C. 1986. *Higher Education and the State in Latin America: Private Challenges to Public Dominance.* Chicago: University of Chicago Press.

Lorey, David E. 1993. *The University System and Economic Development in Mexico Since 1929.* Stanford, CA: Stanford University Press.

———. 1995. The Rise of the Professions, Economic Development, and Identity in Mexico. Paper presented at the American Sociological Association Annual Meeting. Washington, D.C.

Lucas, Tamara, Rosemary Henze, and Ruben Donato. 1990. Promoting the Success of Latino Language-Minority Students: An Exploratory Study of Six High Schools. *Harvard Education Review,* 60(3):315–340.

Macias, Reynaldo. 1989. Bilingual Teacher Supply and Demand in the United States. Los Angeles: USC Center for Multilingual, Multicultural Research and the Tomas Rivera Center.

Madaus, George F. 1999. The Influence of Testing on the Curriculum. In *Issues in Curriculum: A Selection of Chapters from Past NSSE Yearbooks, Ninety-eighth Yearbook of the National Society for the Study of Education, Part II.* Margaret J. Early and Kenneth J. Rehage, eds., pp. 71–111. Chicago: University of Chicago Press.

Mahony, Pat. 2001. 6 Dalton Women Chosen for Scholarships. *Chattanooga Times Free Press,* electronic supplement (Aug. 21). (Accessed on August 21, 2001 at: http://www.timesfreepress.com/2001/aug/21aug01/webdaltonscholars.html)

Massey, Douglas S., Rafael Alarcón, Jorge Durand, and Humberto González. 1987. *Return to Aztlán: The Social Process of International Migration from Western Mexico.* Berkeley: University of California Press.

Maxwell, Joseph A. 1992. Understanding and Validity in Qualitative Research. *Harvard Education Review,* 62(3):279–300.

McFee, Malcolm. 1968. The 150% Man, a Product of Blackfeet Acculturation. *American Anthropologist,* 70:1096–1103.

McQuillan, Patrick James. 1998. *Educational Opportunity in an Urban American High School: A Cultural Analysis.* Albany: State University of New York Press.

Meier, Kenneth J., and Joseph Stewart, Jr. 1991. *The Politics of Hispanic Education: Un Paso Pa'lante y Dos Pa'tras.* Albany: State University Press of New York.

Mencken, F. Carson. 1996. Income and Employment Change in Appalachia During the 1983–1988 Business Cycle Recovery: Locating Differential Effects in North, Central, and Southern Appalachia. *Journal of Appalachian Studies,* 2(1):77–85.

Mendez Lugo, Bernardo. 1997. El Migrante Mexican en EU: De Actor Local a Actor Global. Mexico and the World (September) 6. (http://www.netside.net/mexworld/Issue6/Art2/lugo.html)

Miramontes, Ofelia B., Adel Nadeau, and Nancy L. Commins. 1997. *Restructuring Schools for Linguistic Diversity: Linking Decision Making to Effective Programs.* New York: Teachers College Press.

Mitchell, Douglas E., Tom Destino, and Rita Karam. 1997. Evaluation of English Language Development Programs in the Santa Ana Unified District: A Report on Data System Reliability and Statistical Modeling of Program Impacts. Riverside: California Educational Research Cooperative, School of Education, University of California Riverside. (www.education.ucr.edu/CERCsite/Archives/SantaAna/SAUSD1.html)

Moll, Luis C., Cathy Amanti, Deborah Neff, and Norma Gonzalez. 1992. Funds of Knowledge for Teaching: Using a Qualitative Approach to Connect Homes and Classrooms. *Theory Into Practice,* 31(1):132–141.

Muncey, Donna E., and Patrick J. McQuillan. 1996. *Reform and Resistance in Schools and Classrooms: An Ethnographic View of the Coalition of Essential Schools.* New Haven, CT: Yale University Press.

Murtadha-Watts, Khaula. 2001. Multicultural Curriculum and Academic Performance: African American Women Leaders Negotiating Urban Accountability Policies. In *Policy as Practice: Toward a Comparative Sociocultural Analysis of Educational Policy.* Margaret Sutton and Bradley A. U. Levinson, eds., pp. 103–121. Westport, CT: Ablex.

Nader, Laura. 1972. Up the Anthropologist—Perspectives Gained from Studying Up. In *Reinventing Anthropology.* Dell Hymes, ed., pp. 284–311. New York: Pantheon Books.

Nader, Laura, ed. 1996. *Naked Science: Anthropological Inquiry into Boundaries, Power, and Knowledge.* New York: Routledge.

Nation, Paul, and James Coady. 1988. Vocabulary and Reading. In *Vocabulary and Language Teaching.* Ronald Carter and Michael McCarthy, eds., pp. 97–110. London: Longman.

National Clearinghouse on English Language Acquisition (NCELA). 2002. The Growing Numbers of Limited English Proficient Students: 1991/92–2001/02. Washington, DC: NCELA. (Electronic document accessed July 18, 2003, at http://www.ncela.gwu.edu/states/index.htm)

Oakes, Jeannie. 1985. *Keeping Track: How Schools Structure Inequality.* New Haven, CT: Yale University Press.

Oboler, Suzanne. 1995. *Ethnic Labels, Latino Lives: Identity and Politics of (Re)Presentation in the United States.* Minneapolis: University of Minnesota Press.

Ogbu, John U. 1987. Variability in Minority School Performance: A Problem in Search of An Explanation. *Anthropology & Education Quarterly,* 18(4):312–334.

Packer, Martin. 2001. *Changing Classes: School Reform and the New Economy,* Cambridge: Cambridge University Press.

Padilla, Yolanda C. 1996. The Influence of Family Background on the Education Attainment of Latinos. *New England Journal of Public Policy,* 11(2):25–48.

Park, Robert E., and Ernest W. Burgess. 1970 [1921]. *Introduction to the Science of Sociology: Including an Index to Basic Sociological Concepts.* Abridged Student Edition. Morris Janowitz, abr. Chicago: The University of Chicago Press.

Pastor, Robert, and Jorge G. Castañeda. 1988. *Limits to Friendship: The United States and Mexico.* New York: Random House.

Patton, Randall L. 1999. *Carpet Capital: The Rise of a New Southern Industry.* Athens, GA: University of Georgia Press.

Pierce, Sara. 2001. "World Recognizing Carpet Capital." *The [Dalton] Daily Citizen-News* (Oct. 10).

Piore, Michael J. 1979. *Birds of Passage: Migrant Labor and Industrial Societies.* Cambridge: Cambridge University Press.

Plaut, Thomas. 1983. Conflict, Confrontation, and Social Change in the Regional Setting. In *Appalachia and America: Autonomy and Regional Dependence.* Allen Batteau, ed., pp. 267–284. Lexington, KY: University Press of Kentucky.

Polinard, J. L., Robert D. Wrinkle, and Kenneth J. Meier. 1995. The Influence of Educational and Political Resources on Minority Students' Success. *Journal of Negro Education,* 64(4):463–474.

Poniatowska, Elena. 1971. *Massacre in Mexico.* Helen R. Lane, trans. New York: Viking Press.

Portes, Alejandro. 1996. Introduction: Immigration and Its Aftermath. In *The New Second Generation.* Alejandro Portes, ed., pp. 1–7. New York: Russell Sage Foundation.

President's Advisory Commission on Educational Excellence for Hispanic Americans. 1996. Our Nation on the Fault Line: Hispanic American Education. A Report to the President of the United States, the Nation, and the Secretary of Education, United States Department of Education.

Puckett, John L. 1989. *Foxfire Reconsidered: A Twenty-Year Experiment in Progressive Education.* Urbana: University of Illinois Press.

Pugach, Marlene C. 1998. *On the Border of Opportunity: Education, Community, and Language at the U.S.—Mexico Line.* Mahwah, NJ: Lawrence Erlbaum Association.

Quinn, Christina Lynch. 1997. Mexico Trip Gives Cultural Insights. *The [Dalton] Daily Citizen-News,* July 17: 4A.

Quinn, Matthew C. 1997. NAFTA Partners Boost Georgia Exports. *Atlanta Journal-Constitution,* June 27: D1.

Ramirez, J. David. 1991. Fact Sheet—Longitudinal Study of Structured English Immersion Strategy, Early-exit and Late-exit Bilingual Education Programs. U.S. Department of Education. (Contract No. 300–87–0156).

Recio, Maria. 2002. Recession Hits Hispanics Hard, Study Finds. *Providence Journal* (Jan. 25):A3.

Redfield, Robert, Ralph Linton, and Melville J. Herskovits. 1967 [1936]. Memorandum for the Study of Acculturation. In *Beyond the Frontier: Social Process and Cultural Change.* Paul Bohannan and Fred Plog, eds., pp. 181–186. Garden City, NY: The Natural History Press.

Rehyansky, Mary. 1995a. Raid Nets 108 Illegals. *The [Dalton] Daily-Citizen News,* September 21: 1A.

———. 1995b. Operation SouthPAW Comes to an End. *The [Dalton] Daily-Citizen News.* September 26: 1A.

Reinharz, Shulamit. 1984. *On Becoming a Social Scientist.* Brunswick, NJ: Transaction Books.

Reyes, Pedro, and Richard R. Valencia. 1995. Educational Policy and the Growing Latino Student Population: Problems and Prospect. In *Hispanic Psychology: Critical Issues in Theory and Research.* Amado M. Padilla, ed, pp. 303–325.

Rifkin, Jeremy. 1995. *The End of Work: The Decline of the Global Labor Force and the Dawn of the Post-Market Era.* New York: G. P. Putnam's Sons.

Rippberger, Susan J. 1993. Ideological Shifts in Bilingual Education: Mexico and the United States. *Comparative Education Review,* 37(1):50–61.

Robertson, Tatasha. 2002. An Economic Retreat: Worried About Jobs Some Immigrants Return to Mexico. *Boston Globe* (Feb. 2): A1, A4.

Rogoff, Barbara. 1990. *Apprenticeship in Thinking: Cognitive Development in Social Context.* New York: Oxford University Press.

Rosaldo, Renato. 1989. *Culture and Truth: The Remaking of Social Analysis.* Boston: Beacon Press.

Rosen, Lisa. 2001. Myth Making and Moral Order in a Debate on Mathematics Education Policy. In *Policy as Practice: Toward a Comparative Sociocultural Analysis of Educational Policy.* Margaret Sutton and Bradley Levinson, eds., pp. 295–316. Westport, CT: Ablex.

Rumberger, Russell W., and Larson, K. A. 1998. Student Mobility and the Increased Risk of High School Dropout. *American Journal of Education,* 107:1–35.

Salzer, James. 2001. Georgia Last in Latino Grads. *Atlanta Journal-Constitution* (Nov. 4): E1

Sandel, Michael J. 1996. *Democracy's Discontent: America in Search of a Public Philosophy.* Cambridge, MA: Harvard University Press.

Sarason, Seymour B. 1990. *The Predictable Failure of Educational Reform: Can We Change Course Before It Is too Late?* San Francisco: Jossey-Bass Publishers.

———. 1995. *School Change: The Personal Development of a Point of View.* New York: Teachers College Press.

Sassen, Saskia. 1988. *The Mobility of Labor and Capital: A Study in International Investment and Labor Flow.* Cambridge: Cambridge University Press.

Saville-Troike, Muriel. 1976. *Foundations for Teaching English as a Second Language: Theory and Method for Multicultural Education.* Englewood Cliffs, NJ: Prentice-Hall, Inc.

Schaerer, John W., Neal W. Vickers, Ken E. Hansing, and Art S. Harvey. 1996. *Teacher and Administrator Supply and Demand for the Southeast.* Published independently by John W. Schaerer.

Schlechty, Philip. 2001. *Shaking Up the School House.* San Francisco: Jossey-Bass.

Schleter, Brian M. 1997. Georgia Project Teachers Meet with School Board. *The [Dalton] Daily Citizen-News,* December 17: 3A.

Schnaiberg, Lynn. 1998. Prop. 227 Could Torpedo "Two Way" Language Programs. *Education Week,* May 6:6–7.

Senge, Peter M. 1990. *The Fifth Discipline: The Art and Practice of the Learning Organization.* New York: Doubleday Currency.

Shaheen, Shaheen. 1984. *World Carpets: The First Thirty Years.* Dalton, GA: Lee Printing Co., Inc.

Shaw Industries, Inc. 1997. *Annual Report 1996.* Dalton, GA: Shaw Industries, Inc.

Sherman, Mark. 1997. As District Changes, Deal Tough on Immigrants. *Atlanta Journal-Constitution,* October 31: A10.

Shore, Cris, and Susan Wright, eds. 1997. *Anthropology of Policy: Critical Perspectives on Governance and Power.* London: Routledge.

Short, Deborah. 2000. The ESL Standards: Bridging the Academic Gap for English Language Learners. *ERIC Digest* (Accessed electronically on August 28, 2002 at: http://www.cal.org/ericcll/digest/0013ESLstandards.html)

Snow, Catherine E. 1992. Perspectives on Second-Language Development: Implications for Bilingual Education. *Education Researcher,* 21(2):16–19.

———. 1998. Research on Bilingualism. Symposium. American Educational Research Association Annual Meeting. San Diego, CA.

Spener, David. 1988. Transitional Bilingual Education and the Socialization of Immigrants. *Harvard Educational Review,* 58(2):133–153.

Starks-Winn, Kristy. 2000. Minority Now a Majority. *The [Dalton] Daily Citizen-News,* October 15:1.

———. 2001. First Ever Georgia Project Scholarship Recipients Named. *The [Dalton] Daily Citizen-News,* August 21: 6A.

Stull, Donald D., Michael J. Broadway, and Ken C. Erickson. 1992. The Price of a Good Steak: Beef Packing and Its Consequences for Garden City, Kansas. In *Structuring Diversity: Ethnographic Perspectives on the New Immigration.* Louise Lamphere, ed., pp. 35–64. Chicago: University of Chicago Press.

Stull, Donald D., Michael J. Broadway, and David Griffith, eds. 1995. *Any Way You Cut It: Meat-Processing and Small-town America.* Lawrence, KS: University Press of Kansas.

Suárez-Orozco, Carola, and Marcelo Suárez-Orozco. 1995. *Transformations: Migration, Family Life, and Achievement Motivation Among Latino Adolescents.* Stanford, CA: Stanford University Press.

———. 2001. *Children of Immigration.* Cambridge: Harvard University Press.

Suárez-Orozco, Marcelo M. 1998. State Terrors: Immigrants and Refugees in the Post-National Space. In *Ethnic Identity and Power: Cultural Contexts of Political Action in School and Society.* Yali Zou and Enrique T. Trueba, eds., pp. 283–319. Albany: State University of New York Press.

———. 1999. *Crossings: Mexican Immigration in Interdisciplinary Perspective.* Cambridge, MA: Harvard University, David Rockefeller Center for Latin American Studies.

Surpuriya, Tanuja. 1998a. Georgia Project "Inspiring," May Be State Model. *The [Dalton] Daily Citizen-News,* March 28: 1A.

———. 1998b. State Super Wants Focus on Teaching English. *The [Dalton] Daily Citizen-News,* April 14: 1A.

———. 1998c. State Superintendent Backs Bilingual Education. *The [Dalton] Daily Citizen-News,* April 18: 3A.

Target Tomorrow Task Force. n.d. *Target Tomorrow: "Creating OUR Communities' Future."* Dalton, GA: Dalton/Whitfield Chamber of Commerce.

Teske, Raymond H., and Bardin H. Nelson. 1974. Acculturation and Assimilation: A Clarification. *American Ethnologist,* 1:351–367.

Thomas, Ellen Keith. 1996. The Demise of the One-Room School: School Improvement and Consolidation in the Whitfield County, Georgia, Schools. Ed.D. Dissertation, Georgia State University.

Thomas, Wayne P., and Virginia Collier. 1997. School Effectiveness for Language Minority Students. *NCBE Resource Collection Series,* 9. Washington: National Clearinghouse for Bilingual Education. (www.ncbe.gwu.edu)

Thurston, Scott. 1997a. Delta's Expansion Plans Move with a Latin Beat. *Atlanta Journal-Constitution,* December 9: F1.

———. 1997b. Delta's Latin Project Aiming for 18 Cities. *Atlanta Journal-Constitution,* December 11: F2.

Tienda, Marta. 1989. Looking to the 1990s: Mexican Immigration in Sociological Perspective. In *Mexican Migration to the United States: Origins, Consequences, and Policy Options.* Wayne A. Cornelius and Jorge A. Bustamante, eds., pp. 109–147. San Diego, CA: Center for U.S./Mexican Studies, University of California.

Tienda, Marta, and E. Fielding. 1987. Migration, Preferential Work Status, and Employment: Divergent Paths of Hispanic Market Insertion in the United States. IRP Discussion Paper. Madison: University of Wisconsin.

Todorov, Tzvetan. 1984. *The Conquest of America: The Question of the Other.* Richard Howard, trans. New York: Harper & Row, Publishers.

Toma, J. Douglas. 2000. How Getting Close to Your Subjects Makes Qualitative Data Better. *Theory Into Practice,* 39(3):177–184.

Trueba, Enrique (Henry) T., and Yali Zou. 1998. Introduction. In *Ethnic Identity and Power: Cultural Contexts of Political Action in School and Society.* Yali Zou and Enrique T. Trueba, eds., pp. 1–25. Albany: State University of New York Press.

Trueba, Henry T. 1991. From Failure to Success: The Roles of Culture and Cultural Conflict in the Academic Achievement of Chicano Students. In *Chicano School Failure and Success: Research and Policy Agendas for the 1990s.* Richard R. Valencia, ed., pp. 151–163. London: The Falmer Press.

———. 1994. Reflections on Alternative Visions of Schooling. *Anthropology & Education Quarterly,* 25(3):376–393.

United States Department of Commerce, Economics and Statistics Administration, Bureau of the Census. 1991. County Business Patterns 1989: Georgia. Washington: U.S. Government Printing Office.

———. 1996. County Business Patterns 1994: Georgia. Washington: U.S. Government Printing Office.

Valdés, Guadalupe. 1996. *Con Respeto: Bridging the Distances Between Culturally Diverse Families and Schools, an Ethnographic Portrait.* New York: Teachers College Press.

———. 1998. The World Outside and Inside Schools: Language and Immigrant Children. DeWitt Wallace-Readers Digest Distinguished Lecture. American Educational Research Association Annual Meeting. San Diego, CA.

———. 2001. *Learning and Not Learning English: Latino Students in American Schools.* New York: Teachers College Press.

Valenzuela, Angela. 1999. *Subtractive Schooling: U.S.-Mexican Youth and the Politics of Caring.* Albany: State University of New York Press.

van Willigen, John. 1986. *Applied Anthropology: An Introd⸱⸱⸱⸱⸱⸱* South Hadley, MA: Bergin & Garvey Publishers, Inc.

Varisco de García, Norma, and Eugene E. Garcia. 1996. Teachers for Mexican Migrant and Immigrant Students: Meeting an Urgent Need. In *Children of La Frontera: Binational Efforts to Serve Mexican Migrant and Immigrant Students.* Judith LeBlanc Flores, ed., pp. 153–164. Charleston, WV: ERIC Clearinghouse on Rural Education and Small Schools.

Vasquez, Olga, Lucinda Pease-Alvarez, and Sheila M. Shannon. 1994. *Pushing Boundaries: Language and Culture in a Mexicano Community.* Cambridge: Cambridge University Press.

Villenas, Sofia. 2001. Reinventing Educación in New Latino Communities: Pedagogies of Change and Continuity in North Carolina. In *Education in the New Latino Diaspora.* Stanton Wortham, Enrique G. Murillo, Jr., and Edmund T. Hamann, eds., pp. 17–36. Westport, CT: Ablex Press.

Vio Brossi, G., and R. de Wit, eds. 1981. *Investigación Participativa y Praxis Rural.* Lima, Peru: Mosca Azul.

Wallace, Anthony F. C. 1956. Revitalization Movements. *American Anthropologist,* 58:264–281.

Weber, Max. 1947. *The Theory of Social and Economic Organization.* A. M. Henderson and Talcott Parsons, trans. and eds. New York: Free Press.

Weiss, Melford S. 1994. Marginality, Cultural Brokerage, and School Aides: A Success Story in Education. *Anthropology & Education Quarterly,* 25(3):336–346.

Wexler, Laura. 1999. A Possible Dream. *Georgia Magazine,* 78 (March):32–37.

Williams, John Alexander. 1996. Counting Yesterday's People: Using Aggregate Data to Address the Problem of Appalachia's Boundaries. *Journal of Appalachian Studies,* 2(1):3–27.

Willis, Paul. 1977. *Learning to Labor: How Working Class Kids Get Working Class Jobs.* New York: Columbia University Press.

Winders, Rebecca, Mary Anne Akers, Jan Coyne, Richard Reinheimer, and John Robitscher. 1995. *Migrant and Seasonal Farm Workers in Georgia: Estimates of the Migrant Health Program Target Population Summary.* Athens, GA: Institute of Community and Area Development, The University of Georgia.

Wolcott, Harry F. 1998 [1974]. The Elementary School Principal: Notes from a Field Study. In *Qualitative Inquiry and Research Design: Choosing Among Five Traditions.* John W. Cresswell, ed., pp. 323–356. Thousand Oaks, CA: Sage Publications.

Wolf, Eric. 1956. Aspects of Group Relations in a Complex Society: Mexico. *American Anthropologist,* 58:1065–1078.

Wong Fillmore, Lily, and Lois M. Meyer. 1992. The Curriculum and Linguistic Minorities. In *The Handbook of Research on Curriculum.* Philip W. Jackson, ed., pp. 626–658. New York: MacMillan Publishing Company.

Wortham, Stanton, Enrique G. Murillo, and Edmund T. Hamann, eds. 2001. *Education in the New Latino Diaspora: Policy and the Politics of Identity.* Westport, CT: Ablex Press.

Young, Michelle. 1999. Multifocal Educational Policy Research: Toward a Method for Enhancing Traditional Educational Policy Studies. *American Educational Research Journal,* 36(4):677–714.

Zhao, Yilu. 2002. Wave of Pupils Lacking English Strains Schools. *New York Times* (Aug 5). Electronic document, http://www.nytimes.com/2002/08/05/education/05ESL.html, accessed August 8.

Zuñiga, Victor, and Ruben Hernández-León. 2001. A New Destination of an Old Migration: Origins, Trajectories, and Labor Markets of Hispanics in Dalton Georgia. In *Latino Workers in the Contemporary South.* Arthur Murphy, Colleen Blanchard, and Jennifer A. Hill, eds. Southern Anthropological Society Proceedings Series, No. 34. Athens: University of Georgia Press.

Zuñiga, Víctor, Ruben Hernández-León, Janna L. Shadduck-Hernández, and Maria Olivia Villareal. 2001. The New Paths of Mexican Immigrants in the United States: Challenges for Education and the Role of Mexican Universities. In *Education in the New Latino Diaspora: Policy and the Politics of Identity.* Stanton Wortham, Enrique G. Murillo, and Edmund T. Hamann, eds., pp. 99–116. Westport, CT: Ablex.

# Index

*Note:* This index excludes direct references to Dalton, Whitfield County, Dalton Public Schools, the Universidad de Monterrey, the Georgia Project, and the six profiled architects of the Georgia Project. Each appears so many times that indexing would offer little further guidance.

**About the Author**

EDMUND (TED) HAMANN is Research and Development Specialist, The Education Alliance, Brown University. He is co-editor (with Stanton Wortham and Enrique G. Murillo Jr.) of *Education in the New Latino Diaspora* (2001).